FOOTSO

D0253709

Walks &
Hikes
Around
Puget
Sound

Second Edition

**By Harvey Manning/Photos by Bob & Ira Spring
Maps by Gary Rands/The Mountaineers • Seattle**

*Snoqualmie River • Great Big Western
Tree Farm • Skykomish River*

The Mountaineers: Organized 1906 "...to explore, study, preserve and enjoy the natural beauty of the Northwest."

© 1978, 1981, 1983, 1987 by Harvey Manning
All rights reserved
First edition, May 1978; revised May 1981, May 1983
Second edition, April 1987

Published by The Mountaineers, 306 2nd Avenue West
Seattle, Washington 98119

Published simultaneously in Canada by
Douglas & McIntyre Ltd., 1615 Venables Street
Vancouver, British Columbia V5L 2H1

Manufactured in the United States of America

Series design by Marge Mueller; layout by Bridget Culligan
Cover photo: Mt. Si and the Snoqualmie River
near North Bend

Library of Congress Cataloging-in-Publication Data
(Revised for vol. 2)

Manning, Harvey.
   Footsore : walks & hikes around Puget Sound.

   Includes indexes.
   1. Hiking — Washington (State) — Puget Sound Region —
Guide-books. 2. Puget Sound Region (Wash.) — Description
and travel — Guide-books. I. Title.
GV199.42.W22P835   1982   917.97'79   82-2100
ISBN 0-89886-065-2 (v. 1.)
ISBN 0-89886-126-8 (pbk. : v. 2)

0

5   4   3

CONTENTS 2

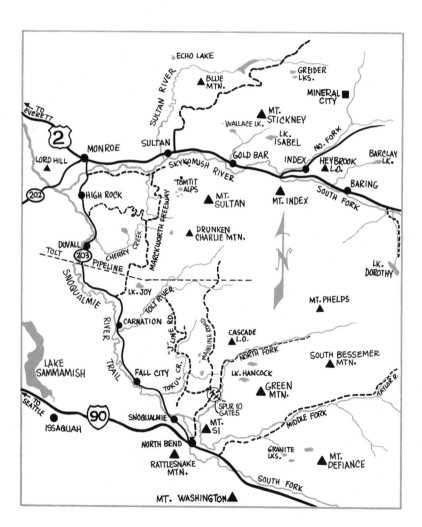

INTRODUCTION 2

For instructions on how to use this book, the reader is referred to Introduction 1 in *Footsore 1,* where will be found explication of the Ten Essentials, the Two-Hour Rule, the Trespassing Code, the difference between summer and winter, and such. Of the caveats stressed there only one will be repeated here: when using this volume as a guide to *Footsore* country, most of which is subject to instant change without notice, keep in mind that the original research was done in 1976-77, with additions in 1981 and 1983. For economic reasons (writing guidebooks is the quick route to the poorhouse) a few of the more remote spots have not been revisited since then on personal boot. Where a government servant had current information, or where a binocular eyeballing from a nearby vantage confirmed the mountain was still there, or when a benefactor provided a firsthand report, the surveyor wasn't always able to justify doing the hike again for this edition, for the sheer fun of it. However, all trailheads were checked in 1985 and all hikes inspected by one means or another, most on foot. As a consequence, two dozen were thrown out (the views have grown in, the motorcycles have arrived in force, the NO TRESPASSING signs have gone up), more than that were so radically revised they're like new, and better than a dozen, all winners, have been newly included. The book structure has been turned topsy-turvy and the introductory matter replaced or thoroughly overhauled.

While remembering the caveat (after all, no guidebook can lead you by the hand and wipe your nose), remember, too, that comments are taken most kindly, and serve not only to help readers of subsequent editions, but to save the surveyor time, which he can use to try to make an honest living — elsewhere than in the guidebook business. The assistance must be mentioned of friends in State Parks, the state Department of Natural Resources, and the Weyerhaeuser Company. The pages of *Signpost* and *Sunset Magazine* are the equivalent of a corps of informants. On the Snoqualmie River Trail a series of seminars on railroad trestles was conducted by J. J. Millegan, a structural engineer licensed by the state of Washington.

The serious *Footsore* traveler wants maps. The U.S. Geological Survey sheets noted for each chapter are the basics. The privately published Green Trails versions are much better for the hiker because they have overprintings (in green) showing current roads and trails, and this data is updated every two years. Both are sold by hiking shops and the two Seattle-area outlets of Metzger Maps (check the white pages).

Robert Kinzebach, an indefatigable and imaginative explorer, issues *Pic-Tour Guide Maps,* aerial photos and GS sheets with his findings overprinted, each summarizing hundreds of hours of poking about.

A number of years ago the surveyor convinced an old fellow traveler, Dee Molenaar, to enlarge his series of pictorial landform maps (Mt. Rainier, the Olympics, state of Washington, and Antarctica) by providing a map of the entire *Footsore* world to let the pilgrim on a mountain top readily identify all visible works of God and man. Dee has been promising the map every year and claims 1986 definitely will be it. Or 1987?

Meanwhile, another fellow traveler, Dick Pargeter, whose series of pictorial overview maps covers the Olympics and Cascades, has produced *Puget Sound Country,* a superb sheet in its own right, and doing much of the job of Dee's.

FREEDOM OF THE FEET

The inexperienced hiker, and the person new to the country, may be nervous about setting forth on any trail, footroad, or shore lacking a prominent "Welcome" sign. In all the *Footsore* hundreds of hikes there are only a few

Russian Buttes and Middle Fork Snoqualmie River

dozen such signs, in state parks, state DNR recreation areas, state wildlife habitat management areas, county and city parks, and national forests (and not in all these, either, where they have not been formally developed for recreation). However, all the walking routes described in this volume were freely open to the public feet at the time of publication in 1986.

The major timber companies, conspicuously Weyerhaeuser, have a standing policy of "tolerated trespassing," meaning they do not restrict foot passage through their lands, except perhaps in fire season. Few of these companies so much as identify their ownership, so that on vast tracts of forest land a person doesn't know if he's on private property — or on free-access public forests of the state Department of Natural Resources or the U.S. Forest Service — and usually it doesn't matter.

Railroads, also, very rarely (if ever) enforce rules against walking their rights-of-way, though if you get squashed they will remind your survivors that you were, at the time of your squashing, committing a crime. Utilities similarly avert eyes from pedestrians on their transmission (power, gas, water) corridors.

Only several trips in this volume are potentially subject to closure by owners, and these are noted in the text. Should "No Trespassing" signs appear at such places, they must be obeyed.

However, also noted in the text are several spots where neighbors have illegally posted "bluff" signs on public property to discourage foreigners, such as you and me. The rule here is to ignore the signs, unless a local comes hollering out of the bushes waving a shotgun, in which case you'll probably have more fun on some other hike.

HOW TO LEARN TO STOP WORRYING AND LOVE CLEARCUTS

Spoiled by the nearness of a hog's share of the nation's remaining wilderness, the typical Puget Sound pedestrian worships virgin forests as temples of Nature, patronizes second-growth woods as ruins soiled by debaucheries of the Hun, and considers a walk in a clearcut as inviting as a vacation in the city dump. An adjustment of attitudes is required for a person to become a contented citizen of *Footsore* country.

In the high mountains, nursery of most local hikers, the land is largely in National Parks, where forests are inviolate, and in National Forests, where forests of National Wilderness Areas also are inviolate and those of undesignated areas are managed under terms of the Multiple Use-Sustained Yield Act to simultaneously produce a continuous supply of wood and also provide water, wildlife, forage, minerals, and whatever else is there that anybody wants, including recreation. On all federal lands recreation has a recognized status. But few *Footsore* trips are on federal land.

State, county, and city parks also contain forests exempted from cellulose production. But most of Washington's non-federal public lands are managed by the state Department of Natural Resources (DNR) for the benefit of the owners (the common schools — thus the often-heard term, "school lands" — and the state universities, various institutions, and the counties, which in past decades acquired many properties through foreclosures for non-payment of taxes.) "Benefit" presently is defined by DNR legal counsel as, substantially, dollar income, National Forest-style multiple-use not permitted. This is not to say the DNR has been blind to recreation: using funds granted by outside agencies, it has built campgrounds and trails, and there are great opportunities for peripatetics on DNR lands, which are wide open to walking. Unfortunately, they are also wide open to everything else. That may change in years ahead but as of 1986 the game is purely laissez faire — four-wheelers and fun-truckers and two-wheel razzers run wild, and pedestrians very often, especially on Sunday, go wild.

As for private lands, a great many *Footsore* trips are in the empires of such companies as Weyerhaeuser, St. Regis, Georgia-Pacific, Boise-Cascade, Scott Paper, and Simpson. Multiple-use also is illegal here, the ban dictated by economic laws which require income to stockholders to be maximized. However, though the policies of the companies differ in detail, all allow walkers, subject to regulations, and the tree farms of the lowland edge-mountain front offer vast — and relatively little-exploited — scope for feet.

In summary, the *Footsore* pedestrian must realize he's not the star of the show on DNR and private lands; indeed he's scarcely in the cast, is really just a member of the audience — an audience, though, that (Elizabethan-style) is allowed on stage, an uncrowded place and with a great view of the action. However, before launching a paean in praise of contemporary clearcuts, a glance at the past is in order.

To generalize, the First Wave clearcutting that commenced at tidewater in the mid-19th century bumped against the mountain front in the 1920s-30s, began climbing the hills in the 1940s-50s, and by the 1970s was reaching ridge tops and/or timberline. The hiker comes upon many evidences of how logging was done in earlier decades of the First Wave. Everywhere are stumps, usually cedar (other species rot quickly), notched for the springboards on which fallers balanced, above the brush and the swollen butt, to wield ax and saw. Still standing, though usually undistinguishable from other snags, are a few spar trees, tall firs that were topped and limbed and rigged with cables to "yard" logs to a "landing." Here was located, on a "skid" of two enormous logs that were rigidly cable-anchored to stumps, the steam donkey engine that provided the power for bringing in the logs and loading them on railroad cars. The landings can be recognized by litters of discarded logs, splintered wood and bark, and rusty junk, and sometimes the left-behind skids (and rarely, ruins of the donkey itself). Until the 1930s most hauling was done by railroad and the old grades remain prominent today, some converted to truck roads, others dwindled to trails, others unused and overgrown, typically with alder, superb routes for adventurous brushbusters. Because the standard locomotive could cope with only modest inclines, the grades meandered all over the countryside on the flat and switchbacked endlessly to gain elevation. But often a hiker is puzzled to see a flat grade abruptly turn sharply uphill; here, normally at the ends of spurs, was the domain of the "sidewinder" locomotive geared for steep grades and heavy loads, so named for having the drive shaft and four big pistons all on one side. Sometimes, too, the hiker comes upon railroad grades high on a mountain, seemingly unconnected to the valley; they were, however — via "incline" railways on the order of the San Francisco (and old Seattle) cablecars.

The last logging railroads shut down in the mid-1950s; by then truck logging, better suited to the mountain slopes the First Wave now was climbing, was dominant. Nowadays the spar pole is metal and the power is from an

Stump with springboard notches

internal-combustion engine, the two combined in a self-contained, self-transporting unit, the "yarder," which decks the logs for a cat-like "loader" to hoist onto trucks. A familiar song in clearcuts is the "poo! poo!" (rendered by some ornithologists as "whoop! whoop!") of the "talkie-tooter," the whistle (modern successor of the steam whistle operated by the "whistle punk") by which the choker-setter, down in the slash attaching cables to logs, signals the yarderman for slack, for tension, or "let's knock off for lunch."

While the First Wave clearcutting of virgin forests proceeds deeper in the mountains, nearing the end of the line, as it is today, Second Wave clearcutting of second-growth is highballing across the lowlands, mingled in older regions with a Third Wave. (It's as appropriate here as anywhere to pause for some definitions. "Virgin" and "old-growth" are mistakenly used as synonyms. "Virgin" denotes the absence of man's saws; the trees may be puny, either from youth, perhaps dating back only to a recent forest fire, or from growing on a poor site. "Old-growth" designates a stand of virgin trees that are very big, usually because they are very old. Some second-growth now being cropped is bigger than some of the virgin. A further confusion to the observer is that in olden days of cheap trees some patches of timber were not logged because they were inconveniently located in "long corners," or had too many limbs ("wolf trees"), or the species was not then of much value; even in lowlands, typically in ravines or on cliffs, a surprised hiker may come upon small stands of genuine virgin old-growth.)

"Tree-farming," a tax dodge and advertising slogan when the term was invented in the 1930s, has neared reality in the last decade or two. Some (not all) state and private land is being farmed. Certain of the agricultural techniques are of interest to a hiker as affecting his sport.

"Clearcutting," the standard harvesting method in the Puget Sound region, is the removal of all trees on a given piece of land. (An alternative is "selective logging," nowadays little used locally except in thinning, as described below.) The sizes of clearcuts vary. In recent years compelled by public opinion to heed esthetics, the U.S. Forest Service tends toward small cuts. Indeed, more and more it is employing "shelterwood" harvesting; the patches are very narrow and shaped to the topography in such manner that adjacent big, old trees left standing can shelter seedlings from heat, cold, and wind during their delicate youth. Private tree-farmers, governed to a minor extent by scandalously weak state regulations (*that* is going to *change* — the scandals are too often on the front pages and the evening news, as fisheries are destroyed and homes flooded out), mainly obey laws of economics as interpreted by company comptrollers, who outrank the company foresters; because big cuts cost less than small, private-land clearcuts typically extend from horizon to horizon,

Clearcuts on Rattlesnake Mountain

or at least to the absolute edge of private property, the boundary of the National Forest. The DNR, dollar-dominated and left pretty much adrift and defenseless by the Legislature, has a variety of policies for a variety of situations.

Most present second-growth forests were planted and nurtured by unassisted nature, but human farmers increasingly are intruding. Where Douglas fir (the most-wanted species) has not regenerated after First Wave logging and the land is covered by fir-smothering deciduous trees, "alder conversion" is sometimes practiced: the forest is clearcut (except for such scattered conifers as may be), the alder and cottonwood are taken, mainly for pulpwood (in the case of alder, about 15 percent for saw timber), the maple and other species are cut and left, except for what little can be sawed for furniture, the slash is burned, and seedlings are hand-planted. Where conifers have regenerated but too thickly, forming a "choked" forest, thinning is sometimes done, the superfluous trees taken for lumber or pulp if big enough, otherwise cut and left, the surviving trees thus given sufficient elbow room to thrive. (Another activity, not truly farming, the hiker will observe is "cedar-mining," done under contract with landowners by honest gypos and in the dark of the moon by professional thieves; logs and snags and even stumps contain sound, clear wood that on today's market is pure gold.)

After clearcutting, whether of virgin or second-growth forest, the slash usually is burned; how long clean-air laws will let this continue is in doubt. Often within days of the logging, seedlings are hand-planted. (The older method of leaving patches of old-growth to seed clearcuts has been abandoned except at higher elevations, mostly on National Forests.) The seedlings come from nurseries, and in some cases the seeds are gathered from dominant, flaw-free trees — and thus the hope for genetically superior "super-trees." The plantations (virtually all Douglas fir, though some hemlock, cedar, and silver fir now are being supplied by nurseries) may be fertilized, may be sprayed with pesticides, and may be protected by poison, traps, or other means from sprout-nibbling mice and deer and bark-chomping bear. On an average lowland site, at about 15 years the plantations may be thinned, the weeded-out trees left, too small for any use. At about 25 may come a "commercial thinning," the logs hauled to the mill. At about 45 to 60 the forest is clearcut and a new plantation started. It is said that through such farming the land yields more than twice the wood volume of a wild forest. (However, this energy-intensive, chemical-intensive, gene-manipulating monoculture is increasingly questioned by scientists, many of whom call it risky to the point of recklessness. The current "high-yield forestry" may well be cited in a few years as another example of yesterday's wisdom becoming today's stupidity.)

That, in sketchy outline, is a tree farm from the viewpoint of the farmer. To the hiker other aspects are prominent.

When harvesting is in progress there are yarders and loaders and tractors to watch (from a safe distance), logging trucks to watch out for, and heard everywhere o'er hill and dale is the song of the talkie-tooter ("poo! poo!"). Afterward there are: land so starkly naked as to reveal every sensuous dip and swell of ravine and ridge; patterns of stumps dotting the slopes, and patterns of draglines radiating from landings; elemental colors replacing forest green — the iron-oxide yellow-brown of road gashes, the carbon black of burned stumps and slash. All very beautiful in its way. And also here in the raw new clearcut are the freedom from claustrophobic greenery, the joy of sunshine when forests are dark and clammy, and the big sky and broad views.

The land appears absolutely devastated, totally barren, utterly dead. Yet a closer look amid black stumps and brown dirt reveals bits of green — the seedlings, the new forest. Forest? For years the young trees seem to the casual passerby scarcely to grow, seem smothered by rank-growing brush. Fireweed and stumps and scraggly fir shrubs, that's all there is to see — except, of course, the continuing wide views.

Then, overnight, the shrubs explode into tall trees, forest-management roads shrink to green tunnels, the views disappear and almost the sky. More years pass, lower limbs die, and the understory and groundcover begin a transition from species that thrive in hot sun to those that like cool moist shadows. The moss time arrives, the fern time, the chanterelle time. And in favored lowland sites the trees grow so large in a half-century a person would swear they are centuries-ancient old-growth — until he spots the monster stumps of the First Wave clearcut. The hiker may reflect, "These wonderful trees are too good to last." He's right. It's time for the Second Wave — which will thoroughly screw up the route described in this guidebook, will destroy the splendid deep woods the surveyor has heavy-breathed about. But look at it this way — the views will now be grand.

A hiker who can't find happiness in a clearcut is as narrow, as maladjusted, as the logger who gets suicidal in a "locked-up" wilderness. A genuine fondness for trees embraces inches-high seedlings, exuberant young Christmas trees, thrifty tall youths, mature giants, broken-top rotten-hearted patriarchs, and silvered snags and logs. And stumps topped by cheery little gardens of huckleberry and salal. To be sure, no apology is required for mourning the massacre of a whole forest of noble old vegetables and one may be excused for considering monoculture monotonous.

But even if a hiker never learns to love clearcuts, as some never become fond of cow pastures, he at least can be consoled that the admitted brutality of the logging, the grimness of the raw slash and dirt, dominate only a year or so; for all the rest of the 40 or 70 years of the harvesting cycle a farm just sits there quietly growing cellulose. More quietly, possibly, than forests on trails of a National Park.

Still and all, no matter how fond an elderly birdwatcher becomes of the haunting call of the Yellow-Shafted Talkie-Tooter, he may be permitted second thoughts amid the second-growth.

Along the mountain front the land managers are not only engaged in as total and drastic a transformation of the landscape as has occurred in the history of the nation, in many places they are conducting a gigantic experiment in forestry at high elevations, in severe climates, on steep slopes, with unfamiliar species — farming for which past experience down low gives inadequate preparation. Can anyone outside the advertising departments of the companies be really sure the experiment will succeed, that this is truly tree-farming? The First Wave has now climbed to forests where the trees often are merely a foot or two in diameter — but are 300 or 400 years old! And at these elevations not nature, not man always can succeed in planting a new forest immediately — often, the forest must creep at a painfully slow pace from the shelter of big trees to fill in the clearcuts; generations, maybe centuries, are required to restock the land, and then more centuries to grow another "commercial" crop. And on these steep slopes a quarter or more of the soil may be lost in the process of harvesting — the basic resource of a farm sluiced down the creeks, not to be replaced except on a scale of eons. When the forest-growing cycle occupies centuries the activity is not properly called tree-farming; a better term is "timber-mining."

MAN DOES NOT LIVE BY PULP ALONE

Little *Footsore* territory is sought for wilderness by preservationists, who are pleased to see tree-farming there, not only because society needs lumber and pulp but because a steady supply from farms reduces the pressure on high-mountain forests that timber-industry extremists are seeking to mine. Further, a tree farm does as much as a cow farm to soften the harshness of urbanization, to enrich the fabric of our living space with stripings and quiltings of green. Indeed, preservationists urgently want a Timberlands Preservation Program, to save certain lowland tree farms from the partnership of the tax-assessor and the land-developer.

Nevertheless, just as much excellent timber-producing land must be sacrificed to build cities, some must be set aside to provide refuge from those cities — places where urban dwellers can go to find quiet, to be quiet, to repair nerves frazzled by the freeway mornings and nights, the shopping-mall Saturdays, the sky parade of jets and helicopters, and the kids' stereo. Were the surveyor for this volume the region's benevolent despot, he would order the affairs of the Cascade mountain front between the Snoqualmie and Skykomish Rivers in the following manner, using these existing agencies:

King County and Snohomish County

Outside the mountain front, the first has newly created Cougar Mountain Regional Wildland Park (see *Footsore 1*) and the second, Lord's Hill Regional Park, both wheelfree, passive, and minutes from the homes of millions. They should now cast their eyes a bit farther east. Snohomish County, for example, might be the proper agency to systematize a series of riverside parks along the Skykomish. King County could revive the old Tolt River Trail, acquire Fuller Mountain from the Weyerhaeuser Company, and undertake the conversion of the CCC Truck Road to the CCC Wheelfree Trail.

State Game (Wildlife) Department

The agency would be instructed by the despot to simply keep on doing what it has been for years — acquiring and protecting wildlife habitats, for non-game as well as game species, and for birders and other hikers as well as hunters and fishers. Formerly the main dues-paying clientele of the department was purchasers of hunting and fishing licenses. Non-consumptive users now have the opportunity to share in supporting the program by purchasing the Conservation License decal, $8.00 a year, displayed on a car when parked in Game Department lots. Ask for the decal at sporting goods stores and hiking shops. Aside from entitling the bearer to be proud, the decal prevents $75 tickets for illegal parking.

State Department of Natural Resources

At various times, in various places, various agency employees have done admirable work in providing campgrounds and trails. They are handicapped by an equivocal mandate from the Legislature, a vagueness of authority, and a lack of funds. Until the DNR philosophical underpinnings are concreted in, not even a benevolent despot can do more than suggest a wait-and-see policy. If, in future, it is allowed to undertake multiple-use management, it can take steps to repair its soiled reputation as the friend of the ATV and ORV and any other contraption that eats gas and belches noise, and to operate mini-parks and wheelfree trails, such as at Cherry Creek Falls and on the Elwell Valley Railroad.

State Parks and Recreation

The agency would be instructed to keep doing (pretty much, if not entirely) what it has been, only more so. Specifically, it would be charged with the development of three super-parks.

The existing *Wallace Falls State Park* would be expanded to the east to May Creek, annexing DNR lands in this area, bordering the (to be) Ragged Ridge Wilderness in Mt. Baker-Snoqualmie National Forest.

Bushtit nest

The existing *Olallie State Park* would be developed for picnicking and nature walks on both sides of the Snoqualmie River, and would be made the focus for trail corridors to Cedar Butte, Mt. Washington, the Snoqualmie Pass Wagon Road, West Defiance, Dirty Harry's Balcony, and, from the latter, eastward through DNR lands to Mason Lake, Bandera Mountain, and the Alpine Lakes Wilderness.

The existing DNR-managed *Mt. Si Conservation Area* would be transferred to State Parks, doubled in size to encompass the entirety of the mountain from the Moon Gorge to the summit ridge, and the trail system perfected, including a high route along the ridge to Teneriffe, Green, Bessemer, and into the Alpine Lakes Wilderness.

Mt. Baker-Snoqualmie National Forest

The manager of the (to be) Ragged Ridge Wilderness and the existing Alpine Lakes Wilderness would coordinate these preserves with neighboring state and county agencies. Particularly it would do more (which is to say, do something) about recreation in the Alpine Lakes Management Area which adjoins the Wilderness. In the Mt. Index area, Persis should have a summit trail, Anderson Cirque a convenient access, and Lake Serene either a decent trail or a stout fence. In the Middle Fork Snoqualmie, a bridge should be built to the Pratt River trail and a route marked up Granite Creek to the Mt. Defiance trail.

FREEDOM OF/FROM THE WHEELS

In the companion to these *Footsore* volumes, the *100 Hikes* series, Ira Spring describes the revolutionary manner in which the U.S. Forest Service is transforming age-old hiker-horse trails to motorcycle roads, giving the tiny minority of noisemaker recreationists a grossly disproportionate share of the public domain.

It may well be said that if fragile ecosystems of the highlands are the wrong place for destructive wheels, tougher lands of the mountain front are the right place, and that's true enough, as far as it goes. It is not the intent here to argue against the ATV and ORV on principle but to declare that they do not, on principle, deserve to inherit the entire near-city earth.

There is no shortage of wheel recreation on the mountain front. Weyerhaeuser, alone, has 2500 miles of roads on its Cascade Tree Farm. Other timber companies, the state DNR, and the National Forests, have thousands of more miles, over and above the roads on the federal, state, and county highway systems.

By contrast, in this entire volume there are barely 100 miles of "trails," and most of these are reclaimed from railroads or trucks, less than a quarter are "trail trails," and of that total, perhaps half are legally or practically wheelfree. The term "footroad" recurs because that is about the only opportunity for exercise the foot gets, other than stomping the gas pedal.

No disparagement is intended of footroads, bless them. Where the agencies of man or nature have halted wheels, we walk quietly and happily, because just as wheels make a trail a road, their absence makes a road a trail. Where there is a good, solid gate policy, as on Weyerhaeuser tree farms, we wave greetings to the occasional logging truck driver or patrolman, content that their machines are the only ones we will meet when the gates are closed. In winter and spring, when snowpatches on the mountain front stop wheels but not feet, we ascend into peace where the snowmelt is roaring and the flowers blooming and the living is easy.

(Sad to say, the sport of snowline-probing extolled in the first edition of this book has next to disappeared, because in the past decade the 4x4 has become America's family car, and to share the fun of the TV commercials the fun trucks, jeeps, and Blazers-Broncos splash through creeks and surf, gouge meadows and squash clams — and especially frolic in the snow. Those who have learned that anything worn on the feet other than boots and socks is costly, complex, and treacherous, and who no longer can tolerate human seas on highways and slopes, tire chains, and yodeling records on the loudspeaker, yet still yearn to walk in clouds of floating flakes amid trees decorated for Christmas cards, through a fluff tracked by a zoo of critters whose presence is never suspected in other seasons, and to teach the kids to throw snowballs and make angels — well, those folks are pretty much out of luck nowadays.)

The surveyor contends it is not un-American (or should one better say, un-Japanese?) to restrict the freedom of the wheels, to give some freedom from the wheels. Among the best hikes in this book are those on roads reclaimed by nature, such as Dirty Harry's Logging Road, the West Fork Miller River road, the Taylor River road, and the like.

In the course of the hike descriptions here, a number of existing fair-to-excellent chances to escape machines are noted; a number of other routes are recommended for protection. In some areas, the Weyerhaeuser gate policy is suggested as the pattern for emulation — especially by the DNR. In others, the Forest Service is encouraged to boulder-block roads to four-wheelers, as it has the Mineral City and Taylor River roads, but to go further and post them against two-wheelers and that wart on 20th-century technology, the three-wheeler. Every agency should stop and ponder: "Is it really written into the Constitution, as the ATV lobby says, that thou shalt not impede thy neighbor's wheels? Or is it in the Bible?"

GEOLOGICAL FUN ON THE MOUNTAIN FRONT

Hiking the mountain front is more interesting if a person knows a few things about the Pleistocene that shaped so much of the surface. Several or more times, most recently a dozen eons ago, a wall of ice came rumbling and grinding down from Canada, at the maximum advances reaching the vicinity of Tenino and pushing far up Cascade and Olympic valleys. (This continental glaciation was separate from the local alpine glaciation, whose work is evident within the mountain front, as in the cirques of Greider Lakes, Lake Serene, Loch Katrine, the troughs of the Middle Fork Snoqualmie and Lake Dorothy, Anderson Cirque, and the like.)

The Canadian glacier, thousands of feet thick, rode over the summits of the Tomtit Alps, Blue Mountain, Fuller Mountain, and Little Si, and high on the sides of Stickney and Sultan and Big Si. On the upstream side of prominences it ground the rocks to smooth slabs; on the downstream side, it plucked the rocks to cliffs, chunks of which later came tumbling down. All along the mountain front are funny little peaklets and clifflets.

Debris carried south on the glacier's back was dumped at the ice front, and where the front was stable for long periods, built huge moraines. One stretches unbroken (except for later stream erosion) from Teneriffe across the Middle Fork Snoqualmie and South Fork Snoqualmie and the one-time valley connecting to the Cedar River, all the way to Rattlesnake Mountain. Another crosses the Skykomish valley from Ragged Ridge to Persis and Sultan.

The moraines dammed lakes which ultimately were partly or entirely filled with sediments from the glacier meltwater and the mountain rivers. Remnants of old lakebeds survive in the Middle and North Forks of the Snoqualmie, Cedar River, the Proctor Trough, Deer Creek Flat, and elsewhere. Some of the lakes remain — Hancock and Calligan.

With the Puget Trough full of ice from the Olympics to the Cascades and north to Canada, meltwater from the ice front and mountain rivers had nowhere to go but south, ultimately reaching the ocean via the modern course of the Hoquiam River. At one time or another rivers flowed in many different channels between Seattle and the mountain front: the "Big Valley" that extends unbroken from Lake Washington to the Nisqually River; the "Marckworth Valley" north of the Tolt River, now used by Stossel, Cherry, Youngs, and Elwell Creeks. Everywhere are "under-sized" streams, little dribbles that obviously didn't dig their "over-sized" valleys.

Erosion by ice and water over several glacier advances-retreats isolated "island mountains," cut off from neighbors by troughs through which the Canadian glacier flowed, and then the "Big River," sum of all the rivers issuing from the Cascades, united in a single torrent larger than the Columbia. Pilchuck and Sultan are notable examples. Rattlesnake is twice islanded, on east and west — as, in fact, are all peaks of the Issaquah Alps — Tiger, Taylor, Grand, Squak, and Cougar.

Now, wasn't *that* fun?

Hark! What is that rumbling, grinding noise in the north?

Harvey Manning
Cougar Mountain

Safety Considerations

Safety is an important concern in all outdoor activities. No guidebook can alert you to every hazard or anticipate the limitations of every reader, so the descriptions in this book are not representations that a particular trip is safe for your party. When you take a trip, you assume responsibility for your own safety. Some of the trips described in this book may require you to do no more than look both ways before crossing the street; on others, more attention to safety may be required due to terrain, traffic, weather, the capabilities of your party, or other factors. Keeping informed on current conditions and exercising common sense are the keys to a safe, enjoyable outing.

The Mountaineers

Harris Creek in the Stillwater Wildlife Recreation Area

SNOQUALMIE RIVER —
FROM THE CONFLUENCE TO THREE FORKS

As the century moved into its second half the lower Snoqualmie valley seemed fated to be fenced off from the public feet by absolute privatization, and not to any special regret, what with the dismal certainty of total Tukwilazation-Issaquazation-Redmondization, whenever the speculators and developers ran out of flat ground to blacktop elsewhere.

The State Game Department struck a blow for the Greens by acquiring expanses of riverbank and floodplain, a comprehensive sampling of riparian-alluvial ecosystems from tidy cornfield to wild swamp. Though originally designated "Wildlife Recreation Areas," the thought arose that wildlife didn't recreate but *lived* there, and that a growing percentage of human visitors come not to shoot or hook but to boot and look. The new name, "Habitat Management Areas," is a significant shift away from anthrocentricity and a recognition of the equality of non-consumptive uses. Hunters and fishermen continue their sport, but in the company of birders, flowerers, and just plain and simple pedestrians.

King County entered the arena from two directions. First, it adopted a policy of snapping up rights-of-way as fast as railroads abandoned them. *Footsore 1* describes the rail trail from Issaquah to Snoqualmie Falls (and from Issaquah to Bothell to Seattle). In these pages is the trail from Cherry Valley to Snoqualmie Falls, 26 miles of cows and strawberries and corn — and farther along, of forests and plantations and clearcuts.

Then, in 1985, the county embarked on a Farmlands Preservation Program, to keep those cows and strawberries and corn on the scene, to be enjoyed walking past, or upon payment of a fee to a farmer, to be picked fresh and enjoyed on the table at home. (Obviously, this applies only to the berries and corn and peas and the like, not the cows.) By purchasing development rights, the county protects the farmer from confiscatory taxes, and from the tempting satchelsful of greenbacks carried by speculators. Thus will be preserved some 5000 acres (sadly, not all) of the broad floodplain over which the river meanders, the flat green plain embellished with cutoff sloughs, oxbow lakes and marshes, and picturesque barns and piles of manure.

Thanks mainly to these two agencies, there's an excellent lot of walking in the valley, the better for being a matter of minutes from major clots of King and Snohomish County population, and at an elevation little above sea level, open the entire year, ready to satisfy any cravings to watch water ripple and fish swim, ducks paddle and dippers dip and herons flap, to scuffle along a gravel bar and skip stones.

The chapter ends at the union of the three forks beneath the scarp of Mount Si. One explanation for this great lump of abrupt mountain is a fault in the earth's crust; another, older, is that this is what became of the Moon when it fell out of the sky. (What's up there now is a substitute.) "Sdoh-kwahl-bu" (or something like that) is how the natives pronounced it. Translated, "Moon River" is what they called the stream, all you huckleberries out there.

USGS maps: Maltby, Monroe, Carnation, Lake Joy, Fall City, Snoqualmie, North Bend

The Great Confluence (map — page 21)

Where the Snoqualmie and Skykomish Rivers end and the Snohomish River begins, a Game Department access (conservation license required) gives close looks at three very different riparian moods.

Drive Highway 522 to 2.5 miles northeast of its bridge over the Snohomish River and take the 164th Street exit. Turn right from the exit road to Tester Road

Snohomish River at the confluence of Snoqualmie and Skykomish Rivers

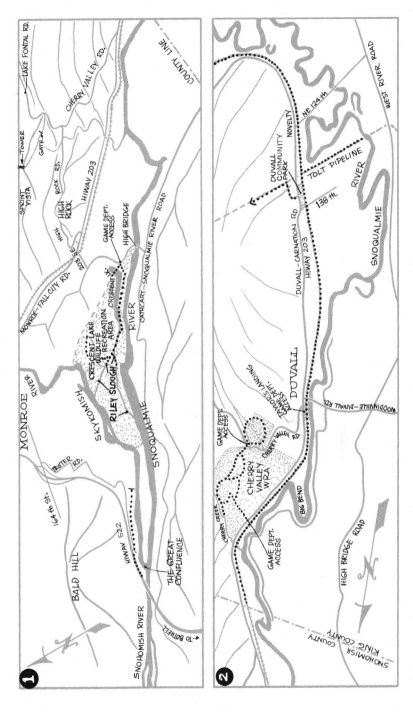

and in 2.7 miles, just short of the highway bridge, park. Elevation, 30 feet.

The barricaded road proceeds downstream under the bridge to a sand bank suitable on hot days for wading, and on any day for contemplating the three rivers. The Snoqualmie is the wild one, bounded on one side by a jungle cliff impenetrable to man, on the other by a floodway swamp probably infested with crocodiles; the gin bottles floating in the stream doubtless are from the *African Queen.* The Skykomish, airy-open between gravel bars, bounces and rattles along with highland energy. At the tip of an island the waters mingle, to flow together to the saltchuck as the Snohomish, a quiet green avenue that cries out for a drifting trip between the farms and the cows and the barns, amid birds flying and swimming. A raft or a vessel of some sort is the only non-automotive means of enjoying the Snohomish valley, which is very lovely but has no trails, nor scarcely a dike that is not a tangle of brambles. Only the water road is freely open and peaceful.

For a more substantial stroll, turn upstream on the path along the Sky-komish. A trench cut through a hellberry hedge leads to ⅓ mile of riverside pasture. Were an easement obtained and a footbridge built over a little creek, the walking could continue on gravel bars another ½ mile.

Round trips 1 mile, allow 1 hour
High point 30 feet, no elevation gain
All year

Lord's Hill Regional Park (map — page 22)

Two valleys connect Monroe and Snohomish. In one, a narrow slot, the Snoqualmie and Skykomish Rivers join to form the Snohomish River. The other, a wide floodplain, has no river at all anymore, which hardly seems fair. Between them a curious little highland rises to an astonishing apex of 737 feet, prominent from miles away, the highest point so far west. A further uniqueness

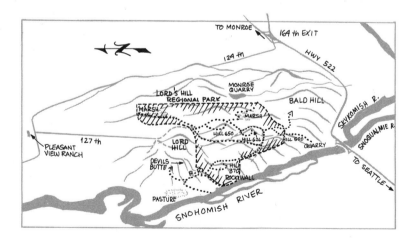

Snohomish River from Lord Hill

in the local area, it is not glacial drift but has a heart of volcanic rock. Dissected into steep little peaks and deep little vales, little rock walls growing gardens of moss and flowers, ponds and marshes and swamps in little bowls, it is altogether enchanting to wildland travelers on two feet or four, or two wings. The beaver continue their engineering, bear harvest the berries, coyote crop the rabbits, deer browse the brush. The great blue heron roosts and may nest, as may (now or in future) bald eagle and osprey and other raptors. Ducks quack and swim, owls hoot and nest, frogs and redwing blackbirds racket. — And all this and more wildlife, and all the wildland paths, are within minutes of Everett and satellite cities and the proliferating subdivisions of south Snohomish and north King Counties.

In 1985 a portion of the area came together as Lord's Hill (Snohomish County) Regional Park, composed of 200 donated acres (the "Seaholt Property") and 160 acres of county trust land (that is, originally and still basically county-owned) "reconveyed" to the county for park purposes by the state Department of Natural Resources. Another 840 acres of county land remain with the DNR and according to existing plans will be logged. They shouldn't be. The timber resource is insignificant compared to the park value. With acquisition of certain other properties, such as a pair of controversial ("KA-BOOM!") quarries, a park of nearly 2000 acres could be established. The surveyor suggests the DNR hold off logging a few years — that will be long enough for the public to rise up and demand the full 2000-acre park.

Meanwhile, Snohomish County Parks is preparing a plan for the 360 acres it has in hand. Watch for announcement of the official opening — in 1987? (If in

23

doubt, call the parks department at 337-2550.) In 1981 and 1985 the surveyor toured the area, where quiet walkers presently are tolerated on rainy weekdays, if not sunny Sundays.

Go off Highway 522 west of Monroe on the exit signed "164th." Drive 124th Street SE northwesterly along the base of the highland 3.6 miles and turn south on 127th (Lord Hill Road). At a Y in 1.8 miles the right fork goes to Turning Point and a microwave relay tower; the left fork is gated, "Private Property." Here, or near, public access will be obtained. The surveyor parked here, elevation 480 feet, and walked the left fork ¾ mile through splendid mixed forest of big old fir, cedar, and maple between Hill 690 and Wetland No. 7 (*Attention DNR:* Do not log. This belongs in the park.) to a Y, 500 feet, at the edge of the "Central Clearing" (a 1980 clearcut). By plan, all motorized vehicles will park here, only feet will proceed. The surveyor did a loop in 1985, with sidetrips then and in 1981, as follows:

Walk the left fork several hundred feet up to a multiple junction on a flat, 600 feet. *Sidetrips:* (1) Take a sharp left, down, ½ mile on the grassy swath of the natural gas pipeline, to the outlet of Wetland No. 7, dammed of old by beaver — which returned in 1985 and commenced logging the alder grown up since they went away. The plan proposes a viewing blind here. (2) Ascend slabs of ice-polished-and-scratched andesite a short bit to Hill 625, to views of the park interior and the countryside around. (3) Go straight ahead on the flat, then down (the way blocked by hellberry thorns in 1985), on a planned major trail to Temple Pond No. 1, which is to be the focal point of the park, with several viewing blinds. From the 600-foot flat the trail will go some ¾ mile to the south end of the large beaver pond.

Resuming the loop, go right on the flat along the side of Hill 650. *Sidetrips:* (1) Take the path right to the summit, the central "territorial" viewpoint. Look south over green pastures of the Snohomish to Tiger and Squak, southeasterly to Sprint Vista in the High Rock Hills and Sultana and Phelps on the Cascade front, easterly up the Skykomish River to Baring, and northerly to Pilchuck, Cultus, and Baker. (2) A bit farther along, ascend right on game traces to Hill 626, another fine viewpoint on a mossy bald above andesite cliffs, a garden of Easter lily and other excellent flowers.

Returned from sidetrips, at ½ mile from the 600-foot flat reach the bottom of a descent at 350 feet in a wetland valley. *Sidetrips:* (1) Proceed straight ahead up Hill 500 and find paths off left into woods to the summit of Bald Hill, 737 feet, the highland's apex; this is in the domain of the Monroe Quarry ("WHAM!"). (2) Continue down the gas line toward another quarry ("BLAM!") beside the Snohomish River.

From the vale bottom, take the right a few minutes to a Y, 356 feet. *Sidetrip, the best part of the whole affair:* Take the left, down the valley and through a notch, then up left, curling around and to the top of Hill 370, which is almost that many feet directly above the Snohomish River and offers the day's most delightful views of water and pastures. This is ¾ mile from the 356-foot Y. Retreat to the notch and descend a road ¼ mile to the river level, opening explorations of a mile of wild sloughs and swamps and a remarkable rock wall that leaps 100 vertical feet from the water. Though now out of the park-as-is, you're in the park-that-must-become.

From the notch descend the logging spur a short bit and just above it in the forest, spot the deadend of an ancient logging railroad. Follow it a wonderful ½ mile in DNR wildwoods. Where it goes through a saddle take a sidetrip left on the rocky ridge that ends in the above-mentioned rock wall. When the rail grade, having been interrupted by several missing trestles, abruptly vanishes at still another gully (a mystery—where did it go?), take a game trail to a cattail pond, a pasture, and out to the river. Climb other game trails to the heights of Devils Butte. On the survey day in March of 1981 the trillium and slender toothwort were in bloom and the creek was tumbling down rock ledges.

To complete the loop, from the 356-foot Y ascend ¾ mile back to the planned parking area.

Loop trip from planned parking area 2 miles, total sidetrips 9 miles, allow 8 hours
High point 737 feet, elevation gain 2200 feet
All year

Sprint Vista (map — page 21)

For generations the short trail to the ice-scraped bald of High Rock was a favorite of hikers from two counties. Thousands upon thousands of picnic lunches and suppers were eaten here, gazing down upon the floodplains of three rivers. But government failed to acquire the de facto park and private

Snoqualmie Valley from Sprint Vista (telephoto)

fences excluded public feet. Now, however, loggers have scraped the adjacent ridges bald and provided a replacement whose panoramas are even more extensive.

Drive 3 miles north of Duvall on Highway 203 and turn right on Cherry Valley Road, which in 1 mile meets High Rock Road, their united way proceeding east as Lake Fontal Road. At .9 mile from the junction turn left on a sideroad obscurely signed "HR 106 and SNO KING 8.1." In .3 mile the road crosses a powerline swath to a gate, often locked. Park here, elevation 1000 feet.

Ascend moderately through pleasant forest (1985, but probably not 1987) into a clearcut of 1980 or so. Nearly a mile from the gate is a Y. The right circles around the clearcut and descends into (temporary) forest toward Barr Creek. Take the left a short way to an always-locked gate, 1300 feet. The road continues a bit to the base of a tower, 1320 feet, from whose top, 250 feet above, SPRINT microwaves relay telephone calls from Tacoma to Bellingham.

The promontory by the gate, atop the first abrupt rise from Tualco Valley, is smashing. Look straight down to the summit of High Rock, cows, inmates of the state reformatory, three rivers, and the town of Monroe. Look north to Pilchuck, Baker, Cultus, and the San Juan Islands. Look west to Paine Field, the Everett waterfront, Whidbey and Camano Islands, and the Olympics. Look southerly to Mt. Selig in downtown Seattle and saltwaterways to Bremerton.

Round trip from powerline gate 2 miles, allow 1½ hours
High point 1300 feet, elevation gain 300 feet
All year

Snoqualmie River Trail (map — pages 21 & 32)

From near-tidewater dairy farms to near-mountain tree farms, this is the quintessential long walking route through a lowland Puget Sound valley. Bring a pad and sketch the barns and cows, or binoculars and watch the ducks paddling and herons fishing. See the water flow and the corn grow, the trees rising taller year by year and falling down in the roar of the chainsaw.

— And listen for the ghostly whistles of the vanished steam trains. That the trail exists is due to the alertness of King County Parks in snapping up an abandoned stretch of the Chicago-Milwaukee-St. Paul and Pacific Railroad before adjoining property owners could buy it and fence off the public. As of 1986 the trail is technically "closed" — but not actually; most of the way is regularly plodded by people and cows and coyotes. (The "Closed" signs were put up purely to discourage motorcycles in the interim before formal "opening" of the trail.) Here and there the hellberries force a detour, or farmers have illegally strung fences, or one of the 33 trestles needs to be planked and guardrailed for the benefit of acrophobes. However, by 1990 or so the route will be open all the way for feet, bicycles, and horses, a link in the Sound-to-Mountains Trail (see *Footsore 1*).

Eventually, too, it may become part of the John Wayne Pioneer Trail. In 1982 the state acquired the Milwaukee right-of-way from Easton east; if it will now obtain the line from Snoqualmie Falls to Easton, the wagons can roll from Duvall to Idaho and onward to Independence, Missouri.

Though long-distance backpackers can include the trail in any number of ingenious journeys, the average walker will do it in pieces on afternoon strolls or all-day tramps, using the many convenient accesses from Highway 203, the Monroe-Fall City Road, and Highway 202, the Fall City-Snoqualmie Road.

King County line to Duvall, 3½ miles

Skip it. Snohomish County failed to acquire the 6 miles north to Monroe and the county line totally lacks mystique. South to Duvall the grade is exactly beside the highway, enjoyed only by joggers. Walkers will find better sport in the Cherry Valley Unit of the Snoqualmie Habitat Management Area.

Duvall to Duvall Community Park, 1½ miles

Maybe do it. If so, start from the south, at Duvall Community Park, off Highway 203 on NE 137th. The way is well-removed from the highway, flood-plain pastures on both sides. Watch for muskrats in murky swamps, blackbirds in the cattails, and redtail hawks patroling the skies on the lookout for stray chickens. Stroll across the fields to the river.

When Duvall gets serious about tourism, the village will clean up the trash and exploit its memories — as at Taylor's Landing, a Game Department access on the north edge of town. Already it has the Duvall Train Depot, preserved as a community meeting place, and the Country Living Deli, famous among loggers and farmers for breakfast and lunch.

Duvall Community Park to Stillwater, 4½ miles

Definitely do it — the south piece, anyhow.

North piece. The 1 mile south from Duvall Park to 124th (Novelty Hill Road) is a good jog, quietly removed from the highway, with broad cross-valley views. A bit south of the park the Tolt Pipeline offers a splendid 1-mile sidetrip to the river. (As described elsewhere in these pages, the pipeline can be walked east to the Tolt River Watershed. As described in *Footsore 1,* a detour via 124th connects to the Tolt Pipeline Trail which connects to the Sammamish River Trail and the Burke-Gilman Trail.) The ½ mile south of 124th is less rewarding and leads to a trail-blocking tangle of hellberries (1986).

South piece. The Stillwater Unit of the Snoqualmie Habitat Management Area (conservation license required) has two accesses. The ¾ mile between the two, located just north of Stillwater Store and at Fay Road, is mainly of interest as a path to cornfields and swamps where the birds live.

The 1 mile beyond Fay Road is arguably the best part of the whole trail. The grade diverges far from highway noise to green peace, bounded for nearly ¼ mile by cattail marsh. It then emerges in pastures and at the site of the railroad station named "Stuart" touches wild river — not channelized, not diked. Do the rotten palisades on the banks date from an erosion-control scheme? Or was there a steamer landing? Views extend up and down the meanders and over pastures to far mountains. Particularly eye-catching are the pink-and-white buildings beyond the green plain — the Carnation Farms. The grade leaves fields and river to enter an enormous grove of huge cottonwoods that produce millions of morels, all eaten by the cows. The miracle mile ends at a slough crossed by a trestle with 12 16-foot spans, some of their crucial timbers missing (1986).

Stillwater to Griffin Creek Road, 5 miles

The 1¼ miles from Stillwater Store (one of the oldest surviving country stores in King County, so stop in and buy something) are quiet because the rail

Tokul Creek bridge

line strikes straight off across the valley floor while the highway hugs the valley wall. Much of the route is used as a farm road; walk slowly to see the strawberries ripening.

The trail then crosses the highway for a 3-mile due-south straightaway through residential neighborhoods of Carnation. The Tolt River bridge is the notable feature of this stretch, which is mainly traveled by local folks.

Griffin Creek Road to Spring Glen Road, 5 miles

Griffin Creek Road, signed "NE 11 Street," crosses the trail ¼ mile from the highway. This is the last public road touching the route for 5 miles and thus is the start of a good, long, lonesome walk. This also is where the grade leaves, the cow-farm valley flats to ascend the tree-farm valley wall. Beyond the Griffin Creek trestle, a handsome structure of 25 16-foot spans, the trail curves into waterfall gulches, out to wide-view promontories. There still is an occasional nearby pasture, here on the hillside rather than the floodplain, and private driveways are proliferating as the suburbs of Puget Sound City advance toward the Cascade Crest, but the mood is mainly forest — mixed forest of big old conifers and maples, monoculture plantations of Douglas fir, and brand new clearcuts. One trestle — a 12-spanner — will be too airy for some customers until planked, but deer don't like it either and have tramped an easy detour around the gulch.

At 3½ miles is the site of Fall City Siding, 293 feet, readily accessible from the car for a shorter hike. Turn off Highway 203 on SE 39th and follow the bank of Rutherford Slough a scant ½ mile to a gate, 120 feet. Park and walk the logging road ¾ mile, up a switchback, to the trail. (Rutherford Slough, a perfect mile-long oxbow, excites the bird-haunted imagination with thoughts of subtle trails to secret viewing blinds, but no such were found by the surveyor, who got his best looks sitting by the road with binoculars.)

Fall City is located at the turn of the river from a westerly to a northerly flow and the view from the siding is over both segments of the valley, the mosaics of man's plane-table right-anglings and nature's hydraulic meanderings and twirlings, the clusters of houses and the ribbons of roads, summits of the Issaquah Alps towering in the background.

Beyond the siding ½ mile is the old Fall City Waterworks, tapping a fine big creek sliced deep in glacial drift. In another scant ½ mile is an 18-span trestle that is slowly toppling and will be demolished, replaced by a trail down to the creek and up again. Scramble paths permit the detour now. Views from the west end of the trestle are among the best of the route: down to Snoqualmie River and Raging River, Fall City, golf course, and highway; across to Lake Alice plateau and Mitchell Hill; and beyond to Rattlesnake and Tiger Mountains. From the trestle a scant ¼ mile reaches the Spring Glen Road.

Spring Glen Road to Snoqualmie Falls Mill, 4½ miles

From Highway 202 the Spring Glen Road, 356th SE, ascends .2 mile to the trail, and the best start for hikes in either direction.

The task of the railroad easterly from here was to climb from the lower Snoqualmie valley to the upper, and with a less abrupt gradient than that of Snoqualmie Falls, whose brink is at an elevation of 400 feet and plunge basin at 120. Cow farms and suburbia are left behind and the way now is mostly in young plantations (that is, clearcuts) with fine views. Note an ancient, narrow track beside the grade — is it a relic of a wagon road from Fall City to Snoqualmie?

At 1½ miles commences the most dramatic portion of the entire trail — the

Tokul Creek canyon. It would've been even more exciting had Europeans arrived a century or two later, because by then Tokul Creek, which used to drain the overflow of Snoqualmie floodwaters, would have captured the entire river. A raw ravine would have been dug in alluvium of the North Bend plain, a Pleistocene lakebed, and a corresponding train of gravel and braided channels deposited downstream of Snoqualmie Falls, which would have been left high and dry, except for seeps and drips, as they are now when Puget Power turns them off.

Views are excellent from the promontory where the grade begins its mile-long swing into the canyon; the 1980s clearcut of the canyon is a stark foreground for Mt. Si and Tiger Mountain. The trestle, too, is impressive — it's perfectly safe but until planks are installed will be too giddy for many people and just about every dog. No reasonable detour is available because the timbers are footed on either side of a slot cut a hundred feet deep in hard rock.

From the trestle the grade swings ⅔ mile out of the canyon, and in another ⅓ mile reaches Tokul Siding, 500 feet. To drive here, go off north from Highway 202, at the east edge of the Snoqualmie Falls area, on Tokul Road SE. Bear left at a Y and in ½ mile, just short of the railroad overpass, park on the shoulder.

The rail line continues 1 mile to Weyerhaeuser's Snoqualmie Falls Mill. The John Wayne Pioneer Trail and the Sound-to-Mountains Trail might follow this former Milwaukee route to North Bend and points east. Alternatively, they could turn south on Tokul Road to Snoqualmie Falls and there join the old Gilman (later, Northern Pacific) Railroad to North Bend.

One way from King County line to Snoqualmie Falls Mill 26 miles
High point 500 feet, elevation gain 450 feet
All year
Bus: Metro 210 to Snoqualmie Falls

Snoqualmie Habitat Management (Wildlife Recreation) Area (map — pages 21 & 32)

The State Game Department has purchased easements on 9 miles of the Snoqualmie River, providing many spots (some but not all identified by such signs as "Public Fishing") to toss a worm to a fish or train glasses on birds. However, until fisherfolk do their immemorial duty of punching paths through the brush, there'll be darn little water-side exercise. Until many bodies and machetes thrust through the greenery, with few exceptions the best bet for intimacy with the river will be to float.

The Snoqualmie Habitat Management Area has three large units with excellent walking in varied and complementary habitats: riverbank, floodway, and floodplain; wildland swamps and sloughs, working farms, and hillside forests. Note: Visitors who do not have a hunting or fishing license must have a conservation license.

Two Rivers

To a pedestrian the name is a fraud, because only by boat can the Snoqualmie be properly enjoyed in this jungle-banked stretch, and the

Misty morning, Stillwater Wildlife Recreation Area

Skykomish can't be reasonably gotten to at all. Forget the rivers, therefore, and wander in wonder through a floodway forest of the sort that once covered hundreds of square miles of Puget Sound lowlands but now is something of a rarity.

From Highway 203 drive west .4 mile on 203rd SE and turn left .6 mile on Crescent Lake Road to the Game Department parking area, elevation 32 feet.

A short path starts behind the privies, follows Crescent Lake easterly a bit, and crosses this excellent slough on a delightful plank bridge through lily pads and blackbirds and ducks.

For the forest, walk north on a (sometimes) gated farm road, a field on the left, Crescent Lake on the right. In ½ mile the road, field, and lake end at a footbridge over the lake outlet. Big cedars and Sitka spruce are scattered about, cottonwoods are numerous and superb, but the noblest tree of all is the bigleaf maple — by the multitudes, huge and tall, boughs arching and intertwining high in the sky, dripping licorice fern. The maze of paths doesn't really go anyplace, except to a forgettable pasture, but fishermen's sidepaths lead to Riley Slough, which cries out for a raft to drift — to where? The map shows it flowing into both the Snoqualmie and the Skykomish. In any event, it definitely discourages ambitions about walking to the Great Confluence.

Round trips 2 miles, allow 2 hours
High point 32 feet, no elevation gain
All year

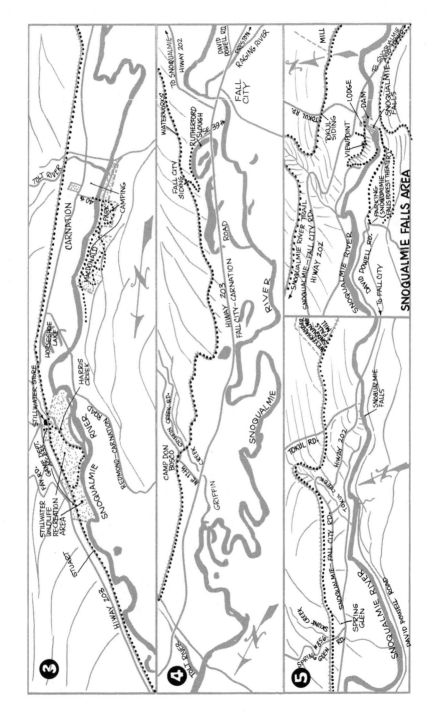

Cherry Valley

A green bay of floodplain curves deep into the High Rock Hills, the fields parklike and kempt, the views broad and the sky big. Enchanting. Liberating.

The walking can begin from the two Game Department accesses beside Highway 203; another access is 1.2 miles from the highway on Cherry Valley Road, at the north edge of Duvall.

From the latter, elevation 40 feet, a 1-mile loop trail ascends hillside forest and traverses in and out of trickle-creek gulches.

From any of the accesses, closed-to-vehicle roads and hunters' paths lead this way and that, up and down and across the valley. A skunk-cabbage swamp features willows and big old spruce. Drainage ditches are thoroughfares for flitting and swimming birds — beware of great blue herons lifting off underfoot with harsh croaks and gangly flappings, very alarming. Footbridges cross the ditches at convenient intervals. Wander the emerald vastness of the 386 acres in any direction, but eventually attain the north side of the valley, where Cherry Creek flows between a dike and the valley wall. Stroll the dike, on the watch for birds in the willow-tangle arching halfway over the creek. Look up to a surprising cliff — and to an amazing white column of water in the trees — McCauley Falls. (The access is via private roads.)

Round trips 3 miles, allow 3 hours
High point 200 feet, elevation gain 160 feet
All year

Stillwater

The public generally isn't allowed to snoop around a farm because people bother the animals, or feet bother the crops, or strangers bother the farmer. But on the 450-acre Stillwater Unit the crops are secondary to recreation — indeed, those fields of corn are designed to lure fowl into shotgun range. When such sport is in season the pacifist ought to stay away. Most of the year, though, the quiet of the floodplain is broken only by whatever racket the birds are making.

Drive Highway 203 to the Stillwater Store. A bit to the north is a Game Department parking area complete with privies. North .5 mile, opposite Fay Road, is a second such. Elevation, 60 feet.

What's to be done in a tract ¾ of a square mile in area, with 2 miles of riverbank, a slough, two creeks, two ponds, cattail marshes, grasslands, brush, and farmland? Prowl around watching for birds and beasts; to further quote the Game Department brochure, there are pheasant, duck, rabbit, snipe, mink, goldfinch, deer, and bear. Absorb the essence of the broad valley between forested highlands, look long and far to Si on the Cascade scarp.

For an introductory walk, start at the southern parking area and go north ¼ mile on the Snoqualmie River Trail to a farm road leading out in the fields. Follow the lane as it climbs onto an old, mostly overgrown dike, drops off it, and after much wandering ends in 1 long mile at a tanglewood guarding a murky slough — Harris Creek. A slippery plank footbridge crosses the creek, a path winds through woods to a gravel bar on the Snoqualmie River. Wild! Remote!

Introductory round trip 2 miles, allow 2 hours
High point 60 feet, no elevation gain
All year

Footbridge over Snoqualmie River at MacDonald Park

MacDonald Memorial (Tolt River) Park
(map — page 32)

The size of this King County park, a "mere" 220 acres, belies the richness and variety of wildwoods and wild-river experiences on its miles (unbelievably many) of trails.

From the south edge of Carnation on Highway 203, drive west .3 mile on NE 40th Street to the parking lot, elevation 60 feet.

Pleasant car-camping sites are carved in the forest. Picnic tables are scattered about wide green fields under the big sky, inviting a romp in the sun to banks of the Snoqualmie River, and downstream to banks of the Tolt River. (The confluence is the site of a village inhabited for — probably — many centuries. The Tolt Historical Society proposes to change the name of the park to make it a memorial to the residents of that village.)

The crossing to the wild side of the Snoqualmie, the largest segment of the park, is alone worth the visit. The 500-foot swinging bridge (no jumping up and down, please, and troops please break step) was built as a Bicentennial project in 1976 by the 409th Engineering Company, Army Reserve, and leads to the hike-in campsites and the trail system. No precise recipe is required for the 10 miles (a guess) of built and just-happened paths. The following perimeter loop (with sidetrips) is a good introduction.

Cross the bridge, pausing to look upstream to Tiger Mountain and downstream to Three Fingers Mountain. On the far side turn right, downstream, on the trail signed "River Road." Taking time out for excursions to the riverbank, where ducks dabble and fish jump and gulls fly, proceed through pristine floodway forest of cottonwoods which are not terribly large, meaning the area was flooded to bare gravel in not too distant a past. The way enters a field and passes North Field Shelter, a large leanto where in event of downpour the patrols can gather from tent sites tucked away in the woods all around.

In 1 mile is a Y, the left fork signed Cottonwood Loop. Before doing that, take the right fork to big gravel bars, the end of the old road, and a path that skirts a deep-woods slough to a wide dike with broad views over river and valley.

The Cottonwood Loop turns toward the valley wall, switchbacks up onto it, and turns upvalley, contouring at just enough distance above the floor to give the sensation of walking through treetops, looking down on the birds. The Lookout Trail diverges steeply right, climbing to a ridge point at some 450 feet, with views to river, pastures, and the Cascades from Three Fingers to Sultan to Index to Si. Traversing over ribs and ravines, it climbs to still better views, then drops back to the Cottonwood Loop. Another trail, signed Railroad Grade (from the days of "lokie" logging), joins in from the sloughs and mixed forest below, and the way drops to fields of Orchard Camp, on the slopes above the swinging bridge.

Perimeter loop and sidetrips 4 miles, allow 3 hours
High point 450 feet, elevation gain 700 feet
All year

Griffin Marsh (map — page 35)

Don't expect to see "a mythical animal with the body and hind legs of a lion, and the head and wings of an eagle." (If you do, report it immediately to the Audubon office.) However, you will view a candidate for the title of largest beaver-dammed marsh in King County, maybe the state — definitely a world-class marsh. Another appeal of the route is the close-to-highway low elevation, open to walking when higher lands are clogged up with white pollution. Under the new Weyerhaeuser policy, the gate on Griffin Creek road is permanently locked, excluding all wheel traffic except logging trucks on business and weekender motorcycles which generally make a quick razz through and then head for Carnation to attend the riot.

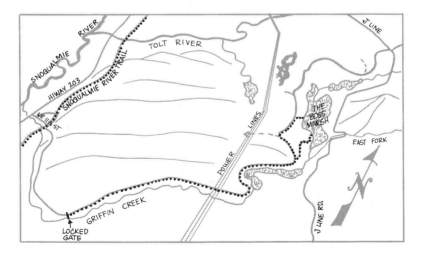

Great Griffin Marsh

Drive Highway 203 to 2 miles south of Carnation and turn east on NE 11th Street. Bear right at a Y and continue 1.5 miles to the gate, just past the end of settlement. Should the gate be open — for the benefit of loggers — and you drive in, it may be locked behind you, without notice, so park here, elevation 300 feet.

The old logging railroad grade converted to truck road is a cozy lane through tall second-growth, for the first 2 miles often so near the creek the banks are handy for rest stops, lying in wait for a dipper or, in salmon-spawning season, a kingfisher, great blue heron, bald eagle, raccoon, weasel, coyote, or cougar. Then the first stretch of marsh appears, and for the next 4 miles that's what the creek *is*.

At 600 feet, 3½ long miles from the gate, the truck road veers left. Go straight ahead right on the old rail grade. The first stretch was the scene of a 1985 crime as heinous as the burning of the Alexandria Library — a Weyerhaeuser customer placed a big order for cottonwood logs and the company, here and throughout the Great Big Western Tree Farm, did in trees that formerly produced millions upon millions of early morels. The cottonwood stumps end as the forest becomes a dense, dank, mossy melange of maples 3 feet at the butt and cedar stumps of 12 feet. So untouched has the grade been since the lokies left that it is still corrugated from removal of the ties. When the grade ends a rude path continues to the brink and skids down to the marsh, 500 feet, reached at ¾ mile from the road. Find a good sitting spot on the sidehill and get out the salami sandwiches and the binoculars.

This is the trip, though 1 more mile up the road a ¼-mile path also leads to the Boss Marsh.

The central and major segment of the marsh reached by these two paths is 1 mile long and up to ⅓ mile wide. Precious little exploring is feasible; even with a boat most of the vast expanse would be impenetrable. But what a spot to sit and contemplate. Secure from invasion by wheels, watch birds, listen to water trickling over a nearby beaver dam — one of the system that created this marsh. Granted that the Pleistocene glaciers left an ill-drained lake-prone landscape, the hiker cannot but be awed by the work done throughout this area by the industrious animals. Everywhere are dams, marshes. But this is the Boss. What satisfaction the vista here must give the ghosts of the centuries of commanding generals of the U.S. Beaver Corps of Engineers.

In this age when primeval wilderness is everywhere under attack by the boots of its lovers if not the bulldozers of its exploiters, here is a wildland that survived the railroad-logging era intact and is sure to survive the Second Wave clearcutting too, a wildland that is now as it was centuries ago and will so remain. It's got nothing for loggers and never did. It's so wild us hikers can't get in it. But the critters can. And we can sit on the shore and look. And think.

Round trip 8¾ miles, allow 6 hours
High point 600 feet, elevation gain 400 feet
All year

Lake Marie (map — page 38)

A nice little walk to a little lake that — typical of the infant post-glacier landscape hereabouts — is well along to becoming a peat bog.

Drive Highway 202 east from Fall City a long 1 mile and turn north on 356th Drive SE. At a Y in 1.5 miles go right on 364th Way SE, and then, at a hairpin turn, right again. In .5 mile, where a driveway goes right to a house, park at the turnaround circle, elevation 962 feet.

(Note: Development may soon close off this access. In that case retreat to the hairpin turn and take the left to the powerline and walk it to intersect the other route.)

Lake Marie

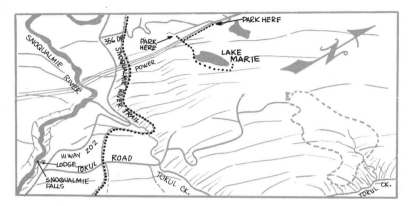

To the left is an unsigned woods road consisting, in season, of linked mudpuddles — a "mud run" churned by play wheels, fair warning that this walk must be shunned on weekends and after school lets out. Shortly it crosses a powerline swath with views to Rattlesnake, and then a creek (the lake outlet). From the end of the mucky road fishermen's paths lead to the shore. An obscure but decent trail goes right, circling the lake, with many sidepaths out on log-peninsulas to peat meadows that have a disconcerting way of bouncing underfoot as if they were floating rafts — which they are. Here and there are holes showing deep water of spooky black depth. Walk with care.

Look for birds — and listen. Sniff the Labrador tea. Come in early June to see acres and acres glowing pink with kalmia.

Round trip 1½ miles, allow 1 hour
High point 962 feet, no elevation gain
All year

Snoqualmie Falls (map — page 32)

In slicing through morainal chaos after retreat of the Puget Glacier, the Snoqualmie River didn't find its buried ancestral bed. Instead it hit a ridge of hard basalt, notched in, and got hung up. Thus, Snoqualmie Falls, as the lower river cut deep in materials easier to erode. Had not we Europeans arrived when we did, along about now Tokul Creek would have extended itself far enough headward to capture the Snoqualmie above the falls, leaving them high and dry. That will not now happen. Puget Power wouldn't stand for it.

Even on days when the falls are turned off to keep the TV sets and scalp-massagers turned on, the dank dripping gorge and solemn plunge basin are awesome. The falls can induce a mystic trance when one stares fixedly at them from any point. However, to place the phenomenon in a full four dimensions, a kinetic view is required.

Start as every tourist does. (The spectacle is said to be outranked in popularity in the state only by Rainier.) Drive Highway 202 east from Fall City 6 miles to pretty little Snoqualmie Falls Park, provided by Puget Power under terms of its FEC license as token compensation for the free use of public water.

Walk the fence-guarded path along the precipice edge to the observation platform daringly thrust into space 300 feet above the plunge basin. Then descend the nature trail, through big-tree forest and views over the lower Snoqualmie valley, to Plant No. 2 Powerhouse, built in 1910, and walk upstream to the viewing platform.

Round trip 1 mile, allow 1 hour
High point 400 feet, elevation gain 280 feet
All year
Bus: Metro 210

Now for something completely different — the wild side of the river.

From the Fall City-Preston Road just south of Fall City turn easterly on David Powell Road, signed "Forest Theater." Drive the slow and lonesome lane between cows and river 3.3 miles (a thoroughly delightful walk for those who come by Metro bus) to where the county road turns uphill right and a private road goes straight ahead. Park outside the gate on shoulders of the county road, elevation 140 feet.

(The Snoqualmie Falls Forest Theater hospitably welcomes walkers-through but can't accommodate parking except for members, guests, and the general public attending events. Return the courtesy by not taking this walk when events are in progress — unless you come to attend the event and thus combine two pleasures.)

Walk the private road ¼ mile from the gate and go off left on an old

Snoqualmie Falls

road-become-trail, marked by a cable or gate to exclude vehicles. In a few steps is a Y, the left leading to the river; go straight, right, soon crossing a small creek. In a bit more the Nature Trail turns off right; save it for the return.

The forest is a rich mixture of lichen-silvery alders, giant maples swollen with moss, and hemlocks growing 100 feet from cedar nurse-stumps, all nourished by rolling waves of spray — a "mist forest." At ¾ mile from the county road the path comes to a bank-top viewpoint which — with removal of a few bushes to open a window — would be the supreme view of the falls, cliffs, tourists atop the precipice, diners gazing out windows of the lodge restaurant, wondering how you got where you are. With such a window there would be little incentive to slither down the muddy bank and risk anklebones and headbones on the mass of slippery logs cast up by floods.

Take the hike in flood time, when the gorge is entirely filled by a drenching cloud that will mock your umbrellas and Gore-Tex. Come in dry time, when the falls are turned off and it is possible for a rational person to walk the logs and clamber the lush-mossy boulders and great hunks of fallen basalt to the tailrace discharge tunnel of Plant No. 1, built in 1898, entirely underground, an engineering feat that had Seattle newspapers gaping.

On the return go left on the (unmarked?) Nature Trail, not completed as of 1986 yet walkable with only a modest amount of mucking around. The way has been thoughtfully designed to sample flora and fauna; among its attractions are great big Sitka spruce, tangles of vine maple that appear to be sculptures in moss, giant nurse stumps from olden-day logging, a swamp that thrills the voluptuary's nose with stink currant and skunk cabbage, a beaver dam and pond. The trail ends with a short ascent into excellent conifer forest and a contour past a small outdoor theater (not the main one) to the entry road.

Round trip 2 miles, allow 3 hours
High point 300 feet, elevation gain 160 feet
All year
Bus: Metro 210, walk David Powell Road 3⅓ miles

Snoqualmie Falls to North Bend Railroad (map — page 42)

Messrs. Burke and Gilman intended for their Seattle, Lakeshore & Eastern Railroad to cross the Cascades to Walla Walla and show those scoundrels of the Northern Pacific that Seattle didn't need them. They built from Ballard to North Bend and quit, and the line eventually was bought by the Northern Pacific, which ran trains on the tracks more than half a century and quit. Part of the route now is the Burke-Gilman Trail, and part (where trains still run) is proposed as a Lake Sammamish Trail, and part is the Issaquah-Preston-Snoqualmie Falls Trail (for all these, see *Footsore 1*). — And on part, where the trains had stopped, they have resumed, under the auspices of the Puget Sound & Snoqualmie Valley Railroad — and long may its steam locomotives go "choo-choo-choo" and whistle up the past.

It is mandatory for every person to sometime take the trip from Snoqualmie to North Bend by train. The Puget Sound Railway Historical Association operates the railroad on weekends, holidays, and some ordinary days, making what ultimately will be a 10-mile round trip in a couple of hours, taking on passengers at each terminus — the 1890 Snoqualmie depot built by Burke and Gilman, and the 1886 North Bend depot, originally and until recently located on the Northern Pacific (Burlington-Northern) line at Lester.

The inveterate pedestrian will also wish to walk the route. This can be done from any number of road-handy spots, but for the full tour drive Highway 202 east from Snoqualmie Falls Lodge .5 mile and where a sideroad turns off to a Puget Power complex, park in the space by the railroad tracks, elevation 420 feet.

The rail grade goes westerly 1 scant mile, past a short missing trestle to a long intact trestle that will be rehabilitated for a posh bike trail when King County Parks gets around to it (1987?); for foot travelers, the route is already open (via a detour down in the gulch) to Issaquah (see *Footsore 1*). A short stroll to the trestle offers springtime flower gardens on rock walls and unusual perspectives on Snoqualmie Falls.

Southeast ¼ mile from the above-noted parking area the Niblock Spur goes off ⅓ mile to the Historical Association's outdoor museum, home of 10 (or is it 16?) steam locomotives, one diesel, some 100 assorted pieces of rolling stock (coach cars, cabooses, snowplows), and a dozen cranes and the like, the largest collection west of the Mississippi. (You can share in the restoration, hands-on or by cash contribution.)

Beyond the spur ¾ mile (on the way, sidetrip out on the railroad bridge over the river) is Railroad Place Park, centered on the Snoqualmie Depot, restored to Gay Nineties condition. (The volunteers who run the trains also are dressed in Gay Nineties condition.)

The competition between the twin towns for the tourist trade bodes well for

Steam engine in Puget Sound and Snoqualmie Valley Railroad yard

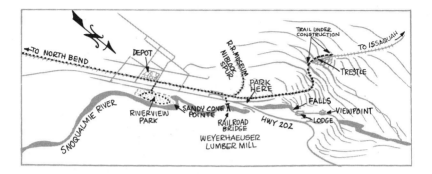

the visitor. Snoqualmie's Riverview Park, handy to the tracks, is a good place to watch ducks swim, and the site of the planned Sandy Cove Pointe (sic) is famous for the wading.

The 3 miles of grade to the end of rails at Ballarat Avenue are a quiet walk on the flat, mostly in woods, partly in broad views to Rattlesnake and Si. North Bend is plotting various ways to trap the tourist dollar. The Snoqualmie Valley Museum south of the depot in Weeks Park definitely is on track.

Complete round trip (with sidetrips) 12 miles, allow 7 hours
High point 442 feet, elevation gain 22 feet
All year
Bus: Metro 210

Three Forks State Park (map — page 44)

Though only a proposal at the moment, creation of the park is just a matter of time; even knee-jerk anti-preservationists can find nothing worth exploiting in these hundreds of acres of floodway forests and sloughs where the three forks of the Snoqualmie deviously unite. On the other hand, though a park's marked paths would enable more people to more easily enjoy the area, existing trails lead to any number of gravel bars for picnicking, sand bars for castle-building, side channels for wading, and marshes and thickets and oxbows and fields for bewilderments of birds.

Another constant attraction is a stupendous piece of real estate — the 3500-foot fault scarp of Mt. Si. A perambulation in the Three Forks area is a series of gasps and exclamations. Again and again a person has to haul out the camera for yet another portrait — close-up and faraway, full face and profile, in bright morning and afternoon shadows, framed by railroad bridge or cottonwood forest, foregrounded by pasture or river. A climber can spend hours plotting Class 5.11 routes on the Great Buttress.

Homes block some routes to the rivers. Vast expanses of tulgey wood are best left to private whifflings of the Jabberwock. Often the walker finds himself longing to be a kayaker. However, a plenty of short paths offer delight. The following sampler is presented in order upstream.

From the east end (old downtown) of Snoqualmie, drive Reinig Road over the river and .5 mile to the railroad bridge over road and river. Park on the shoulder, elevation 400 feet. Climb to the Milwaukee Railroad tracks, which nowadays deadend just north at the Weyerhaeuser mill, and cross the bridge "Built by the Pennsylvania Steel Co. Steelton Pa. 1910." Take a Si photo. The tracks parallel the river, then diverge. A path invites picnickers to belly up to a bar. A long ½ mile from the bridge a farm lane goes ¼ mile over a pasture (another Si photo) to a larger bar. The tracks can be followed 1½ more miles by Meadowbrook Slough, Mt. Si Golf Course, and a thousand birds to North Bend. However, the larger bar makes a nice turnabout. **Round trip 1½ miles.**

From the bridge drive Reinig Road 1 mile and park on the shoulder. Across the river the South Fork emerges from the largest and most tangled of Three Forks wildlands. Wish for a kayak. In the lack, walk the gravel bars that start a bit upstream from the confluence. Another Si photo. **Round trip 1 mile.**

Drive Reinig Road .5 mile from the confluence, about .3 mile short of the junction with North Fork County Road, spot a cable-barred woods road, and park. The lane goes through a grove of huge maples to a huge gravel bar and the confluence of the North and Middle Forks. Fly a kite. And yes, Si again. **Round trip ½ mile.**

From Reinig Road turn south on North Fork County Road .2 mile to the bridge over the North Fork and park. On the north side of the bridge walk the dike upstream to its end, then proceed on gravel bars. Change film and shoot. **Round trip 1 mile.**

Drive North Fork County Road .4 mile to the new bridge over the Middle Fork. (The old Norman Bridge, the last remaining timber-truss vehicular bridge

Snoqualmie River and Mount Si

in King County, has been preserved as a pedestrian-only County Landmark.) Park on the shoulder just south, where a lane enters the forest — and an undeveloped, 56-acre, King County park. In springtime beware of false morels leaping out from under the cottonwoods. In ⅓ mile the lane ends at the river. With a modest amount of pain a walker can beat on a short way, by a cattail pond, to a big bar in sight of the North Fork confluence. Shoot again. **Round trip 1 mile.**

The next two walks can be reached by continuing south on North Fork Road. However, the access from North Bend is quicker. From North Bend Way (former Highway 10 through downtown) turn north on Ballarat Avenue (which later throws off this disguise and reveals itself to be the North Fork Road). Several blocks from downtown turn right on 6th Avenue E which becomes SE 114th Street and follow it to a deadend on the Middle Fork, directly across from Little Si. Si's Haystack and Spire are neck-bendingly straight up, but the views of the Great Buttress and the back side of Little Si, route of the brand new (1985) summit trail, are worth a few snaps. The dikes can be walked upstream and down. **Round trip ¾ mile.**

From North Bend drive the North Bend-Snoqualmie Road (ancient Sunset Highway) to the west edge of town and the bridge over the river. Park on the shoulder, elevation 440 feet.

Walk the dike downstream ¼ mile to the railroad tracks. These continue east to Tanner as the route of the Sound-To-Mountains Trail, and west by many a birdy slough to the Mt. Si Golf Course and the Weyerhaeuser mill. However, for the river walk leave the tracks just across the South Fork bridge and follow a path to sprawling bars, sand and gravel. A rickety footbridge crosses a small slough to more morels, more bars, then veers from the banks through woods to the railroad tracks, whence another path heads through floodway forests to the river and still more bars. Look for beaver dams and fresh tooth-logging. **Round trip 2 miles.**

Allow an hour or all day
High point 440 feet, elevation gain 40 feet
All year
Bus: Metro 210

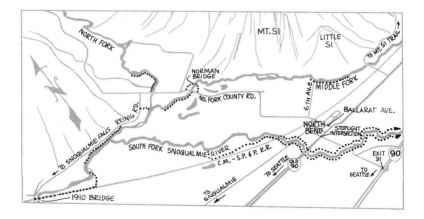

SOUTH FORK SNOQUALMIE RIVER

The South is the Fork of the Snoqualmie everybody knows. The valley, route of the "Main Street of the Northwest," is so crowded by freeway, sometime railroad, logging roads, powerlines, coaxial cables, and microwave relays there's barely space for the river — which indeed has been shoved aside to permit free flow of automobiles. Summer and winter, swarms of these are going and coming, side by side and bumper to bumper, to and from highland trails and ski slopes. Summer and winter they more and more often are stacked up in miles-long, hours-long jams, and even when the freeway truly is,

South Fork Snoqualmie River from McClellan's Buttelet

the decline of civility characteristic of our times means that increasingly it's a jungle out there, east of North Bend. The "front country," closer to home, is easier on the nerves — and the sorry state of these, after all, is largely what hiking is all about.

The North Bend plain, bed of a Pleistocene lake, appears doomed to follow the model of the Issaquah plain, another lakebed, and become a link in the "I-90 Corridor" master plan, the speculators' and developers' vision of continuous shopping centers from Lake Washington to Ellensburg. Even the South Fork dikes, built by public funds, are only tenuously public — by toleration, not government policy.

The situation is better in the uplands. The 7-mile ridge of Rattlesnake Mountain, the connection of the Issaquah Alps to the Cascades, has walking routes from both ends and the middle. On the opposite side of the plain is the Mount Si Conservation Area, treated in the next chapter. A fit companion for that super-park-to-be lies at the east end of the plain, where the portal peaks of Washington and West Defiance guard the entry to the hanging valley of the South Fork. Olallie State Park, in the terminal moraines of the Canadian glacier, can become another "super," hub of a network of trails to Cedar Butte, Rattlesnake, Washington, Defiance, Dirty Harry's Balcony, Bandera, and the Alpine Lakes Wilderness.

Though elevations range high, the snows don't pile to mountain-interior depths and can shrivel overnight in a warm January storm; some or all trails are walkable the winter through.

USGS maps: Fall City, Snoqualmie, North Bend, Bandera

South Fork Dikes (map — page 47)

Granted, a channelized and diked and riprapped river is man's drainage ditch, not wild living room for the children of Nature. Nevertheless, the water ripples and rattles and in floodtime has a roar that may be as wildly pleasing as frightening to those without houses nearby. Fish swim and therefore fisher-birds fly and dive. The walking is flat and easy and when the brush is kept cut and the motorcycles banned, as here, has neither messiness nor annoyance. On these dikes the views of mountains, notably the stupendosity of Si, compete with the river for attention.

Note: Though built by public funds, the dikes are private property — of abutting owners — and legally-technically not open to the public. However, along some of the river the abutting owner is the public — the City of North Bend — and elsewhere the "trespassing" is widely tolerated. Indeed, residents so much enjoy the dike-walking they recognize it as one of the major civic assets, its preservation essential to development of the tourist industry. If you are challenged, though, turn back — and try another access to the dikes.

Go off I-90 on Exit 31 and drive North Bend Avenue to a block short of North Bend Way, the town's main drag (old Highway 10), and park at Gardiner Weeks Memorial Park, which contains the Snoqualmie Valley Museum and Mt. Si Senior Center. Elevation, 440 feet.

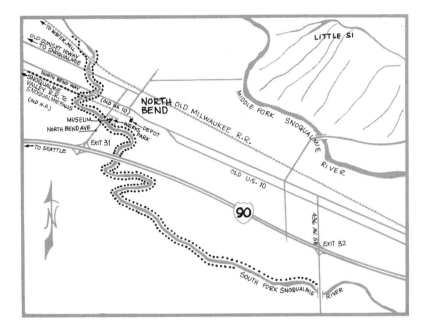

Dikes go downstream on both banks of the river 1 mile, through the west edge of town and under old Highway 10, older Sunset Highway, and the still older Northern Pacific and Milwaukee Railroad grades — a museum of transportation history.

Dikes also go upstream on both banks, that on the true right (the right side of the river, facing the direction of flow) all the way to Cedar Falls Road — 2¼ air miles, 3 miles as the river goes. (It has been channelized but not straightened, not yet.) That on the true left stops somewhat short, the need obviated by a cliff. Both pass under the monstrous I-90 bridge, newest chapter in the transportation history.

To start the walk from the upstream end, go off I-90 on Exit 32 to 436th Avenue SE (Cedar Falls Road), park on either side of the bridge, and get on the true right dike.

A favorite time to do the dikes is on a spring day when the intent in Seattle was to hike higher — and upon reaching the North Bend plain, the peaks are seen to be white to their very bottoms. The views then are particularly dazzling over the plain (bed of a huge Pleistocene lake) to Rattlesnake, Washington, West Defiance, valleys of the South Fork and Middle Fork, and the absolutely inescapable Si. Especially for a person who recently has spent a lot of time in the deep woods, there is a marvelous sense of abundant air and big sky.

Total length of all dikes 9 miles, allow 1-12 hours
High point 480 feet, elevation gain 40 feet
All year
Bus: Metro 210

Rattlesnake Mountain — West Peak (map — page 49)

The 7-mile-long ridge of Rattlesnake Mountain, easternmost peak of the Issaquah Alps, has feet in three valleys. (That may make it a monster, but no reptile — the name came from the rattling of dry seed pods in a wind that made members of a pioneer party nervous.) On the west it belongs to the Raging River, on the south to the Cedar, on the north and east to the Snoqualmie. As another distinction, it is the link between the near-city "Old Mountains" and the Cascade front that upthrusts from North Bend. Of the four Rattlesnake hikes described in this book, West Peak is the least lovable. The route is entirely on high-speed, hard-surface road. The distance is too formidable to be fun for anyone except a hiking machine or a jogger wanting a good stretch of the legs. If pleasure is your goal, take the North Scarp Vista trip.

Rattlesnake Mountain, West Peak

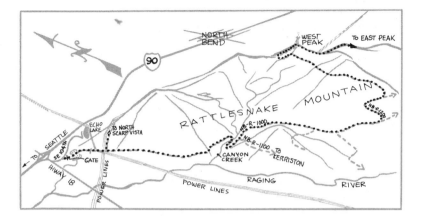

Exit from I-90 onto Highway 18. About .2 mile from the cloverleaf turn left (east) on SE 104th Street. Where that road bends left to Echo Lake a logging road proceeds straight ahead. Park at this junction, elevation 900 feet.

Walk to a lovely marsh of Lake Creek. Here is the gate; even when open it is closed to public vehicles. To drive beyond is to risk getting locked in overnight — or until Monday morning — and nobody to take pity on your scofflaw brashness. So, *walk.* That's legal.

At ¾ mile are the broad swaths of two intersecting powerlines, elevation 1000 feet. (Here is the alternate takeoff for Rattlesnake Mountain — North Scarp Vista.) Views begin of Tiger and Taylor across the valley of the Raging River. In 1½ miles more the road swings into the valley of Canyon Creek, soon crossed at 1300 feet. Shortly the hiker spots, up on the summit, the orange-silver telephone company microwave tower — so big it appears close. It ain't. At 1396 feet, ¾ mile from the entrance to Canyon's canyon, a road (maybe) signed "NB-R-1100" goes downhill right. Go left on NB-R-1000.

In another ¾ mile, at 1636 feet, is a road downhill right; stay left. In ¼ mile, at 1677 feet, is a Y; go left. In ½ mile, at 1800 feet, is a junction where the ascent begins in earnest and the views expand by the minute.

Go left, uphill, on NB-R-1200. The summit tower is in sight and that's good, because logging spurs go off constantly in all directions. The rule is to stick with the most-traveled road, on the theory that the parade of service trucks to the summit installation will keep a track well-beaten. Keep an eye on that summit tower. Switchback under it, choosing forks that trend in its direction. At about 2800 feet is a Y where the tower is directly above but neither road heads directly toward it. Take the left, which makes a long detour northward to the ridge, then switchbacks and returns to the summit, 3262 feet, some 3½ miles from the 1800-foot junction.

The views are from sites of the various microwave and FM radio towers — Pacific Northwest Bell, King County Police, logging companies, tow-truck companies, and your Aunt Nelly. (In this age of overcommunication everybody's got to have a telephone, a C-B radio, and if he can afford it, his own network.) To previous views over the Raging River valley to the Issaquah Alps, Preston, I-90, and the Olympics, south over the Cedar River to MacDonald,

Enumclaw, and Rainier, now are added views north to towns in the Snoqualmie valley and to Pilchuck, Three Fingers, Baker, Glacier, Sultan, Index, Teneriffe, Si, Defiance, and Washington, to name a few prominent peaks. Also in view, 1¼ air miles distant, is the East Peak of Rattlesnake, a long up-and-down walk on a snarl of roads which fail to connect neatly, though the route has been done and a rude path flagged.

Round trip 16 miles, allow 10 hours
High point 3262 feet, elevation gain 2400 feet
April-November

Rattlesnake Mountain — North Scarp Vista (map — page 50)

From a point directly below the West Peak of Rattlesnake most of the summit view can be obtained with half or less the effort. In fact the view is partly better: this is precisely the perfect spot to comprehend the incredible bulk and tallness of Si and appreciate how astoundingly it towers above the houses and pastures of North Bend.

Go off I-90 on Exit 27 and drive Winery Road, following signs for Snoqualmie Winery. Continue to the winery, if desired, to sample the semillon, or the early-release chardonnay, amusingly presumptuous; here at the edge of the City of Snoqualmie Watershed eventually will be located a highway rest area and hotel. For the walk, however, at .2 mile from the exit spot a narrow, steep, gravel road switchbacking uphill to the right (west). Your vehicle may request you to park here, elevation 950 feet — especially if the road is gated. However, walkers wanting views more than exercise, and owning tough little vehicles, often prefer to drive .7 mile and park on a turnout at the start of a 1976 clearcut, elevation 1100 feet.

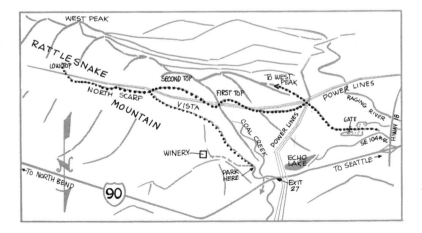

The views instantly are staggering. A newspaper wine columnist wrote, to describe his impressions as he emerged from the tasting room, "...the late afternoon sun began to paint Mt. Si pink and then almost magenta..." — resembling, perhaps, the "cabernet sauvignon and merlot slowly aging in the barrels." The panorama extends from the west face of Mt. Si over the North Bend plain (lakebed, once) to the village of Snoqualmie and the sprawling Weyerhaeuser mill, and north to Fuller Mountain and Baker and west to the Olympics. In 1 mile pass a logging spur switchbacking up right. Leave the clearcut and at 1⅓ miles, elevation 1394 feet, pass the powerline service road switchbacking up right. (This service road goes west on the heights, climbing in ½ mile to Second Top, 1840 feet, continuing ¾ mile to First Top, 1800 feet, both with grand views, then plummets ¾ mile along the powerline swath to the road from Highway 18 to West Peak Rattlesnake, an alternate approach.)

The road quickly climbs back into views and mainly stays there the final 1¼ upsy-downsy miles to Low Top, 1550 feet. Here the road ends on the brink of a cliff (with flowers that bloom in the spring) that provides wide, unscreened views of mountains north to Baker and Three Fingers and Sultan and Index, and up the three forks of the Snoqualmie, and up the Cedar River. And views 1000 vertical feet down to cars on I-90, trains on tracks, cows in pastures, houses in North Bend.

Above all, from this platform just high enough to see it all but not so high it begins to lose grandeur, there is Si, the 3600 feet of rugged cliff standing hugely over the green plain.

Round trip from clearcut to Low Top 5 miles, allow 3 hours
High point 1600 feet, elevation gain 900 feet
February-December

Rattlesnake Ledge (map — page 53)

In rounding the east end of Rattlesnake Mountain the Canadian glacier ground off the tip, shaping the formidably vertical cliff that causes climbers driving along I-90 to snap their carabiners. Not only is Rattlesnake Ledge a remarkable phenomenon rewarding close inspection; the view from the top is superb. Moreover, winds sheering around the corner and sun blasting the naked rock constitute so severe a microclimate that flowers of the Ledge are — despite the low elevation — amazingly alpine.

Go off I-90 on Exit 32 and drive 436th Avenue SE (Cedar Falls Road) 2.7 miles to Rattlesnake Lake. On approaching the shore, turn right and follow the gravel road (if the gate is closed, on foot) .2 mile to the Game Department picnic area, elevation 950 feet.

A person new to the trip, stretching his neck up at the cliff from the parking lot, may wish he had some carabiners to snap. However, a volunteer-built path (never really finished) ascends a route somewhat less abrupt. A concrete post, a few feet north of the privies, marks one of many entries to the trail, which gently climbs a short bit to an old logging road. Turn left 70 paces to a large boulder on the left and find the trail resumption uphill on the right.

Big stumps are passed in the second-growth, as are great mossy-ferny boulders tumbled from the ice-oversteepened Ledge. The path grows steeper,

Mount Si from Rattlesnake Mountain

with several pitches of muddy rock and awkward logs so mean to clamber over that myriad detours have been built by boots, and with stretches of three-point suspension up the rubbly volcanic crud of the Ledge. The best thing that can be said about the "trail" is that it's short. Soon comes a scramble out of the forest onto a rock nose and the first views, and thenceforth — though the ascent is in one or another boot-eroded gully, slippery and messy, fortunately provided with many a thank-God shrubbery handhold — the spectacular airiness of the scene keeps hikers' language relatively clean.

Botanists are fascinated by the array of subalpine herbs and shrubs, the colors particularly gay when the phlox and lupine and penstemon and paintbrush and tiger lily and California tea are blooming. Both kinnikinnick and manzanita grow here — and also the hybrid of the two.

At ¾ mile from the parking lot is the top of the Ledge, 2079 feet. What an appalling place! Enough to give acrophobia to a mountain goat. Definitely not a spot for kiddies to toddle about — nor for teenagers to play chicken, seeing who dares make the closest approach to the brink, which for some 400 feet is vertical. A narrow cleft 20 feet deep reminds of the huge chunks of former Ledge down in the woods.

Sit for a while on the north side of the Ledge and look down to the Wilderness Rim subdivision, out to I-90 and North Bend and gigantic Si. Move

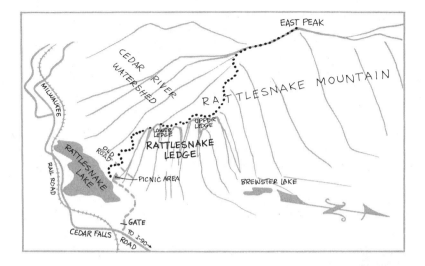

to the east brink and look up the Middle Fork to Russian Buttes and Garfield, up the South Fork past the portal peaks of Defiance and Washington, and dizzily down down to Rattlesnake Lake and the tidy community of Cedar Falls and up the Cedar River to Chester Morse Lake, the Seattle City Water reservoir. Note the "gravel cirque" (now aldery) in the moraine. This is the site of the Boxley Burst, which occurred in 1918 when Seattle attempted to fill the reservoir behind its Masonry Dam and the water burst through the moraine, washing 2,000,000 cubic yards of glacial drift into the valley, obliterating dozens of homes — an entire town. Move to the south side and look out the Cedar to MacDonald and Enumclaw.

Round trip 1½ miles, allow 3 hours
High point 2079 feet, elevation gain 1100 feet
February-December

Most hikers will feel the first knob ("Lower Ledge") quite suffices and that any spare time is best spent soaking up the views. Others will be tantalized by the Higher Ledge and forced to go on.

From Lower Ledge dip a bit to a saddle and find a rude path sneaking through dense-limbed young forest dating from an old burn. It is a rude path indeed, easy to lose, but by sticking near the cliff edge, and by exerting patience eked out by profanity, a hiker soon attains another bald at 2350 feet and another appalling cliff. And pretty much the same view as before.

Rattlesnake Mountain — East Peak (map — page 53)

The tippy-top of Rattlesnake Mountain, the East Peak, also has the biggest views in all directions, mainly because it is logged absolutely naked, no summit forest to get in the way.

Ascend Rattlesnake Ledge (which see) and continue to Upper Ledge. The rude path reenters forest, in several hundred feet emerging into a 1976 clearcut. Stay high on the right side, picking a relatively easy way upward through slash and brush to a clearcut of the early 1970s. Continue up, at 2850 feet reaching a logging road on the ridgecrest. Follow the road system, at all junctions picking the forks that promise to lead onward up the bare crest. At about 3 miles from the Rattlesnake Lake trailhead is the summit of the East Peak, 3517 feet, marked by the Washington State Patrol radio house, from within which speak disembodied voices, very disconcerting to a lone hiker wrapped in a cloud.

On his first trip the surveyor saw nothing but the hoarfrost crystallizing from the wind-driven winter cloud, whitening the tower, the bushes, and his eyebrows and beard. He soon departed, disturbed by finding himself talking back to the disembodied voices. On the second visit, however, the view extended from Rainier to the Olympics to Baker to the peaks of Snoqualmie Pass, absolutely the most enormous to be had from Rattlesnake.

Round trip 6 miles, allow 6 hours
High point 3517 feet, elevation gain 2600 feet
March-November

Olallie State Park (map — page 56)

Exploiting a frontier anachronism of a law that permits individuals to preempt public waters for private gain, the "small hydro" entrepreneurs are roving the landscape, squeezing kilowatts out of any river, creek, or dribble they can grab. Exhibiting the mentality and morality of miners on a gold rush, they are even invading parks. Two firms have staked out Weeks Falls and the Twin Falls Natural Area in Olallie State Park. Construction of the Weeks Falls project began in 1986; what "amelioration" — required by law — there will be that is of interest to hikers is not known at this writing. As for Twin Falls, the developer, the State Parks Commissioner, the State Ecology Department, the State Legislature, and the Sierra Club and Friends of the Earth and the courts have the project on hold. The situation as of 1987 cannot be described — or predicted. The next printing will bring the status up to date. However the case comes out in court, ultimately there will be two entries.

Exit 34 (How It Is in 1986)

Twin Falls Natural Area is a sublimely beautiful place, a cathedral of old-growth forest, rock-walled canyon, and a river that thunders and murmurs. The developer would turn it off at his pleasure. It is also a terrible place where legs turn to jelly and the throat constricts too tight to shriek. However, some of it is great for little kids to play in the sand and wade quiet pools.

Leave I-90 on Exit 34, signed "Edgewick Road." From the interchange go right on 468th Avenue SE .5 mile and just before the river crossing turn left on SE 159th Street. In .5 mile is the roadend turnaround, elevation 700 feet.

The park is totally undeveloped but boots have been active and occasion-

Lower Twin Falls

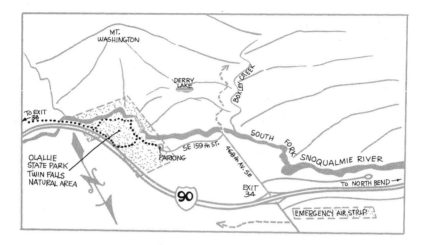

ally an ax and a saw. The first ½ mile is a toddler's delight, through superb old second-growth forest, by river bars that invite picnicking, watching the water ouzels and kingfishers. This mild aspect ends at a huge "lawn" — the grassy outwash of a blowout caused by construction of I-90, which is directly up the gravel fan at an elevation of 1000 feet. (Keep that in mind.) The wading and lunching are particularly fine here in the sun-open sandbars and the meadows where the corydalis and toothwort bloom.

Gentle spirits need not quit yet, not quite. Indeed, though the path grows rude it remains safe enough and lets the walker savor sky gardens of moss in groves of vine maple, 5-foot-diameter trees of old-growth forest, and green pools and churning foam. (The powerhouse would replace the trees, and a service road the trail to this point.) However, when the path starts up the precipitous valley wall the time has come to think things over. If a spot makes you nervous, turn back, because worse is to come.

Nevertheless, there is no real danger, provided one doesn't faint, and shuns the plummeting sidetrails. The path tops out above the canyon wall beside I-90 and there — ½ mile from the gravel-wash meadow but seeming thrice that — comes to what was, in the days of old Highway 10, a turnout-parking area and trailhead down to the falls. Now signed "Emergency Parking Only," getting there legally puts us to all these terrible troubles.

Actually, the old trail down to the falls never was suitable for dogs or toddlers. A number of paths lead to a number of overlooks, varying from chilling to suicidal. In flood time the earth shakes, the human voice is lost, in the Judgment Day of pounding waters, splintering logs, swirling spray. River aside, the forest is glorious, as are the rock walls hung with licorice fern and maidenhair spleenwort. And actually, some of the overlooks are safe, though they don't feel like it. If you can't tell which are safe and which are not, you've no business here (or just about anywhere ⅰɪ this book).

A person distraught at the thought of the return may be tempted to cheat. By skulking along the cleared swath beside I-90 one can quickly reach the top of the gravel wash, slip through the barbed-wire fence where folks have been doing so ever since it was erected, and descend the wash. This way may be technically illegal, but it's safe.

Round trip to falls 1 mile, allow 2 hours
High point 1000 feet, elevation gain 500 feet
All year

Exit 38 (How It May Be in 1987 or so)

Leave I-90 on the west end of Exit 38, turn right over the river, and instantly right on the gravel-blacktop (?) road .2 mile to the new (1987?) trailhead, elevation 1200 feet.

The trail is, for the first scant ¼ mile, along the route pioneered by the Mountaineers volunteers who opened the Mt. Washington trail (which see). It then will turn west on new construction some 1½ miles to Twin Falls.

Presumably there also will be paths along the river to Weeks Falls, and whatever other mercies the kindly capitalists bestow upon us peasants. Watch these pink pages for the latest news.

Grouse Ridge (map — page 57)

A highway traveler more than normally observant may wonder why a ridge crosses the South Fork Snoqualmie valley at right angles. Aren't ridges supposed to parallel valleys? Ah, says the geomorphologist, you reckon without the glaciers. This is a moraine marking a long-stable terminus of the ice, a dumping ground. Here, said early geologists, was the end of a glacier descending the South Fork Snoqualmie. However, a professor at the University of Washington, Dr. J. Hoover Mackin, was bothered by fractious evidence. To make a long scientific detective story short, he proposed the preposterous notion the glacier hadn't come down the valley but up. And he proved it. The moraine was none other than that of the Puget Glacier intruding from Canada and pushing deep into the Cascades.

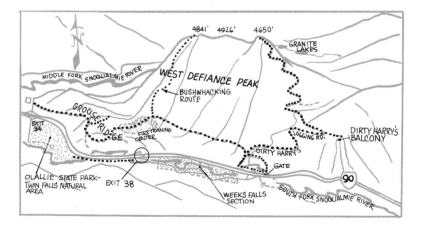

West Defiance from Grouse Ridge

That's one fascinating thing about Grouse Ridge, as the moraine is called in this segment. The other is that it was on the route of the first road from the lowlands over Snoqualmie Pass. A construction start by Seattle pioneers in 1859 was aborted by the Civil War. In 1865 some $2500 was subscribed by boosters and a Snoqualmie Pass Trail or Wagon Road cleared nearly to the pass — though as late as 1872 an actual crossing by a wagon rated a newspaper item. Such Seattle entrepreneurs as A. A. Denny and H. L. Yesler realized the government wasn't going to help; in 1883 was organized the Seattle and Walla Walla Train and Wagon Road Company which for a decade operated the Seattle-Walla Walla Toll Road, the first cross-Cascades road link between Seattle and Eastern Washington. But there wasn't much call for it when built, and even less after completion of the cross-mountain line of the Northern Pacific Railroad; in 1892 the 14-foot right-of-way was signed over to King County in a quit-claim deed; the county promptly commenced a long neglect, letting logs fall and creeks gully and weeds grow. But time was marching on, or wheeling on, and the nation was falling helplessly in love with newfangled machines. As a promotion event for the Alaska-Yukon-Pacific Exposition of 1909 an automobile race was held from New York to Seattle, requiring the over-mountains road to be made at least temporarily passable. Soon everybody was getting wheels and in 1913 a primary highway, part of the transcontinental system, was designated over Snoqualmie Pass. However, the Sunset Highway, formally opened in 1915, followed a new line east from North Bend, the line that remained in use until the coming in the 1970s of I-90.

As traffic grew on what in the 1920s was called the Yellowstone Trail (a reflection of the popularity of the national park as a goal for the new American sport of auto-touring), a 6.2-mile stretch of the pioneer route was forgotten. Private companies, assuming they owned the right-of-way, reopened it for hauling gravel and logs. And then came the freeway-builders, and the fire-fighters. Though the way no longer resembles a wagon road, the view is much what the pioneers saw from the moraine slopes — the flat valley around North Bend falling away below, the far-west near-saltwater lowlands receding, and then, atop the moraine flat, the mountains guarding the way to Snoqualmie Pass appearing. Walk and muse.

Leave I-90 on Exit 34, signed "Edgewick Road," turn left to pass under the freeway, and just beyond turn right on a paved road signed "Forest Inns" 250 yards to a gate, elevation 650 feet.

The gate is posted, "Unauthorized motorized use not permitted. Non-motorized use permitted. Gate locked without notice." Therefore, even if the gate is open, park here and praise the authorities for making this a footroad. (Yes, there occasionally are illegal two-wheelers, but you can yell at them, "Scofflaw! Scofflaw!" and ostentatiously write down their license numbers and watch them scoot.)

The first scant 1 mile is virtually flat and totally clearcut, the site of the future metropolis of East North Bend. Views are of Teneriffe, Si, Rattlesnake, Wash-ington, West Defiance — and the moraine, straight ahead. Arriving there, the way turns steeply up, switchbacking, narrowing nearly to olden-day width. Dodge sideroads left and keep heading for the powerline. (However, a sideroad left at 1300 feet climbs ¼ mile to the flat crest of a spur ridge at 1500 feet and a T. The left goes a short bit to a clearcut and a stunning view up the Middle Fork valley, the right a short bit to a clearcut and a view of the South Fork.)

The main road goes under the powerline at 1350 feet, through up-leaping firs of a plantation to a clearcut of the early 1980s, and at 1500 feet, a scant 2 miles from the gate, comes to a promontory landing and the climax views. See the South Fork Snoqualmie below, in Olallie State Park, and look out to where the river plunges, via Snoqualmie Falls, from the old lakebed of the upper valley. See lanes of I-90, tree-mining clearcuts high on valley walls, smog of Puget Sound City. See Rattlesnake, Si, and Teneriffe. It's enough. Bring out the pickles and grapes and beef sticks and ponder. Listen for wagon wheels. The putt-putt of AYP road-racers. The original settlers on the way to attack the new settlers in Seattle. The glacier dropping boulders.

Round trip 4 miles, allow 3 hours
High point 1500 feet, elevation gain 1000 feet
All year

The road shortly tops out, at 1600 feet, on the flat plateau of Grouse Ridge. Splendid (but temporary) conifer forest pretty well blocks views, but the quiet is worth the walk. As new clearcuts and new roads confuse the issue, remember to keep generally on the flat and aim for the ridge of West Defiance. By picking the correct forks, some 3½ miles from the gate a person will come to a fence at the edge of a gravel pit thought to be the largest in the Western Hemisphere, a major source of the raw material of I-90. It now is the site of a "No Trespassing Fire Training Center." Firemen come from around the state to set fires and put them out, which sounds more exciting than it is and never will become a great spectator sport, not even on cable TV.

On the far side of the ½-mile-wide gravel pit, on the slopes of West Defiance, the old wagon road resumes — as the paved access road to the training center. Despite the "No Trespassing" sign, it is illegal for the state to block the county route, so if you desire and have your attorney present, proceed to Dirty Harry's Logging Road (which see), at about 5½ miles from the gate. The gravel road that here goes off right ⅓ mile to the Snoqualmie River and I-90 is the route of the old wagon road. At the freeway the 1865 and 1986 routes coincide for a while.

Dirty Harry's Balcony (map — page 57)

Driving I-90 along the South Fork Snoqualmie above the moraine, a person paying attention to more than concrete and machines notes that at a certain point the valley, quite wide upstream and downstream, is constricted to a slot by a ridge thrusting from the side of Defiance. And a person with an eye for rock may look up and judge this a most impressive collection indeed of precipices and chimneys. If that person has a taste for pedestrian exercise, he may wonder what it's like to be up there on the top. Well, he ought to go find out. Ought to look down from bald buttresses, and down and down, more than 1000 exceedingly vertical feet, to a most impressive collection of concrete ribbons and busy machines. But the view down is only a fraction of the breathtaking vista from "Dirty Harry's Balcony." And in season there is a brilliant rock garden of blossoming herbs and shrubs. In the years since the first edition of this book brought it to the attention of the hiking community, the Balcony has become one of the most popular jaunts in the North Bend area.

Drive east on I-90, go off on the west end of Exit 38, and follow old Highway 10, now a recreation-and-rest road, 2 miles to the east end of Exit 38 — at all times following signs, "State Fire Training Center." Go under the freeway and, for one possible start, park here, elevation 1300 feet. For the better possibility, drive the training center road 150 yards more to a gate, and park.

From the first start (technically illegal, but so minor a crime the police are not known ever to have arrested anyone), cross the Snoqualmie River on the westbound freeway bridge — be careful and do it fast, no loitering, and don't sass any police you may encounter. (Claim ignorance, preferably in a foreign language, with many gestures.) At the west end of the bridge note a woods road. This is the upper terminus of the 6.2 miles of the old wagon road (see Grouse Ridge). Follow it ⅓ mile to intersect the training center road at 1350 feet. Directly across the pavement starts Dirty Harry's Logging Road. (For explanation of the name, see West Defiance Peak.)

From the second — and better — start, walk ½ mile to Dirty Harry's Logging Road, crossing the river on a one-lane bridge (lovely gravel bar here) and passing "No Trespassing" signs. Actually, these are merely to keep Sunday gawkers from the fireworks shows and nobody ever has interfered with hikers on the way to visit Dirty Harry. In fact, hikers who feel lucky often drive the ½ mile, trusting the gate won't be locked behind them. But why bother, to save a few minutes afoot?

Dirty Harry's Logging Road doesn't see wheels from one year to the next,

McClellan Butte from Dirty Harry's Balcony

being practically if not technically undrivable, and Harry hasn't operated in these parts since the 1970s, so the route is more a creekbed than a road. Only the water is noisy, inviting hikers toiling upward in the hot sun of the small second-growth to cool their fevered brows.

In 1½ miles from the Wagon Road, at 2500 feet, Dirty Harry's Road switchbacks west. Go off right on a rude but obvious path to a saddle and campsite between Defiance slopes and Balcony Ridge. Just past the camp turn right and follow the path through snags of a silver forest, shrubs, and salal onto the mossy, craggy bald top of Dirty Harry's Balcony, 2550 feet.

Zounds! Look east to Bandera, south to McClellan's Butte, west to Washington, and — from other viewpoints nearby — farther west to Rattlesnake, the lower Snoqualmie valley, and the Olympics. But especially look down the giddy crags to the concrete swath of I-90, where bugs chase each other's tails east and west, to and fro, and to the gravel channels of the river, and to the railroad and the gashes of tree-mining roads that climb so high, almost touch the sky — and would be hauling logs from there, too, if Nature could grow them.

From the first bald top explore others, stepping *very* gingerly along the brink, admiring airy pillars and deep-incised chimneys and scary cliffs. In spring the knobs and pillars and chimneys and cliffs are a glowing garden of penstemon and paintbrush and beargrass and much more.

Round trip 5 miles, allow 4 hours
High point 2550 feet, elevation gain 1300 feet
February-December

West Defiance Peak (map — page 57)

Guarding the entry to the above-moraine South Fork valley are two portal peaks, Washington on the south and, on the north, "West Defiance," the name applied here to the group of summits on the ridge extending westward from the West Peak of Defiance into the angle between the South Fork and Middle Fork valleys. The views from on high are airplane-wing lofty, fully the equal of those from Si.

From the switchback at 2500 feet on Dirty Harry's Logging Road (see Dirty Harry's Balcony) continue west. The road ascends in growing views 1¾ miles to a promontory at 2800 feet — far enough for many hikers, and probably all on an early-spring snowline-probing trip. The view is grand across the valley to McClellan's Butte, down to I-90 and railroad and river, east to the Snoqualmie Pass peaks, and — especially — out the portals to the lowlands.

A bit farther, at 3000 feet, the road crosses a tumbling creek. Continue climbing, avoiding roads (cat tracks) that go off right into the valley of the creek and its 1970s clearcut; at all junctions take left turns except those obviously deadending in a hurry. Views become bigger and bigger, absolutely immense, until in about 1½ miles from the tumbling creek the road tops out on a 4650-foot summit of West Defiance. All the way to here have cats been pushed, chainsaws hauled, by the gypo known to his friends as "Dirty Harry," whose business and pleasure for many years was mining the trees from this private land.

Walk this way and that in the clearcut and the lingering remnant of lovely mountain hemlocks, and heather and beargrass, taking in the scenery. To the west, beyond the other two peaks of West Defiance (4926 and 4851 feet), made inaccessible from here by a cliffy notch, are North Bend, Rattlesnake, Issaquah Alps, towers of downtown Seattle dim in smog, the smoke pall of invisible Tacoma, Green Mountain (the one near Bremerton), and the Olympics. South, beyond Washington, is Rainier. North is Baker. Easterly are Glacier, Kaleetan, Chair, Chimney, and all. Beyond the Middle Fork valley are the amazing clearcuts on Bessemer. Straight down beneath cliffs (watch your step) are the clearcut basins of Granite Lakes.

Round trip to summit 11 miles, allow 9 hours
High point 4650 feet, elevation gain 3400 feet
May-November (to lower points, in March)

What's badly needed, when some group of doughty volunteers (see Mt. Washington and Little Si) recognizes the potential, is a trail up from the

Snoqualmie Pass Wagon Road at Grouse Ridge. This spine of West Defiance, burned bare by a forest fire of the 19th century and still largely meadowy-naked, has a southwest exposure and frequently melts free of snow in March or April, when all the country around is white. The hiking season would be long and the view, from the very tip of the portal ridge, would be a stunner. The route can be done now, at the cost of some brushfighting down low.

Mount Washington (map — page 63)

One of the grandest viewpoints of the Cascade front is attained via a most entertainingly devious, but very easy, trail pioneered and maintained by Mountaineer (and other?) volunteers. Climb to the summit for the big picture — or partway, to the "Owl Hike Spot," for a picture so big many hikers feel no need for more.

Leave I-90 on the west end of Exit 38, turn right over the river, then right again on the first road. Drive it west .2 mile, on gravel, then old blacktop (1985) to the end, elevation 1200 feet.

In 1987 or so this may become the trailhead for a new route to the Twin Falls Natural Area. Construction of the trail — and of the "small hydro" projects which may be screwing up Olallie State Park (which see) — may create confusion hereabouts. However, because the railroad tracks provide a surefire baseline, it will be impossible to miss the way. If the scene is a mess, simply scramble straight up to the rail grade.

Ascend the grassy flat westward and find the trail at the edge of the woods. It switchbacks twice, climbing to a bench and there intersecting an ancient roadway. The new Twin Falls trail will proceed west; turn sharp left, east, on the

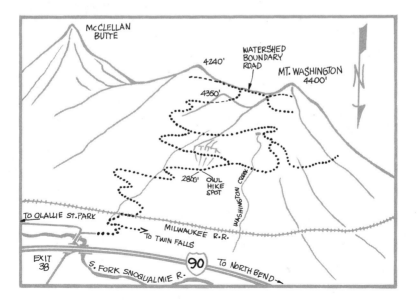

Frozen waterfall on Mount Washington Trail

ancient road, which switchbacks west at the famous Junked Buick and climbs to the Milwaukee Railroad tracks, 1400 feet, a long ⅓ mile from the road.

Walk west on the tracks 40 to 50 paces and go off left on a well-maintained, highly visible (but totally wheelfree) trail along what the old map calls "jeep trail." Actually it's a gypo logging road of the 1950s or so (one of Dirty Harry's jobs?), and a clever little road it is, picking a devious and ingenious way under and over and between cliffs, gaining elevation steadily and steeply, switch-backing east three times and west three times, finally traversing westward toward the objective. The way is largely in young alder but partly in virgin hemlock, with several groves of old-growth Douglas fir snagtops (beware of the golden eagles). The cliffs are great fun, plummeting below, beetling above — some overhanging, forming impressive caves (beware of the jaws that bite, the claws that scratch). Springs gush from crevices and nourish hangings of maidenhair fern and saxifrages. In season the icicles are dazzling.

Windows open in the forest, first down to the freeway and across to Grouse Ridge, West Defiance, and Dirty Harry's Country, then up the Middle Fork from Si to Bessemer. Finally, about 2 miles from the trailhead, the little old road (picture a logging truck on it!) rounds a cliff corner into the broad valley of "Washington Creek." Here, at 2800 feet, is the famous Owl Hike Spot, so called because since 1959 it has been a favorite evening hike of The Mountaineers, who cook a picnic supper, watch the sunset, and descend by flashlight. The panorama is a three-star gasper, from Rattlesnake over the North Bend lakebed (South and Middle Forks meandering along either side, freeway slicing through the middle, towns of North Bend and Snoqualmie sprawling) to Little Si and Big Si and Teneriffe, out the Snoqualmie Falls notch to lowlands and Olympics — and straight down precipices to the gorge of Twin Falls.

Round trip to Owl Hike Spot 4 miles, allow 4 hours
High point 2800 feet, elevation gain 1600 feet
March-November

The summit beckoned the surveyor, who has gazed there longingly many years, but the November night was near and the snow was bleak and the dogs were whining and the book deadline was at hand. For the next printing he will report his personal progress to the pinnacle, but here will quote the clear and authoritative description published in the September, 1985, *Signpost* by Jim and Ginny Evans, who pioneered the Owl Hike Spot in 1979. (The map also follows that of Jim Evans.)

Continue on the trail ½-mile to the junction with an abandoned road which you follow uphill to the left (northeast). This junction is easy to miss; if you get to the creek, you have gone past it.

Follow the roadbed past a boulder and around to the north side of Peak 4350, then switchback up to an in-use logging road. At this point, go left (east) directly away from the summit, and follow the road through recent clearcuts clockwise around the north and east sides of Peak 4350 to the "Great Wall of China." Avoid roads which go up toward the top of Peak 4350. Walk along the Great Wall, then turn right (west) on the watershed boundary road ¼-mile to a fork in the road. From here, follow a cat track up the ridge to the summit, with views of Chester Morse Lake and Mount Rainier.

Round trip to summit 10 miles, allow 8 hours
High point 4400 feet, elevation gain 3200 feet
May-October

McClellan's Buttelet (map — page 66)

Huge stumps of very old trees and sizable quite-old trees, cataracts of Alice Creek, the wire-wrapped wooden pipe that once carried water to Camp Mason, a railroad grade with broad valley views, virgin forest of Douglas firs and hemlocks and cedars up to 7 feet in diameter, and ruins of an ancient mine — that's a lot of action for so short a trip.

Leave I-90 on Exit 42, signed "Tinkham Road" — and also "McClellan Butte Trail," which due to this advertisement by the State Highway Department has become one of the most famed pedestrian thoroughfares in the Northwest. Turn right, south, from the interchange, in a few yards crossing the South Fork and coming to a trailhead parking area, elevation 1500 feet.

The way begins at the site of historic Camp Mason, once the last outpost of

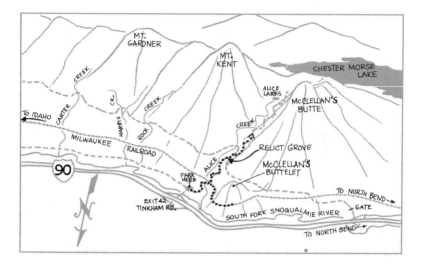

civilization east of North Bend, and wanders through cool, mossy forest grown up since the 1920s; note centuries-old stumps and chunks of trees that apparently were too big to haul to the mill. The way crosses a little picnic creek and follows the pipeline to Alice Creek, crossed on a 1985 bridge that replaced an older, Scout-built span broken up by rot and flood. The trail begins to climb, leaves mossy woods and returns, passes a splendid waterfall gushing from a railroad culvert, and intersects an old rail grade, probably the temporary line built early in the century. A few steps to the left are remains of the trestle over Alice Creek.

A few steps higher is the modern railroad, discussed below. The trail crosses into young forest grown up since clearcutting in the 1960s and follows above the gorge of Alice Creek to old-growth Relict Grove. How has it survived? Perhaps it lies on a patented mining claim, owned by someone who has not yet sold out to the tree-miners? The mine and its portable artifacts have vanished but some heavy chunks of machinery can be found. Just above mine and grove at 2200 feet, 1 mile from the trailhead, is the mainline log-haul road that is carrying the vegetative cover of the mountaintops to the docks for shipment to lumber mills abroad, in order that our nation can afford the motorcycles that racket about the valley. (Close by, the Forest Service is proposing to turn over much of a mountain to the wheels as a regional ATV park.)

The trail continues 3 more miles to the 5162-foot summit of McClellan's Butte, but that's another story, told in *100 Hikes in the South Cascades and Olympics*. This trip turns back at Relict Grove, retreats to the Milwaukee Railroad, 1750 feet, and sets out west for McClellan's Buttelet.

The Milwaukee trains no longer run, of course, and though the Burlington-Northern has acquired the grade, neither do its trains use the rails more than once in a blue moon. The way is therefore lonesome and quiet — if sad — along the rusty rails, weeds growing between. In ¾ mile the grade rounds The Nose of the Buttelet, a 2250-foot pimple peak erupting from the valley wall. On the left are splendid cliffs, on the right a concrete rampart plunging to more cliffs, to the river. Flowers in the crannied wall brighten the spring. The views are down to I-90, east to Bandera, west to Dirty Harry's Balcony, up to the nut-brown nakedness of burned and/or logged and/or avalanche-denuded slopes.

The rail avenue can be walked west to North Bend and, via connections, to Issaquah and Seattle, and east to Idaho and Milwaukee. Think of it as the western addition to the John Wayne Pioneer Trail. In proper time, stick out your thumb and hitch a ride to Independence, Missouri, on one of Happy Jack's wagon trains.

Round trips to Relict Grove and The Nose 3½ miles, allow 3 hours
High point 2200 feet, elevation gain 700 feet
March-November

Bandera Mountain from McClellan's Buttelet

Mount Si Trail

MIDDLE FORK SNOQUALMIE RIVER

The center ring, the big business, the heart of the matter, is the Middle Fork. One need only scan a map and note from what great peaks it flows, what a vast basin it drains, how long is its valley and — in the lower reaches of the U-shaped glacial trough — how wide, to realize this is the main show. Fittingly, upon debouching from the Cascade front onto the North Bend plain shared with the other forks, it wraps around the foot of Mt. Si and claims that choice chunk for its own.

As a hiking province the Middle Fork is divided by the terminal moraine of the Canadian glacier, a sprawl of ridges and lakebeds. So awesomely enormous is the valley above the moraine that it draws throngs every fine weekend except in the depths of a cold winter; most of the hikers come only once, because low-elevation trails are non-existent, as is any federal, state, or private control over off-road vehicles.

However, if hikers–horseriders can come together and find the correct federal-state-King County buttons to push, there is a glorious opportunity to convert a rotten, useless road to a splendid, famous trail. If closed to public vehicles, and gated and barricaded to repel scofflaws, 5 miles of the ancient CCC Truck Road could be made a trail, open through most of the winter, the loudest sounds made by the score of tumbling creeks, idyllic picnic spots for families and camps for backpackers.

Below the moraines, in 1977 the Legislature authorized a 2360-acre Mt. Si Conservation Area; as of 1986, 2000 of those acres have been acquired. It is a typical example of getting half a loaf (The Mountaineers wanted 1900 more acres, and State Parks as manager, rather than the Department of Natural Resources the Legislature chose), with a general expectation that a second effort would obtain the other half. But that effort has not been forthcoming, and as one result motorized vehicles have invaded Haystack Basin, degrading a high-in-the-sky refuge to a romper room. A state park is wanted here — a *super-park*. (As has often been said, were Si anywhere east of the Rockies, it would have become America's first *national* park, somewhat after or before the Revolution.) To demonstrate the effect volunteers can have, and to revitalize the drive for the Big Park, a trail was built to the summit of Little Si, and it's such a stunner it soon will be competing with the most-hiked trail in the Northwest — the one to the summit of Big Si.

USGS maps: Snoqualmie, North Bend, Mt. Si, Bandera, Snoqualmie Lake

Little Si (map — page 73)

Mt. Si's footstool peaklet is as old as the Canadian glacier that rode over and around it, smoothing and plucking, as old as the seismic shakings that thrust up the Moon Wall and this lesser byblow, and for a century (or eons?) people have been scrambling to the summit to gaze out upon the North Bend plain. However, until 1985 there never was a real trail, only the boot-scrubbed rocks of the scrambling route. Then your surveyor decided the peak was needed in this new edition to publicize the Mt. Si Conservation Area; having, himself, other business to attend to, he asked Will Thompson, one of the Original Hard-Core Ptarmigans, famed for explorations in the North Cascades in the 1930s, to take a look. Will looked — and flagged — and built an enchanting ¾ mile of new trail to the summit. In October he led "Thompson's Army," recruited from the Issaquah Alps Trails Club and The Mountaineers and the Volunteers of Washington, on a general cleanup and improvement of the previously existing mile of boot-beaten path. The group assembled on top to hoist the flag and sing the anthem, celebrating the inauguration of what is sure to become the most popular summit hike in the area, combining the spooky green cleft between Big Si and Little Si, beneath the Great Overhang, and the magnificent summit views — all on a hike easily done in a lazy afternoon, and open to walking the year around.

Take Exit 31 from I-90 into North Bend and drive east through town on North Bend Way. From the point where it splits in two, continue on the left half (North Bend Way) a scant 1 mile and turn left on Mt. Si Road NE .3 mile to the bridge over the Middle Fork. Immediately past the bridge turn left on 434th Avenue SE and immediately left again into the parking area by the bridge, elevation 500 feet.

Walk 434th ¼ mile, to just past a green-and-white house numbered "12222," and turn right on a woods road — a public road, within the Mt. Si Conservation Area. A short bit from the paved road is a one-car parking spot usable on lonesome days, and on such days a few cars also can park on the shoulder of the county road without bothering the neighborhood. The rude little woods road probably will be gated or otherwise blocked; even if not, were two vehicles (necessarily 4x4) to meet, one would have to self-destruct. So walk, steeply. At ⅓ mile, just beyond an ancient Y, the road levels out and makes a sweeping turn left; here, at another Y the route to Moss Vista goes off right. Follow the left-sweeping fork to its end at a creek, 700 feet, in ¼ mile — ¾ mile from the bridge.

The trail shortly becomes impassable to wheels in any number as it leaves the mixed forest grown up since a 1960s logging show and enters virgin forest grown up since the fires that swept most of Little and Big Si in the 19th century. The trees are not big, but none are "farmed." In ¼ mile the trail rounds a swampy bowl, old beaver ponds, to a camp, 840 feet. From here the scramble route climbs left to the rockslide that leads to the gullies, where in olden days the Climbing Course of The Mountaineers annually sent mobs of novices upward to their fates. (A prominent buttress in the middle of the gully system used to bear the lettering, "Manning's Perch," because that's where the surveyor, when Climbing Chairman, was wont to position himself to scream at stupid novices and idiot instructors.)

Keep right, ascending into the rift where the little fault block split off from the big one, and the glacier squeezed through. The ice seems scarcely to have melted out, so chilly it is here, where the sun so rarely shines. Giant boulders tumbled from above are strewn through the dark forest, and under the boulders are trogs, and if on a gloomy winter day a hiker peers down to the interiors, he may see troglodytes peering back. One becomes aware of the cliff close left — and then of a cliff *overhead!* It is the Great Overhang, often admired from I-90, but a shocking surprise to be discovered hanging heavy heavy over thy head!

The path tops out at an 1100-foot saddle, then descends a haunting glen of old hemlocks and mossy splinters of fault scarp. At 1000 feet, ¾ mile from the camp, begins the ¾ mile of Will's (1985) Trail. Setting out up a rift that Will diagnoses as probably dating from a great quake of about 200 years ago, the way alternates between steep leaps and gentlings, climbing the north ridge of Little Si, from small but tall Douglas firs to spindly fir. Windows open out this way and that. One investigates a brink to the left — and shrinks back from the straight-down view to the bottom of the rift. Soon beyond, the way emerges on the summit, 1576 feet.

The mossy balds have grown very little vegetation since the times of ice and fire, mainly shrubby lodgepole pine, copses of manzanita, sprawls of kinnikinnick, clumps of serviceberry and ocean spray; when last the surveyor was here in spring, in the 1950s, he scarcely knew the flowers from the birds, but plans to return to study a marvel (no doubt) of May blossoms. The views are up up up the Si scarp to the Haystack, north to the Great Buttress, and beyond to

Tuesday Hikers on Little Si

Fuller Mountain; from McClellan's Butte and Grouse Ridge and Mt. Washington to the long stretch of Rattlesnake and out to Tiger and Cougar and Grand and the Olympics. But the main show is down, to the Pleistocene lakebed and the towns of Snoqualmie and North Bend, old Highway 10 and new I-90, the river, the lumber mill, the cows.

Round trip from bridge 5 miles, allow 3 hours
High point 1576 feet, elevation gain 1200 feet
All year

Moss Vista (map — page 73)

In sliding around the corner of Mt. Si the Canadian ice rode over rock buttresses, smoothing their tops and plucking their sides. Subsequently

Moss Vista

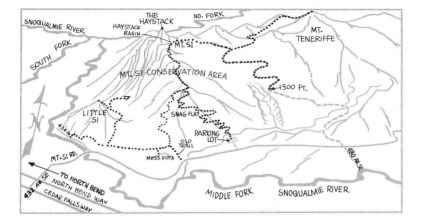

grown up in deep carpets of moss, these tilted slabs hanging high above the North Bend plain, on the edge of the big sky, long have been favored for sunbathing by hikers too lazy to take the 6000 steps to the top of the Big One. Spring is a favorite season for snoozing and viewing, but sunsets the year around have fans, as do the moonshine and starshine.

The route diverges rightward from the Little Si trail (which see) at the 700-foot Y ⅓ mile from 434th Avenue SE and ½ mile from the Middle Fork bridge, elevation 500 feet.

The 1960s logging road, rarely explored by wheelers, contours and then ascends easterly, switchbacking from the clearcut's brush into firs that are not big but tall, a virgin forest grown up since a fire of the semi-remote past. The way goes through a mossy cleft, under a mossy cliff, by gigantic mossy buttresses and moss domes. At ¾ mile from the Y is a saddle, 1200 feet, in a spur ridge.

(The road descends to the 1960s clearcut that obliterated a stretch of the Old Mt. Si trail — see Mt. Si.)

Cross the saddle and in about 100 feet turn right to a path that scrambles up a 1250-foot blip on the spur ridge and there emerges from deep forest to big sky. Walk (softly) down the moss lawn, amid serviceberry shrubs that in spring are great white bouquets. Hang onto the dogs and kids! Stay back from the brink! It overhangs! Look straight down to the Mt. Si Road and the Middle Fork Snoqualmie, then retreat.

Don the sunbathing costume of choice and lie (gently) in the moss. Nibble grapes and pomegranates. Look out to the peaks from Grouse Ridge to Washington to Herpicide Spire to Rattlesnake, and down to I-5 and old Highway 10 crossing the North Bend plain. Visualize the lake that once was here, dammed by the Canadian ice, and the ice front which at another time dammed the Middle Fork and South Fork valleys and deposited the enormous terminal moraines.

Round trip from bridge 2¾ miles, allow 3 hours
High point 1250 feet, elevation gain 800 feet
All year

Mount Si (map — page 73)

In 1964 Tom Miller presented the Literary Fund Committee of The Mountaineers with a plan for a guidebook that was fated to cause quite a commotion. The plan adopted, he proceeded to implement it, and more than any other person or combination of persons was responsible for the pioneering *100 Hikes in Western Washington,* published in 1966. That fame was not his aim is evidenced by his willingness to let others take the credit. His motivation was something else: As he explained to the committee, his career was suffering because come sunny spring he couldn't get any work done. From all over the company a parade of visitors marched through his office, everybody wanting directions on how to climb Si. And so The Mountaineers got into the guidebook business.

Almost since this majestic hunk was named for an early settler, Josiah Merritt ("Uncle Si"), it has drawn hikers. After its being for generations the best-known (well, perhaps second to Rainier) and most-climbed (by some

Nurse log, Mount Si Trail

20,000 folks a year) mountain in the state, in 1977 the State Legislature created a Mt. Si Conservation Area. Proposed for future development is a whole system of trails on and around Si. For now there's the existing "New Trail," maintained by Volunteers of Washington, what with the state being so short on funds; the route provides short trips to modest but satisfying viewpoints and to a splendid grove of big old firs, and a long trip to the high-in-the-sky views from Haystack Basin.

Take Exit 31 from I-90 into North Bend and drive through town on the main drag, North Bend Way, old Highway 10. At the east end of town the highway divides; stay on the left segment, North Bend Way. At 1 mile from the split, turn left on Mt. Si Road, which crosses the Middle Fork Snoqualmie and swings right; in 2 miles from the bridge turn left to the huge trailhead parking lot, elevation 750 feet.

How far do you want to go? That depends partly on the time of year. Some of the Si trail is always walkable — and often it is entirely snowfree in the dead of winter.

From the lush low-valley green of hardwood-conifer forest (and the brown of fresh clearcuts) the trail ascends the steep valley wall and enters a 19th-century burn featuring a new forest of firs up to 2 feet thick, plus large black snags of the old forest. In 1 long mile, at 1600 feet, a rock slab-cliff provides a wide window out to the valley floor, to I-90, to the Puget Moraine sweeping in an arc from the Middle Fork valley over the South Fork to the Cedar River, and to Washington and McClellan's Butte.

In ¾ mile more, at 2100 feet, the way levels at Snag Flat, a bench with a stupendous grove of tremendous Douglas firs; though fire-blackened, they were big enough to survive the conflagrations that denuded most of Si in the 19th century, and remote enough to escape the loggers. However, they at last are succumbing, weakened by the fire, and most are snagtops. Here in the virgin-forest gloom, beside the lovely creek, is a pleasant spot for picnicking. From the creek a spur trail contours east to a viewpoint.

Usually in March or April (often earlier) the snow melts on the higher slopes. The steadily steep trail can then be climbed 2¼ more miles to Haystack Basin, 3900 feet, 4 miles from the parking lot. Clamber around the great boulders under the imposing wall of the Haystack, the 4167-foot final peak of Si. (But don't climb it unless you know what you're doing on rock — and even if you do, don't climb it when other people are around; there is danger of being hit by falling bodies.)

From the edge of the gigantic fault scarp plunging more than 3000 feet to the valley, admire the pretty green pastures, the geometry of streets in North Bend and Snoqualmie, the bugs scurrying along I-90, and the panorama from Rainier to Rattlesnake to the Issaquah Alps to towers of downtown Seattle to Olympics.

Round trips 2, 3½, 8 miles, allow 2, 4, 8 hours
High point 1600, 2100, 3900 feet, elevation gain 850, 1350, 3200 feet
All year (partway)

The above is the New Si Trail, built in the 1960s by the DNR (aided by volunteer Mountaineers and others) to replace the Old Si Trail, which had been partly clearcut. However, the Old Trail is, for the most part, as good as ever, and indeed has its own crew of volunteer maintenance workers, who like it because it's much lonesomer, at least to the 3000-foot junction with the New Trail, and shorter by a mile, thanks to a steeper grade. The trailhead parking area is unsigned but plainly visible, 1.6 miles from the Middle Fork bridge on Mt. Si Road.

The Old Old Si Trail, used until the late 1950s, ascended from what is now 434th Avenue SE to an alder-forest campground by a creek — none other than the creek at the 700-foot Y described herein for the trails to Little Si and Moss Vista. There was a Y then, too, the left to Little Si, the right to Big Si. Reports have been received that some of the tread is intact in the vicinity of Moss Vista; check it out, history buffs. The Moss Vista road definitely is used as an access to the Old Trail.

The Old, Old Old Si Trail by which the Mountaineers made the club's first mountain ascent, in 1907, probably went upward from the rift between Little Si and Big Si. Rumor has it that volunteers are talking about constructing a New New Trail up a timbered ridge from the rift to Haystack Basin.

(We refuse to recognize or countenance the motorcycle razzerway punched through the woods to Haystack Basin from the Teneriffe logging road, and demand that the DNR block it off to prevent machine intrusions on a scene that ought to be purely quiet, saving only the thudding of thousands of boots.)

Mount Teneriffe (map — page 73)

Si is the tip of the ridge forming the north wall of the Middle Fork valley. Next in line, and higher, is Teneriffe. Yet on a day when the Si trail is bumper to bumper from parking lot to Haystack Basin, Teneriffe may be quite lonesome. It thus is an alternative much worth considering, even though the way is on a road sometimes polluted by razzers. The view is different but no less impressive. And, as with Si, one needn't go to the top to have a fine walk. Indeed, it's an excellent snowline-prober — in such season the wheelers are halted by snowbanks and the early flowers are brilliant.

Drive the Mt. Si Road (see Mt. Si) 1.5 miles past the Si trail to where 480th Avenue SE goes off right. Make a reverse turn left on a woods road to a gate, elevation 950 feet. Weyerhaeuser used to lock the gate, while it was completing liquidation of the company's inventory here, but neither Georgia-Pacific, owner of the highlands, nor the DNR, manager of the lower slopes, is partial to locks. Drive on, therefore, through big-view clearcuts, the last completed in 1984, to the edge of forest, 1300 feet.

Parking is recommended here, where the old map shows "jeep trail" crossing a nameless intermittent stream. In the mid-1960s this creek was destabilized by Georgia-Pacific logging (the point of destabilization plainly identifiable on the hiking route) and staged a hell-roaring blowout flood that gouged a canyon and destroyed the jeep trail. For renewed ridge-scalping a replacement road was built, refraining from crossing Hell-Roaring Nameless Canyon — until the point where it caused the blowout. Hang-gliders and owners of tough, dispensable machines drive higher than 1300 feet, bouncing and grinding and churning, and they are the reason Teneriffe is not recommended for weekends.

At 3200 feet, 2 steep, switchbacking miles from the 1300-foot level, there is

West Defiance from Mount Teneriffe

a consciousness-expanding experience. The road emerges from forest into the 1970s Georgia-Pacific clearcut so shockingly visible from I-90. Preservationists come here to take Horrible Example photographs. It's a scene so ghastly it's beautiful. And the view! The Si-like panorama westward is lacking but there's a grand spread from Rattlesnake to Rainier to McClellan's Butte. And I-90 climbing the moraine exerts its special sort of fascination, the roar loud even this high.

Far enough? If not, continue switchbacking up in the devastation. Avoid a spur left toward Si, whose Haystack soon appears, doubtless with a thicket of people visible on the summit. (The wheel route to Haystack Basin, which we insist must be closed, is sometimes used as a different route, via the Mt. Si trail, to Teneriffe.) At about 3700 feet the route heads east. The routefinding trick here is to pay close attention to the map and *not* climb too high too soon. *Do not* take spur roads toward the top of the ridge; rather, choose the one and only road that swings around a prominent spur ridge at 4000 feet, to a promontory with a big view and in season a big snowbank that halts sportdrivers who have spun wheels this high. Dropping to round the head of a small valley, the road then climbs to a 4200-foot saddle, 2 miles from the 3200-foot viewpoint. Now is added the view down to Rachor Lake and out to the North Fork. For many hikers this is quite far enough.

At last the route leaves road and clearcut, proceeding along the forested summit ridge east on a very faint trail, the way easy and safe on the rounded crest. With ups and downs and a final up, in 1 mile the trees grow small and yield to the bald summit, the mossy rocks sprinkled with phlox, lupine, paintbrush, and other alpine flora. The 4788-foot summit (which unlike Si's Haystack requires no dangerous scrambling) is a simple walk and has a view guaranteed to shut your mouth.

The plunge to the valley is longer and thus more impressive than from Si. And there is Si to look at, and Rattlesnake and Issaquah Alps. And Rainier and

Washington and McClellan's Butte. And Green, Garfield, Russian Buttes, peaks of the Cascade Crest, Glacier, and the North Cascades.

Round trip to summit from 1300 feet 10 miles, allow 9 hours
High point 4788 feet, elevation gain 4000 feet
May-November

CCC Truck Road (map — page 81)

Virgin forests of the Middle Fork were logged in the 1920s-30s by valley-bottom railroad. The job done, trestles began to collapse and grades to sink into the swamps. To provide a new valley access, not for logging or any other good reason except it then was an article of faith in the American Way that every portion of God's earth was meant to be available to man's wheels, the Depression–New Deal Civilian Conservation Corps (CCC, or "Three C's") built a truck road, starting high in terminal moraines of the Puget Glacier, only well up the valley dropping to join the rail grade. As the forests regrew the rough and narrow track became a green tunnel. Then, in the 1960s, loggers returned to cut the second-growth and the scattered patches of virgin forest, and to climb valley walls beyond the reach of railroads. To accommodate the new supertrucks a new Middle Fork road was built in the valley bottom. The CCC Truck Road was pretty much abandoned, until Second Wave clearcutters put it to work. By the mid-1980s the overseas log-export industry had so thoroughly skinned the moraines and adjoining slopes as to "create" the most magnificent scenic drive so near Seattle. Mind you, it's a *rough* drive on a *truck* road, but navigable much of the way by the standard family street vehicle. However, portions have deteriorated (improved) to such rudeness they never see any but sport wheels — and other parts are so regularly washed out in winter that far into spring they are as lonesome and quiet as a misanthrope could wish.

There is an opportunity here, if the Forest Service and the state and King County are listening, for the supreme *trail* in the lower valley. Much of it is a delight to walk now — in winter-spring, and on weekdays the year around.

West Entry
Drive Mt. Si Road 3.4 miles from North Bend Way to the turnoff to Mt. Teneriffe (which see). From here the road climbs steeply through the frontier of suburbia into tree farms. Observe (with the economic, ecologic, and esthetic eye) the red-brown of fresh slash and the stark black of recent slash-burning, the light greens of seedlings and youthful plantations, contrasting with the dark green of virgin forest on the valley walls, where tree-farming stops and tree-mining has begun. Note the logging roads switchbacking to the ridge summits, so high that until late spring, when flowers are blooming in the valley, they retain snowbanks, forming white zigzags up through the brown clearcuts to the cliffs and crests. Dominating all views is the enormously wide and long Middle Fork valley, trough of the glacier that came down from the Cascades, and of the other glacier that came up from the lowlands, the latter depositing boulders and gravel and sand and lake-floor clay to form ridges and hillocks jutting far out in the valley. Along the way are distant views to the North Bend plain and

Rattlesnake, over Grouse Ridge to the South Fork valley framed by Defiance and Washington, over the Middle Fork gulf to boggling mine-clearcuts in Granite Creek and on Teneriffe and Green and the unbelievably scalped Bessemer, and to rugged peaks of Russian Buttes and the Yosemite-like granite cliffs of Garfield.

To stay on the CCC Road through a maze of subdivision and logging roads demands attention, and perhaps a few mistakes that lead to deadends (but more views). The following description is valid for 1986: From the Teneriffe turnoff drive .9 mile to a triple split; go straight, on the middle fork. In .5 mile is a Y; keep left, climbing steeply. In .5 mile the road levels to a triple split; go straight down the middle. In 1.6 miles pass the turnoff left to Green Mountain. In .5 mile is a brawling creek, the suggested parking place, 7.4 miles from North Bend Way, elevation 1520 feet.

This creek and its many companions are excitingly torrential in spring snowmelt, and the more appreciated because they can be trusted to rip up the road every bad (good) winter. *Attention Government:* The road ought to be gated here, closed to recreational wheels, made a footroad, a trail, the glory of the Middle Fork. No rational person can enjoy *driving* it — unless his joy comes

Pratt River Valley from CCC Truck Road

from a bruised bottom and many little hemorrhages in the rattled brain.

So, afoot: At ⅓ mile from Brawling Creek the CCC blasted a narrow ledge across a wall of granite slabs polished smooth by the ice. Good views. In ⅔ mile more, at a very unruly creek, slabs and forest end in a gigantic mid-1970s clearcut. In the next short mile are big views, more creeks, a sideroad that once connected down to the valley road, and then, at 1250 feet, a sideroad out on the Puget Moraines.

(The Moraines are a fine excursion. The sideroad dips to a Y; go right, on or near a moraine crest ⅔ mile south, straight across the broad valley to the other side. On the way are looks down to creeks and marshes. At the far end is an abrupt drop to the Middle Fork road and the river. Everywhere are views up to mean bluffs of Russian Buttes, downvalley to Defiance and upvalley to Garfield, and superb spots for staring in disbelief at the deforestation of Bessemer.)

The CCC Road continues ⅓ mile to Big Blowout Creek, 1280 feet. Destabilized by the clearcutting near the summit of Bessemer, the stream flows sometimes in a canyon a dozen feet deep, sometimes through a tumble of boulders very kicky for sport-drivers, and rarely is passable by rational wheels. Just beyond the creek is the connector road to the valley road.

One way from Brawling Creek to Big Blowout Creek 2¼ miles
High point 1520 feet, elevation loss 240 feet
February-December

Middle Entry

Drive the Middle Fork road (see Middle Fork Strolls) 5 miles from Vallley (*sic*) Camp and turn left on the unsigned Bessemer road which climbs through the moraines 1.1 miles to intersect the CCC Road at Big Blowout Creek. This connector road sometimes is blown out by Big Blowout, and sometimes its clay portions slump out. It ought to be gated and closed to all public wheels.

Afoot: Turn right on the CCC Road ⅓ mile. Here the Bessemer road, engineered for big trucks, turns uphill left and the CCC road reverts to 1930s primitiveness. Rarely or never used as a haul road, this stretch mainly serves sport-drivers; one suspects the maintenance is done by Good Joes, volunteer jeeper engineers who do Good Deeds, such as keeping this road open to wheels, when God plainly wishes it to be traveled afoot only. *Note to Government:* There is a plenty of sport roads hereabouts, a paucity of foot trails. Correct the imbalance. *Close this road,* with boulders and moats.

The way tunnels through young forest, then emerges to views. It crosses a saddle in a spur ridge, rounds a rock corner, and at 1 mile from the Bessemer road comes to a tall moss cliff and, below it, a landing promontory, 1350 feet. The views are superb straight down to the river, along the valley, to the lowlands and to Garfield's cliffs, and into the Pratt River valley.

One way from Big Blowout Creek to Tall Moss Cliff 1⅓ miles
High point 1520 feet, elevation gain 300 feet, loss 170 feet
March-November

East Entry

Drive the Middle Fork road 2.3 miles from the Bessemer connector and spot a sideroad left, signed "CCC Road 1" — odd, because this *is* the CCC Road, elevation 960 feet.

Nobody's wheels need this road and it ought to be blocked. As a foot trail it would become a very popular family stroll, ascending a forest tunnel through big second-growth and old virgin stands, crossing pretty creeks, and emerging to the grand views at Tall Moss Cliff.

One way from Middle Fork road to Tall Moss Cliff 1⅓ miles
High point 1350 feet, elevation gain 400 feet
March-November

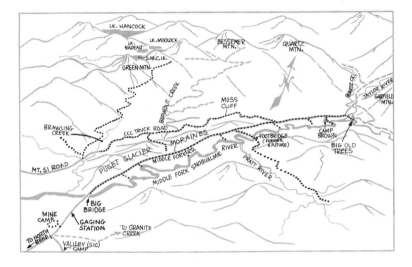

Green Mountain (map — page 81)

The next mountain east from Teneriffe is Green. Because the 4824-foot summit is forested and thus relatively viewless, and because it has no trail and is thus a bit of a battle, perhaps only a bagger would hunger for the peak. But the walk to a high promontory with a panorama of the Middle Fork valley is the finest low-elevation broad-view walk in the vicinity. The slope was so thoroughly skinned in the late 1950s that alders have by no means closed the windows. And the abandoned road quickly becomes so rough that four-wheel playboys can't get through, only the most callused two-wheelers. Even on Sunday peace and quiet is possible.

Drive the CCC Truck Road (which see) 3.5 miles to a white survey post on the right and, just beyond, a sideroad left. If the gate is closed, park here, elevation 1514 feet. If open, drive .1 mile to a Y and go right, past a borrow pit and over a creek a short bit to another Y. (The left climbs a 1980s clearcut on a slope so steep one almost marvels trees ever were able to grow on it, and loggers to wield chainsaws. In a scant 1 mile it deadends at a matchless viewpoint of stumps and valley and peaks.) For Green Mountain, take the right fork, on foot.

The way begins in dense second-growth, switchbacking, climbing to alder-screened glimpses out. In early spring, the ideal season for this trip, a

Mount Garfield from Green Mountain as it looked in 1968. Hikers of today will note vast new clearcuts everywhere

splendid snowline-prober, meltwater is splashing everywhere and flowers rioting. Granite slabs invite admiration, and big old stumps, and at ½ mile a surprising patch of virgin forest.

At 1 mile, 2300 feet, at a big ravine, are the first wide-angle views down to the U-shaped glacier trough of the Middle Fork, the rolling moraine ridges out in the trough, and the rough buttresses of Russian Buttes rising beyond. The creek sheets over granite slabs, suggesting drinking, foot-washing, and other water sports. If snow gets too deep, this makes a highly satisfactory turn-around.

In four more switchbacks, at 2 miles, 2900 feet, the road nears the top of the old clearcut and commences contouring. Here, beside an esthetic granite outcrop, is Far Enough Promontory, featuring a granite bench designed for sitting and gazing. Sit and gaze out the valley to Rattlesnake and Rainier, across to Defiance and Granite Creek clearcuts and Russian Buttes, and up the valley to the Pratt River and the Yosemite-like granite walls of Garfield.

Far enough, yet one ought not quit. Contour another ¼ mile to Absolute Last Promontory, 2800 feet. Here are views east to the Taylor River — and especially to the staggering system of raw clearcuts on adjacent Bessemer.

Round trip to Absolute Last Promontory 4½ miles, allow 4 hours
High point 2900 feet, elevation gain 1500 feet
February-December

South Bessemer Mountain (map — page 83)

Thanks to its eminence as the apex of the ridge that starts with Mt. Si and continues through Teneriffe and Green, and thanks to some of the most savage logging of the past quarter-century, South Bessemer is the supreme grandstand of the Middle Fork. The devastation is hideous — the Forest Service cringes at the sight and reminds the visitor, "Don't blame us, blame the Northern Pacific Land Grant, blame private industry." At lower elevations the second-growth since 1950s clearcutting is doing well enough. On high the 1960s clearcutting is a catastrophe on the geologic scale. Trees 450 years old and only as big as lowland trees grow in 30 years were cut — and fewer than a third were hauled away, the rest left to rot. Streams destabilized by the logging have gone crazy, flushing the mountain's soil to the valley in blowout floods. If this be "tree-farming" then ARCO and Shell and the Arabs can call themselves "oil farmers." Don't come here for the trees, come for the views.

Drive Middle Fork Road (see Middle Fork Strolls) 5 miles from Vallley (*sic*) Camp and turn left on the unsigned Bessemer road 1.1 miles to the CCC Road. Turn right .3 mile to a Y at 1280 feet and go left, uphill, on the Bessemer road.

The question is, on wheels or afoot? A car less agile than a beetle isn't going to want to start up this road at all and soon will be whimpering. Eventually even a beetle gets hysterical, spooked by the bleached bones of wrecked jeeps and the vultures circling above. In any event the road repeatedly crosses a destabilized gully-gouging creek that may settle the matter very quickly — perhaps before reaching the CCC Road. Finally, there's snow — which inspires the realization that this is a classic snowline-probing walk, offering shut-my-mouth views at no great distance from the valley. So, study the situation and improvise.

Assuming the road, the vehicle, and your nerves agree, drive up and up a series of switchbacks, dodging spurs, sticking with the steady-up grade. At

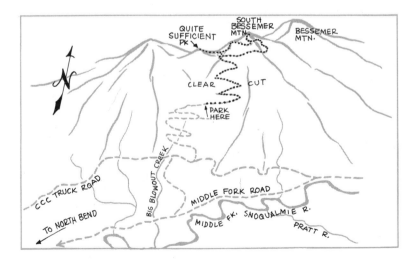

2500 feet, 2 miles from the CCC Road, the way abruptly emerges from 1950s second-growth into raw stumpland of the 1960s and the views become total and flabbergasting. Park and walk. (Drive bravely on and you risk getting into a sticky spot with no room to turn around. The vultures then start gleefully croaking.)

To summarize the views: Early on the feature is the broad trough of the Middle Fork and the intricate dissection of the bed of the Pleistocene lake dammed by the glacier from Canada. Next the broad trough of the Pratt River dominates, the catkin-brown (in spring) lines of alder in green second-growth forest plainly showing the logging-railroad grades of the 1920s-30s. Then the "Low Sierra" walls of Garfield capture the eye, and the row of icy peaks on the Cascade Crest from Daniels to Chimney Rock to Lemah, and smaller peaks of the Snoqualmie Pass area. Finally there is the around-the-compass panorama from the summit — Rainier and Baker, Olympics and Puget Sound and towers of downtown Seattle, Cougar Mountain and the Snoqualmie River valley. No trees get in eyes' way.

Though the network of logging roads on Bessemer looks formidably intricate from a distance, there's no confusion. Always choose the option that proceeds meaningfully upward and you can't miss. At about 2 miles from the 2500-foot level the main road comes within a few feet of a 4000-foot saddle. If you like, continue on the main road around a spur and to the top. However, for the shortcut go to the saddle. A spur climbs left to the 4200-foot top of Quite Sufficient Peak, as it may be judged when snow is soft. If not sufficient, take the rude track climbing right from the saddle. As it runs out to end in the sky, switchback right — climbing a washed-out bank to do so. When this spur meets the main road, switchback left on the latter and at about ¾ mile from the saddle attain the scalped, bulldozed-flat top of South Bessemer Mountain at 5000 feet. Actually, the tippy-top is 5028 feet and a stone's throw away but its

Bessemer Mountain in early May

views are plagued by a group of scrawny trees that shamed even the brutes who ravaged all else. North Bessemer, 5166 feet, is a rough mile away and not worth it.

Round trip (from 2500 feet) 5½ miles, allow 6 hours
High point 5000 feet, elevation gain 2500 feet
April-October (summit)

Middle Fork Strolls (map — page 87)

The great long wide Middle Fork valley inevitably draws throngs of folks in spring to see if the mountains are still there, and where (if any) is the snow. They always are and it sometimes isn't. But where are the trails? Mainly in the fevered imaginations of guidebook writers to whom Government turns a deaf ear. Nevertheless, a day's pedestrian entertainment, suitable for mixed company (that is, the very small and young and the somewhat elderly and gimpy, as is the average guidebook writer), is easy to find.

Go off I-90 on Exit 34, signed "Edgewick Road," and turn left under the freeway on 468th Avenue SE. Pass Seattle East Auto Truck Plaza and turn right on SE Middle Fork Road. The road splits in two pieces, which proceed through the frontier of suburbia and rejoin at Vallley (*sic* — Lutheran Laymens League) Camp, 3 miles from the freeway exit.

At .3 mile from the camp is the second of several entries to Granite Creek road, a good springtime stroll (see the description, following). In 1.1 miles more is the DNR Mine Creek Camp and Picnic Area, featuring a River Trail and a Nature Trail, the two good for an hour or more. In .9 more mile, just past a stream-gaging station, is a marvelous large gravel bar accessible on foot by a woods road. In .7 mile is a big concrete bridge over the river.

Onward from Big Bridge, which is 3 miles from Vallley Camp, the route offers many nice little things to do. A snowline-probing excursion may find the snowline on the valley floor, providing machine-free exercise on Middle Fork Road itself, plus all the snowballs the children can throw and all the snow angels they can make. Look for remnants of old trestles of the logging railroad; Middle Fork Road largely follows the mainline rail grade, which sprouted many a spur up toward the Puget Glacier moraines. Beaver dams and beaver logging are ubiquitous; no kid need come home without a "beaver stick" to take to school for Show and Tell. Numerous sideroads take off riverwards. Don't drive them — that's a waste. Park and walk through the trees and birds to the sunny sandbars and the sparkling waters.

At .2 mile from Big Bridge, stop to explore a fresh slice into blue clay of the Pleistocene lakebed. In .7 mile more is the connector road to the CCC Truck Road and Bessemer Mountain (which see); just beyond are trestle remnants. In 1.6 miles more, park to explore the area near the great wide Pratt River valley, which joins the Middle Fork from the other side. Fans of Li'l Abner used to come here to gather schmoos; latterly the place has become notorious among weird geologists for X-rated concretions. Until a couple of decades ago a swinging bridge crossed the Middle Fork to the Pratt River trail, which is still

Abandoned footbridge over Middle Fork Snoqualmie River

there but presently requires wading to get at it; the Forest Service expects to install a new bridge someday, opening a wonderful low-elevation long-season walk. One hopes they also will then build (rather, rebuild) a Middle Fork Trail on that quiet and wild side of the river.

At 4.2 miles from Big Bridge is the east entry to the CCC Truck Road (which see). In 1.7 miles more, note a clearing on the right, and a concrete slab, foundation of the old Camp Brown Guard Station. Just before the slab a mucky sideroad leads to a path down through fine mossy forest to a gravel bar with an astounding view of the granite walls of Garfield. In .3 mile more is a Y. The left is the Middle Fork Road to the Taylor River and beyond; stay straight, in several hundred yards coming to the Taylor River, an old abandoned campground, and a stunning grove of colossal ancient Douglas fir and cedar, and more views of Garfield granite. This is 6.3 miles from Big Bridge, at an elevation of 1030 feet.

Allow an afternoon or a weekend
High point 1030 feet, no elevation gain
All year

Granite Creek (map — page 87

The Granite Creek road is gated at the very bottom and the gate is closed — or open — or swinging — and who knows when it will be which? Weyerhaeuser has finished liquidating its inventory in the valley and removed its locks from the gate. St. Regis, which never had any policy whatsoever, only whims, has sold out to Champion International, which as the new boy on the scene says it will generally follow Weyerhaeuser practice. However, repeatedly the surveyor checked the gates in the spring, summer, and fall of 1985, weekends and weekdays, and never found them open. Other hikers had better luck, but on no consistent pattern. A hiker planning a serious expedition might call Kerry Pershing, in the Tacoma office of Champion, 577-8300. The surveyor was going to do that, but then the snows shut him down, so a revision must await another year, another printing. The following is from the previous survey.

Drive to Vallley Camp (see Middle Fork Strolls) and .3 mile more to an unsigned road turning off right and up. This is the Granite Creek road. Elevation, 800 feet.

For a winter-spring walk, enjoy the low valley. The road parallels the Middle Fork Road 1 mile, then begins ascending steadily in fine forest of big maples and mixed conifers. At 1½ miles, 1200 feet, is a good view to the valley and moraines and from Rattlesnake to Si and Teneriffe and Green and Bessemer. At 2 miles, 1600 feet, is another and better view, a good turnaround for a snowline-prober since not much new happens in the next stretch.

For a longer, late-spring hike, continue to where the road turns sharp right into the Granite Creek valley at 1700 feet, 2½ miles from the Middle Fork Road. Follow the road as it crosses Granite Creek and ascends 1½ miles to a Y at 2800 feet. The right fork contours and drops, then climbs the opposite valley wall. The left fork climbs a scant ½ mile to a second Y, 3100 feet. The right fork contours in ½ mile to Lower Granite Lake, 2950 feet, and ½ mile more to Upper Granite Lake, 3100 feet, 5½ miles from the Middle Fork Road. Both lakes have been logged to the shores.

For the longest hike, at the 3100-foot Y take the left fork. Shortly switchback left. In a bit is a junction from which the good main road proceeds straight ahead; turn right up a rough, undrivable, unsigned road. In about ⅓ mile is a Y; go right, at the sign "Mt. Defiance Trail." In another long switchbacking ⅓ mile the road switchbacks left and is blocked by a heap of dirt. Off the spur to the right, perhaps marked with part of an old sign, "Mt. Defiance," the trail begins. Don't feel bad if you don't find the trail; few people do. It doesn't matter a whole lot because wherever you end up the views are grand over the awesomely naked lake basin and out to the Middle Fork valley and horizons beyond. If

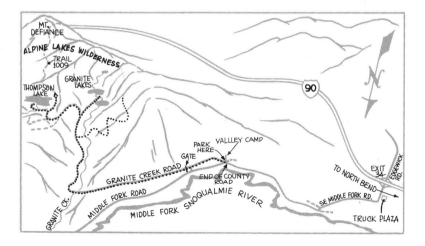

Green Mountain from Granite Creek Road

found, the trail leads out of the clearcut into forest and ascends to a 4300-foot saddle, 2 miles from the 3100-foot Y, 6½ miles from the Middle Fork Road. From here the trail descends to Thompson Lake. No views to compare with those from the clearcut. But nice and cool in the virgin shadows. And notable because here the Sound-to-Mountains Trail at last moves from humanized land to wildland at the edge of the Alpine Lakes Wilderness.

Round trips 4, 11, and 13 miles, allow 3, 8, and 11 hours
High points 1600, 3100, and 4300 feet, elevation gains 800, 1900, and 3100 feet
All year, one trip or the other

Taylor River Trail (map — page 89)

A trail wide enough for side-by-side sociable sauntering, a forest partly half-century-old second-growth and partly centuries-old old-growth, and a profusion of creeks brawling and splashing down granite slabs from green pool to green pool. The Forest Service has done something good, has actually closed a road and reclaimed a valley for trail country! Unfortunately, it's done only half the job, eliminating four-wheelers but not two-wheelers. When writing the supervisor of Mt. Baker-Snoqualmie National Forest to applaud the closing of the Taylor River road, remind that motorcycles have 100 other miles of roads in the Middle Fork to razz and can well afford to give up this route. Also remind that there presently are no low-elevation foot-only trails in Middle Fork country.

Drive Middle Fork Road 9.7 miles from Vallley (*sic*) Camp (see Middle Fork Strolls) to the Taylor River bridge, which comes and goes at the whims of floodwaters. At the Y just beyond, go left, straight ahead, .4 mile, to where a vehicle bridge recrossed the Taylor River until vandals burned it. The replacement (1986) is two-wheeler- and foot-only. Park here, elevation 1200 feet.

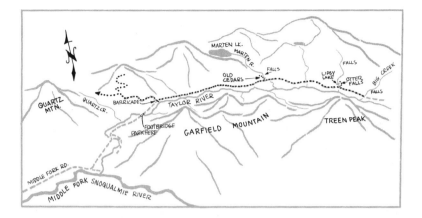

In ⅓ mile pause to inspect a beaver dam (inactive) and pond on the left. At the Y here, the Quartz Creek road goes off left and steeply up, climbing to clearcuts at 4000 feet and above and probable paths to summits and lakes. So long as the 10-odd miles of roads are free from four-wheelers they are much worth exploring on foot but were not surveyed for this guide because of a suspicion a new bridge soon will bring back the sport drivers and return the Quartz Creek to its former uproar. Pedestrians might well ask the Forest Service its intentions — and then complain.

For the trip in hand, take the right fork, the former Taylor River road, now barricaded. The river tumbles along close below, accessible by short sidetrips. Peaks of Garfield soar sharply high. The varied thrush trills, the winter wren twitters. The forest floor is carpeted with deer fern, elkhorn moss, teaberry, and bunchberry. Massive granite blocks invite scrambling.

At a long 2 miles from the blockade is the first of the big creeks, Marten, with falls churning a pool of limeade. For the best experience — actually, the hike climax — find a mean little old trail a hundred feet before the plank bridge and climb through an awesome forest of ancient cedars, some more than 12 feet in diameter. Take careful sidetrips for close views of a whole series of superb cataracts and plunge basins and clouds of spray.

Return to the road-trail and proceed by several little creeks to the next big one, in another long 1 mile. See a falls high above on the valley wall. Otter Falls, however, is lower down; to get there find a rude trail over a rotten log 500 feet beyond the creek.

Return to the road-trail for another ½ mile to Big Creek, 1700 feet, and more falls, by the concrete bridge, snow water sheeting down smooth granite. This is a neat spot to eat lunch, imagining otters sliding the slabs.

If more exercise is wanted, Snoqualmie Lake is a couple of long, steep miles away at 3147 feet in the Alpine Lakes Wilderness.

Round trip (with sidetrips) 8⅔ miles, allow 5 hours
High point 2000 feet, elevation gain 800 feet
March-November

North Fork Snoqualmie River flowing through old lake bed

NORTH FORK SNOQUALMIE RIVER —
VIA NORTH FORK COUNTY ROAD

The North Fork is three stories: the Cascade mountain front; the plateau west of the front; and the valley to the east, inside. As a hiking province it is further divided into trips that can be done comfortably by parking on the North Fork County Road, subject of this chapter, and those best done when Weyerhaeuser's Spur 10 Gates are open to public vehicles, subject of the next chapter.

The southern section of the front is the great wall of The Mountain that Was the Moon, destined to be famous among hikers when the Mt. Si State Superpark is established, the boundaries of the present Conservation Area expanded to take in the entirety of the Moon Wall and Moon Gorge, as well as the high, wild cirque of Crater Lake and adjoining ridges.

The front north of Si is a series of lake basins and ridges in the Great Big Western Tree Mine, whose lofty clearcuts offer wide-screen views that will not shrink for generations, so slowly do the trees grow at these elevations.

West of the front sprawls the Tokul Plateau, heart of the Great Big Western Tree Farm, where elevations, slopes, and soils are ideal for growing commercial forests on a harvest cycle of half a century or less. The plateau is scant on geographical drama, but when the Spur 10 Gates are closed (as they are weekdays the year around and weekends from the end of hunting season to the start of fishing season), long on solitude. Aside from the Fuller Mountain vicinity described herein there are many circlings about to do within easy foot reach of Gate 10, amid clifflets and peaklets and hillocks, creeks and creeklets, lakes and marshes and swamps and bogs. Obtain the USGS maps and the (free) Weyerhaeuser map. Note the maze of roads and roadlets, including a few historic old logging railroad grades not yet obliterated and still marvelously walkable. Much of the plateau offers nothing better than lonesome walking in forests of ages from 0 to 50 (no older, nevermore), only the occasional patch of cattails and blackbirds to disturb inner reveries. Talk to yourself, if you please. If you can't handle the quiet, sing. Play the flute. Bang a tambourine.

Within the mountain front the walking is mainly on the awesomely moonscapy clearcuts that climb from farmland to the tree mines, at elevations where Nature will be so long growing another forest that forest science will have time to catch up with the loggers and tell them to leave the summits alone.

The chapter ends in a shock. After clearcuts and plantations, upon entering the Alpine Lakes Wilderness the hiker is stunned to see that vegetables can grow so tall and huge. The mind reels, the very reason is threatened. But it's worth the risk.

(Note: The City of Bellevue may, or may not, build a dam on the North Fork at river mile 6.7, reservoirizing the stream to river mile 11.2 — roughly the stretch from above the Moon Gorge to Spur 10. A pipeline would carry drinking water near the confluence of the Snoqualmie River and Tokul Creek, just below Snoqualmie Falls, and onward to the North Fork Issaquah Creek and a reservoir on Cougar Mountain. If Bellevue doesn't build the dam, Seattle says it will, though not until well into the next century. Residents downstream from the damsite are very nervous.)

USGS maps: Mt. Si, Index, Snoqualmie, Lake Joy, Sultan

For a free copy of the company's road system, write Weyerhaeuser Company, Box W, Snoqualmie, WA 98065

Hawk's Rocks (map — page 94)

In the 1950s the surveyor starred in a movie produced by Jim Hawk. The climactic scene shows the hero standing on the summit of Mt. Shuksan, waving arms and flapping mouth as if in friendly greeting to Jim, who — at the controls of a Supercub float plane — had cut his engine, hung momentarily like a falling leaf, and leaned out the window to yell, "Hey, Harvey! Want a ride home?" Harvey, expecting the craft to pancake down upon him, actually was not the least friendly, was screaming, "Get *out* of here, you maniac!"

North Bend residents said much the same to Jim in the 1980s, when he reopened an ancient quarry at the foot of Mt. Si, stimulating a fear his blasting might shake the Great Buttress loose and bring tumbling down upon the city this entire portion of what used to be, according to former residents, the Moon. The matter ended amicably in 1983, when Jim sold his rocks to the state for addition to the Mt. Si Conservation Area.

Go off I-90 on Exit 31 into North Bend. Turn east on the main drag, North Bend Way, former Highway 10, 2 blocks and turn north on Ballarat Avenue. Follow the thoroughfare through its many changes in name/number (in all these disguises it is the North Fork County Road). At 2.2 miles from downtown, just past the Middle Fork bridge, turn right on SE 92nd Street. In .5 mile this jogs left to become 436th. A couple of hundred yards past the jog is a fenced utility enclave on the right. Immediately beyond, a narrow lane enters the woods. Park on the county road shoulder, elevation 430 feet.

Ignore "Keep Out" signs (this lane is public), clamber over wheel-barring barricades, and in several minutes pass a truck engine on blocks and a power takeoff. This artifact of the quarry era ought to be preserved; the junked cars are dispensable. Turn left a few steps to a greensward amid talus boulders as big as bread boxes, refrigerators, Volkswagens, and gazebos. The quarry never attacked the bedrock of Si, was confined to busting up these boulders, and thus did next to nothing to molest the pristinity.

Little kids will want to scramble around the boulders. Older kids may wish to explore the talus and brush upward to the base of the wall, some 450 vertical

Hawk's Rocks and Mount Si

feet above. Middling kids likely will be content to unpack the tuna fish sandwiches and picnic dills, get out the binoculars, and inspect the buttresses above for mountain goats, who feel perfectly secure in this sprawling empire of verticality. They will not be seen on the face of the Great Buttress, which in large part overhangs and from base to top is 2000 vertical feet, at an overall angle of about 75 degrees. Geologists say the fault responsible for this scarp is not presently active. So relax and enjoy your olives.

Round trip ¼ mile, allow 1 lunch
High point 430 feet, no elevation gain
All year

The Moon Wall (map — page 94)

The highway millions and the trail thousands know large portions of The Mountain that Was the Moon and the Moon River. One side of the mountain, though, and one stretch of the river, are known to more goats and coyotes and bears than people — despite the fact that an excellent trail crosses this Moon Wall and has for — how many years? The surveyor speculates the "jeep trail," as the map labels it, may have been scratched into the precipice, perhaps in the 1920s, as access to a mine in Rachor Creek; it was used subsequently or originally, perhaps in the 1930s, by gypo loggers. Except at the very start, the trail's forest never has been clearcut, was merely high-graded, and a half-century after departure of the double-bitted axes and misery whips and

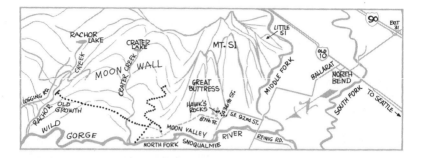

donkey engines has an exquisitely virgin feeling to it — and in fact is partly magnificent old-growth. On his first exploration, the surveyor followed fresh tracks of cougar through the snow. On his latest, he found the path well-beaten — but as shown by fallen logs across the way, mainly by walkers no taller than 3 feet and innocent of shoes.

For the greater glory of the Mt. Si Conservation Area, two things must be done: (1) Volunteers must build a trail around private property at the start of the route; (2) The state must acquire from Weyerhaeuser the route from Crater Creek to Rachor Creek, and all lands above to the cliffs and below to the wild waters of the North Fork in its gorge and Rachor Creek in its canyon.

Drive 1.5 miles from the Middle Fork Snoqualmie bridge (see Hawk's Rocks) on SE 92nd, which becomes 436th, then 87th, and finally Moon Valley Road. Spot a woods road on the right. Ignore the "No Trespassing" sign (the road is public) and drive up it a few feet to a parking turnout, elevation 475 feet.

Attention Volunteers: A few yards from the county road is a Y. (Between the forks, note the enormous logs, the skid on which the donkey engine was mounted.) The right fork is public; the left is private across 5.28 acres recently closed to walkers. The DNR is negotiating to buy a property some 500 feet farther north on Moon Valley Road, and when this happens volunteers can build some 700 feet of trail there to intersect the "jeep trail." In the meantime, hikers must take the right fork, walk up it and due east 820 feet from the county road, turn due north 254 feet to pass the private acres and house. Even before a half-dozen volunteers spend a morning flagging and brushing a bypass, hikers will find the going easy on moderate sidehill in open forest, on state land. In a dozen-odd minutes they will pass above the house and angle down to a gravel pit and there join the jeep trail.

(*Attention Volunteers and Government:* The first edition of this book described "Three Forks Vista," a walk up the right fork 1¼ miles to the end at 1350 feet, giving a view down to the North Fork Snoqualmie coming from the right, the Middle Fork from the left, the two proceeding west ½ mile to where the South Fork, invisible in floodway forests, completes the Three Forks union. The views extended beyond to pastures, barns, the town of Snoqualmie and the swath of I-90, the Issaquah Alps, Seattle, the Olympics — and close at hand, the Great Buttress of Si, in awesome profile. The right fork still is a peaceful, wheelfree woods walk, and in winter has screened views. However, it could become a famous feature of the Conservation Area if volunteers, with government permission, would take a chainsaw to several dozen scrappy alders and maples to reopen the window, and build a short trail from the road-end to a picnic spot beside the marvelous tumbling creek that plunges down the chasm beside the Great Buttress.)

Having beaten through the public woods to the public jeep trail, the hiker ascends a steep bit to a flat, 950 feet, beneath imposing cliffs. See the Great Buttress, the white thread of Rachor Creek, Fuller Mountain, and Tokul Plateau. At the bouldery, brawling cataracts of Crater Creek, 1040 feet, many a picnicker (once the route is made family-easy) will get out the meatloaf sandwiches and turn the kids loose to wade. Just beyond is the rotting jackstraw of a small clearcut of the late 1970s; a very short but exceedingly mean path squirms through to a resumption of jeep trail.

Attention Government: At exactly this point the Conservation Area is left for Weyerhaeuser property which continues to Rachor Creek. The company has expressed a willingness to make a land exchange and meanwhile has deferred logging — but will not wait indefinitely. The state must act *soon* or lose what lies beyond Crater Creek.

What lies beyond is instant grandeur, the old road totally wheelfree and unmolested in half a century or more, yet open and easy walking in deep forest, by big boulders that have fallen from the cliffs over the centuries — and some that fell in 1984, bashing down big trees. The way goes through groves of alder-maple, mixed forest, impressive conifer forest of fir, hemlock, and cedar up to 3 feet in diameter and more, very virginlike. The bouldery fan of Wowfow Creek is passed, and two blowout fans of the 1980s. The ear harkens to an awesome roar — Moon River, directly below in its thundering gorge. And suddenly the firs are 5 feet in diameter, old-growth beauties, mingled with even larger snags, veritable bird condos. Another roar is heard — Rachor Creek, pure white water all the way down its canyon from the hanging valley to the river.

The jeep trail swings into the Rachor canyon to brush that can be penetrated to a safe ford, leading to a short scramble up gravel to the modern logging road (see Rachor Vista). Most walkers will find the old-growth grove at 2½ miles, 2000 feet, a satisfying turnaround, completing a memorable visit to cougar country.

Round trip 5 miles, allow 4 hours
High point 2000 feet, elevation gain 1600 feet
March-November

The Moon Gorge (map — page 102)

Before the North Fork Snoqualmie settles down to meander through cow farms it has a last wild fling in tree farms, dropping a tumultuous 400 feet in a deep gorge, joined on the way by waterfalling Rachor Creek, and through the length of the 2-mile (as the river runs) gorge cutting the foot of the Moon Wall. Here is still another glory that must be added to the Mt. Si Conservation Area.

Go off I-90 on Exit 31 into North Bend. Turn east on the main drag, North Bend Way, 2 blocks and turn north on Ballarat Avenue. Follow the thoroughfare through its many changes in name/number until at last, 4 miles from downtown, at a Y where the right fork is Ernie's Grove Road, the left fork throws off disguises and reveals itself to be the North Fork Road, signed "Dead End for 24 Miles." Drive its chuckholes and washboard 1.5 miles. As the road is completing a switchback left near the top of a 1975 clearcut, take the unsigned two-entry road going right. Elevation, 1000 feet.

At .3 mile from the North Fork Road, enter a 1980s clearcut. Immediately note that the gorge brink is close to the right; park and walk one or another easy path through rotting slash. Look down down to the North Fork, 400 vertical feet below, and up up the Moon Wall, rising 4000 feet from the river. A gravel chute makes an easy and safe skid down to the river, a hard trudge back up to the car.

At .5 mile from the North Fork Road is a Y; go right .5 mile, then right again .2 mile more on a narrow sideroad into forest (1986) to the end, where cedar miners worked in 1980 or so. Park here, elevation 1050 feet. A rude track enters the forest and in several minutes reaches the brink. A fishermen's mad path plummets down the cliff, exceedingly steep but with plenty of trees to hang onto, yet dangerous nevertheless. In 250 vertical feet of descent the path hits the river — exactly where it emerges in cataracts from a rock slot, joined there by Rachor Creek tumbling down the wall into a boiling cauldron. How wild! How loud!

Two round trips ½ mile, allow 2 hours
High point 1050 feet, elevation loss (and gain) 650 feet
All year

Fuller Mountain (map — page 97)

A footstool peak isolated from the Cascade front, the haystack of Fuller towers (well, that's going a bit strong) nearly 1000 feet over the Tokul Plateau, prominent from miles away in all directions and providing a lordly view of surrounding forests and lakes.

At the Y 4 miles from North Bend, where Ernie's Grove Road goes right, keep straight ahead left on North Fork County Road (see The Moon Gorge). Taking care to dodge logging and firewood-cutting spurs, stick with the chuckholes and washboard past the rows of shooting galleries 3.8 miles to the intersection with Weyerhaeuser's famous Spur 10. Turn left the short bit to the West Spur 10 Gate and park, elevation 1003 feet.

Walk by the gate, cross Weyerhaeuser's Mainline log-haul road, and spot the boot-beaten, flag-marked path into a 1984 clearcut. In woods at its edge runs Ten Creek, crossed by a volunteer-built (Green River College) bridge. Emerge from woods to a logging road; the route to Klaus and Boyle Lakes turns left on this road; a few feet down it to the left, spot a cairn-marked trail through a 1984 clearcut to a second logging road. As of 1986, what with the start of the ascent route on Fuller having been obliterated by a new clearcut, the way turns left on this road to join the first road that was crossed, turns right on the latter, and continues to where the sharp eye will spot, at the top of the clearcut, a cairn, a white plastic bottle, a mass of ribbons, and whatnot, to mark the start of undestroyed trail. Flags more or less guide the way through the slash. In future, volunteers will improve the trail but may relocate the start at the small quarry, in which case the route will turn right from the second logging road, then left on the quarry road to its end, above the quarry. So stay alert for meaningful-looking ribbons and perhaps signs.

Having got boots on trail, don't expect a boulevard. The Green River College students who built the trail in 1975 as a classroom exercise engineered the route beautifully but for purposes of defense against intruding wheels left the tread with many small obstacles of roots and rocks. Ascending across steep west slopes of the mountain in fine mixed forest, the trail attains the north ridge at about 1600 feet and turns south to the summit — dense woods with no view.

However, views there are. First, partway up the mountain, on a rockslide, is a look down to Klaus Lake. Second, on the ridge the trailbuilders have cut a window in the forest, opening out north on Boyle and Bridges Lakes, Metcalf Marsh, various bumps and vales, the North Fork and Tolt valleys, and east to the Cascade front. Third, they have cut another window opening west over Klaus Lake and the Tokul Plateau to the Issaquah Alps and Mt. Selig and the Olympics. Finally, for the climax vista, just before the final rise to the summit go left down a grassy glade and through woods, following orange dots on trees, to a mossy bald, a flower glory in spring and in all seasons offering a stunning panorama of the Cascade front from Lake Hancock to Si to North Bend.

Round trip 2½ miles, allow 3 hours
High point 1850 feet, elevation gain 850 feet
February-December

Fuller Mountain Lakes and Looks and Loops (map — page 97)

Much of the Tokul Plateau is mainly notable for lonesome walking in forests of every age from 5 minutes to 50 years, with little except the cattails and blackbirds of occasional wet spots to break the train of thought. The walker

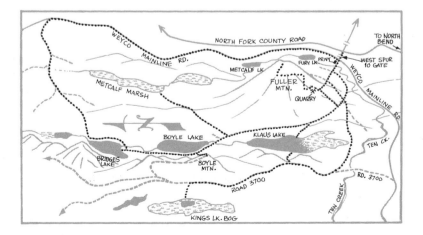

Boyle Lake and Fuller Mountain

who wants more action than that can find plenty in the Fuller Mountain vicinity — and on most days of the year can find peace and quiet too, what with the West Spur 10 Gate being closed to public four-wheelers.

Kings Lake Bog

Though a spot of open water has been given the name of "lake," the bog is the attraction, ⅔ mile long and ¼ mile wide, the biggest and best sphagnum bog of the region. Come in late spring when the entire bog is a pink sea of kalmia in bloom, in summer to sniff the aromatic Labrador tea and watch the meat-eating sundew have lunch, and in fall to pick a hatful of wild cranberries.

From West Spur 10 Gate, elevation 1003 feet, walk the route to the four-way intersection at the foot of Fuller Mountain (which see). Turn left a scant 1 mile, then right 1 long mile on road 3700. Find the location of the bog by the tall cedar snags (drowned by beaver floods) above the screen of trees bordering the shore. Pick a short but mean route through the slash of the 1985 clearcut; fishermen, whose previous paths were obliterated, in time will beat new ones, so look sharp.

Round trip 5 miles, allow 3 hours
High point 1003 feet, minor elevation gain
All year

Klaus, Boyle, Bridges, and Metcalf Lakes

The somber lakes curving in a chain around the foot of Fuller Mountain make a fine walk in themselves or combine with the peak to fill out a day. The half-lake, half-marsh openings in second-growth forest (which will be left intact to screen the waters, even after the clearcuts have let daylight into the rest of the area) offer splendid birdwatching and much-appreciated freedom from wheels.

From the four-way intersection at the foot of Fuller Mountain go straight north, close under the peak, on an old railroad grade converted in the 1980s to a logging road. At ⅓ mile from the four-way, a spur ascends a short bit left to a deadend. Find the fishermen's path dropping to the shore of Klaus Lake, 983 feet, 1 mile from the Spur 10 gate. Gaze through reeds and grasses over quiet waters, watch ducks swim, perhaps hear a loon call. Search for (but do not disturb) a beaver lodge with an entry that is not only underwater but underground, through a tunnel beneath the boggy surface.

Beyond the Klaus spur the logging road bends left to a deadend. At the turn go straight ahead, down into the woods, to hit the surviving stretch of rail grade — surviving, that is, until the logging road is extended, in 1987 or so. Pass a spur rail grade making a reverse-turn right; this leads in a scant ½ mile to fish-bearing waters of Metcalf Lake-Marsh, which occupies the course of Ten Creek for better than 2 miles. In a short bit from the spur the new road will turn right, uphill, from the main rail grade, leaving the last few hundred feet untouched, by agreement with the State Game Department. In a few more steps, a scant 1 mile from the Klaus Lake junction, is the outlet of Boyle Lake, 1034 feet.

The best part of the hike now begins, following the Great Lakeshore & Northern Railroad an enchanting 1¼ miles. The open, parklike grade closely follows Boyle Lake, with many a path out from big second-growth cedars and firs to good spots for watching birds and gaping at the lofty mound of Fuller Mountain; at a Y of grades take the right. Beyond the lake-end marsh is the lovely little inlet creek, at one point beaver-dammed to a marshy pond. From the outlet of Bridges Lake (a wet-foot crossing in winter) the rail grade continues by more reeds and birds, petering out in marshes at the end of the lake.

Round trip 6½ miles, allow 4 hours
High point 1034 feet, elevation gain 200 feet
All year

Boyle Mountain

The crest of a ridge rising abruptly from Boyle Lake has the most sweeping views of the area, not excluding Fuller Mountain. They are guaranteed to last well into the 1990s, when the 1985 clearcut will begin to brush in.

Just after coming to the south end of Boyle Lake, leave the trail and climb the steep woods (still there in 1986) a scant ¼ mile to the summit, 1350 feet.

Gaze to Fuller Mountain, the Si scarp and Little Si, the North Bend plain, Rattlesnake and Tiger Mountains, varied-aged forests of the Tokul Plateau, the vacuity marking the unseen Snoqualmie valley, the East Sammamish Plateau, Mt. Selig and the Olympics.

Round trip from Boyle Lake ½ mile, allow 1 hour
High point 1350 feet, elevation gain 300 feet
All year

The Fuller Circle

The network of logging roads behind the West Spur 10 Gate offers excellent exercise for long-leggitty joggers. A loop that demands a minimum of huffing and puffing completely circles Fuller Mountain, via a batch of lakes and ponds and marshes and creeks.

At the inlet marshes of Bridges Lake, 1055 feet, find a fishermen's path from the rail grade up through a mid-1980s clearcut to a landing at the end of a logging road, 1160 feet. Walk northerly, through vales amid cliff-sided hillocks, in forests of many ages, some grown to fine dark woods and not due for the next harvest until 2020. At all junctions take the right (except for obviously deadend reverse-turns); a short 2 miles from the landing intersect the Mainline. Walk it south 3½ miles along Ten Creek drainage (Metcalf Marsh and Lake and Fury Lake); at 5¾ miles from Bridges Lake return to West Spur 10 Gate.

Loop trip 9 miles, allow 6 hours
High point 1300 feet, elevation gain 500 feet
All year

Mount Si from route to Lake Hancock

Lake Hancock (map — page 102)

During its retreat, the Puget Glacier built moraines that dammed streams issuing from the Cascade front, thus creating lakes. Most of the streams have breached the dams and drained the lakes, but Hancock remains, resembling the hundreds of cirque lakes in this section of the range but having a quite different origin. Sitting in a bowl perched above the low country at the foot of the mountains, it's a fine blue puddle in the green trees ringing most of the shore. On the way are magnificent views to Seattle and all.

Drive the North Fork County Road to Spur 10 (see Fuller Mountain) and park near (but not blocking) the East Spur 10 Gate, elevation 1000 feet.

Spur 10 heads east, bends north, and in 1 long mile crosses the North Fork. A few yards uphill is a junction with a water tower and a mess of signs. To the right is 4200, the route to Rachor Vista (which see). To the left is the main road, signed "Spur 10, Spur 14." Go straight ahead, uphill, on 4300. (In an older numbering system, 13.)

Ascending steadily in second-growth firs that have blocked the view, at 1800 feet, 1¼ miles from the North Fork bridge, the road to Hancock switchbacks right; going left from here is road 14A (unsigned) to Calligan Lake (which see). Views begin, from Fuller to the Olympics, Si to the Issaquah Alps and downtown Seattle.

At subsequent switchbacks keep to the obvious main road. The trees shrink and the views from steep hillsides grow, the Puget Sound lowlands spread out like a map. The grandest panorama, featuring the North Fork and sun sparkling on faraway lakes and saltwater, is from the moraine at the basin lip. In ¾ mile from the Calligan junction is a Y; go right. In ¼ mile, when dropping toward Hancock (Black) Creek, turn left just past an old gravel pit and follow a road-path a few hundred feet to the lakeshore, 3½ miles from the East Gate.

Though this west approach to the lake is clearcut, a few old cedars were left on the shore. Sitting under them on the gravel beach, listening to waves, looking over the water to virgin forests on the peaks, one can forget the logging. Just don't look over your shoulder.

Round trip 7 miles, allow 5 hours
High point 2172 feet, elevation gain 1200 feet
March-November

Calligan Lake (map — page 102)

Why should Lake Hancock get all the business? Calligan is a near twin, also dammed by the glacier, also offering broad vistas from clearcuts.

On the road to Lake Hancock (which see), at 1¼ miles from Watertower Junction turn left on road 14A (unsigned) and go north 1 mile to cascades of Calligan Creek, then ¾ mile more to join road 14, coming from the north. Follow 14 in switchbacks up the hill ½ mile to the basin lip. The view from here over the Snoqualmie Tree Farm to the Snoqualmie valley and Puget Sound and the Olympics is a crackerjack.

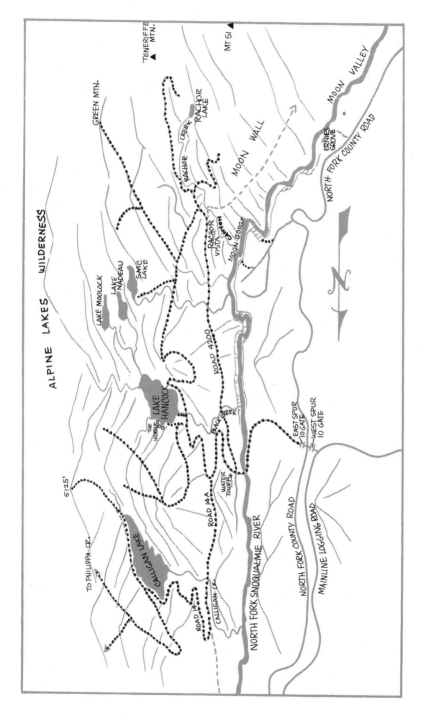

Lake Calligan

For the quickest way to the lakeshore, turn right here on 14E. Alternatively continue on 14 the 1 scant mile to the lake, 2222 feet, 4½ miles from Water-tower Junction.

Most of Calligan's shores have been logged, just one patch of timber remaining, so amid the naked slopes the lake lacks Hancock's semi-pristine quality. But the views out are the full equal.

The logging road follows the shore to the head of the lake, more than 1 mile long, and sprouts spurs that climb the skinned, wide-view ridges to more than 4000 feet. Amazing.

Round trip to lake 11 miles, allow 8 hours
High point 2222 feet, elevation gain 1222 feet
March-November

Rachor Vista (map — page 102)

Rachor Creek is the first of the three major valleys north of the massive bulk of Si. The next two are occupied by Lakes Hancock and Calligan, but the Rachor valley lost its moraine-dammed lake centuries or eons ago. At higher elevation it does have a little cirque lake close under the peak of Teneriffe. And it has Cascade-front views matching those from neighbor valleys to the north.

Waterfall near Rachor Vista

Walk Spur 10 from East Gate, elevation 1000 feet, 1 long mile to cross the North Fork to Watertower Junction (see Lake Hancock). Turn right on road 4200. In 1¼ miles, at 1200 feet, the excitement begins as the road tilts steeply upward to climb the front scarp of the Cascades. Three creeks are crossed, each in such a tumble as to be more air than water, any one of them a delirious spot to eat an apple and a can of kipper snacks, take off the boots and freeze the feet in snow juice.

As for the views, they grow by the step, climaxing on a 2200-foot promontory with a panorama down to the North Fork Gorge, west to Fuller Mountain,

Tokul Plateau, Issaquah Alps, Seattle, and the Olympics, and north to the High Rock Hills, Mt. Sultan, and the San Juan Islands.

Round trip 8 miles, allow 6 hours
High point 2200 feet, elevation gain 1200 feet
March-November

Phelps Ridge (map — page 106)

Phelps is a mountain hardly anybody has heard of, and just about everybody has seen. So impressive is the haystack summit from Seattle, people suppose the peak is famous. In fact, they think it's Index. A high ridge thrusts westward from the haystack, separating the valleys of the North Fork Snoqualmie and the South Fork Tolt, the latter a Seattle water supply. The tip of the ridge, jutting out in the sky on the edge of the Cascade front, provides a panorama over the intricate tangle of drainages north to and beyond the Tolt River and west and south to the Snoqualmie. And that's not the half of it. With nary a stick of big timber the whole route, views are virtually continuous, mostly enormous.

Drive the North Fork County Road 6 miles beyond Spur 10 (see Fuller Mountain) to where narrow woods roads go right and left, neither signed. The right goes a short bit to the DNR's abandoned (but still used) Wagner Bridge Campground, on banks of the North Fork. Take the left, road 30B (unsigned), and drive 1.2 miles to a gate, never open to the public, elevation 1250 feet.

Walk the few yards to intersect Spur 30. Directly across is 30A, marked by blue paint on a large log.

When West Spur 10 Gate is open, this point can be reached by car. From the gate drive the Mainline north 5.2 miles. Turn right on Spur 30 and continue 1 mile, there passing Spur 32 on the left, taking the right, signed Spur 30 and perhaps "Cascade Lookout." In .3 mile is a three-way junction. Park here, elevation 1300 feet. Spur 30 goes straight, 30A left, uphill, to Cascade Lookout, and 30B right.

Let it be noted that 30A is a perfectly good, solid road that ordinarily can be driven by your family sedan clear to the summit. If that's your pleasure, go ahead. But first throw away this book and your boots. Walking's our game. And unless the views are built step by step they're as phony as aerial photographs (interesting to mapmakers and eagles but showing an Earth never intended for man to see and thus not real). Nevertheless, on a summer Sunday when the parade of sport drivers is unbearable, it is ethically permissible to drive partway, to the point noted below. Yet keep in mind that when Spur 10 Gates are closed, the hike still can be done via the Wagner Bridge approach and is then molested only by two-wheelers.

Ascend steadily steep 30A, through medium-young second-growth, 1¼ miles to a window at 2000 feet and views south to Si and the Issaquah Alps. The suggested alternate parking spot is in a flat ¼ mile beyond, at 2150 feet. To drive farther is foolish, no matter how heavy the traffic, because the views don't quit, can only be digested at footpace, and are liable to send a goggling driver plunging off the precipice.

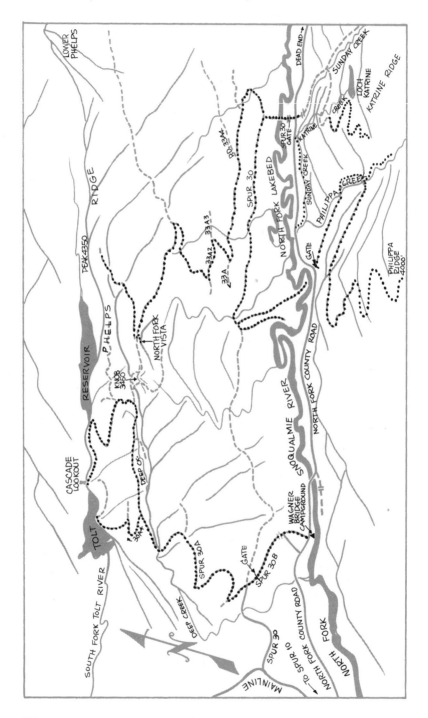

Blue grouse giving mating call on Phelps Ridge

The road climbs through a saddle between the main slope and a 2400-foot knoll west and attains a promontory with vistas across the Deep Creek valley (an old glacier trough) to Beaver-Tokul-Canyon Creeks, the Tolt valley, the Snoqualmie, downtown Seattle, and the Olympics. Here, too, the lookout tower is first spotted.

Now on a steep sidehill beneath cliffs of gaudy sedimentary-volcanic garbage, the way comes to another stupendous view promontory and swings east into the hanging upper valley of Deep Creek, which is crossed at 2550 feet. In ¼ mile more, 2½ miles from the three-way junction, at 2700 feet, a washed-out and overgrown spur (30A4, but probably unsigned) switchbacks left; this is the way to go to leave the Sunday drivers behind. It doesn't quite make the summit but attains views that are much better.

(However, on a quiet day the route to the summit via 30A is only 1½ miles longer and adds a fascinating look down to the old lakebed of the North Fork Snoqualmie valley. For this route simply stick with the obvious good road up Deep Creek, which is recrossed; go well east of Cascade Lookout, climb to the

107

ridge, and return west to the summit. Many junctions are met but by keeping the position of the lookout in mind one hardly can get lost. The rule is, take all the lefts that are good road — because good road continues all the way to the top. By the 30A route the distance from 30A4 to the summit is 3 miles.)

Meanwhile, back on 30A4, this lesser road climbs into more recent logging and thus shrub-size second-growth. Lying all the way on the steep west slope, its views are constantly dramatic. In ½ mile the road switchbacks twice; at the second a spur right deadends; take the left, switchbacking. At 3500 feet is a corner with a straight-down view to the South Fork Tolt and Seattle's reservoir. Here the road switchbacks south to a deadend. Forget it. Look up, see the lookout tower a short way off, on the ridge summit at 3700 feet, and forget that too. The lookout tower has been leased from the DNR for scientific research and is thus private property, off limits. Rest content with what you have: Look north to Sultan and Baring, and west over Mainline and J Line to Skykomish and Snoqualmie valleys, Puget Sound and Everett and Seattle, North Bend, Si, Rattlesnake, Fuller, Issaquah Alps. And more, more.

Round trip to 30A4 vista 6½ miles, allow 5 hours
High point 3500 feet, elevation gain 2250 feet
May-November

From Cascade Lookout the Spur 30 system of logging roads runs all over the top of the ridge east, extending very near Little Phelps and up to some 4200 feet. Having earned the lookout views, on another day one may wish to drive to the ridgecrest and wander eastward, on top of the naked world.

Keep in mind that since the great views begin long before the summit, as low as 2000 feet, this trip can be done partway far earlier than May. It makes a superb snowline-prober in March. A few good snowbanks do wonders for the peace and quiet.

Philippa Ridge (map — page 106)

The views from Philippa Ridge are much the same as those from Katrine Ridge and North Fork Vista (which see), except there are no ridges westerly to frame the window on the lowlands; the lowlands are all and entirely there, north and south to the horizons. The second distinction of the route is a gate at the very bottom, barring public wheels, making for a walk that is quieter than the others — and much longer. The surveyor has not yet done it on foot, only by eyeball, but definitely has put it on his to-do list and emphatically recommends it for yours.

Drive the North Fork County Road a long 8 miles beyond Spur 10 (see Fuller Mountain) and spot a rude sideroad climbing right, the gate visible. Park here, elevation 1550 feet.

The footroad begins with a flat ¾ mile easterly to the Philippa valley and over the creek. It then ascends the valley a scant 1 mile to 2000 feet. A spur continues upvalley to the Alpine Lakes Wilderness and possibly a fishermen's path to Lake Philippa, 3350 feet.

The main road turns right, recrosses the creek, and ascends to the north end of the ridge, to a first switchback at 2300 feet, 1½ miles from the valley spur. The story now is switchbacks, some 2 miles of them, from one big-view landing to another, culminating on the scalped-clean ridgecrest at 4000 feet, nothing in the way of views to Mt. Selig and the Kingdome and the rest of the civilized world.

The road system continues to a still higher naked knob, 4400 feet, and on through and over and down the tree mine to Calligan Lake.

Round trip 10 miles, allow 8 hours
High point 4000 feet, elevation gain 2500 feet
May-November

North Fork Lakebed (map — page 106)

Moraines dumped by the big glacier from Canada dammed all the valleys of the Cascade front hereabouts. Still remaining are Lakes Hancock and Calligan. But the largest lake in the vicinity was that of the North Fork Snoqualmie, some 6 miles long and up to 1 mile and more wide, extending up both the main valley of the North Fork and that of a major tributary, Sunday Creek. The lake lasted long enough to be partly filled in, then (by a break in the moraine dam) was drained. Through the eons the North Fork and Sunday Creek have meandered over the flat lakebed; presently the two run on opposite sides of the broad valley, the North Fork between walls of green, Sunday Creek over wide gravel bars. On a hot Sunday the valley rings with laughter of little children — for this is the favorite water-play spot in the area. In addition there are meander-cutoff sloughs, oxbow lakes, marshes loud with birds. Lying below 1600 feet, the lakebed is open for walking when ridges above are largely white.

Drive the North Fork County Road past Spur 10 (see Lake Hancock) to where the road enters a canyon through the moraine and climbs into the hanging North Fork valley. Continue on, past a series of roadside views down to the river and sloughs, up to the peaks. Then choose between — or combine — two quite different experiences of the lakebed.

Sunday Creek
For more than half the length of the old lake Sunday Creek meanders independently along the south side of the valley, the whole way on a swath of white gravel a hundred or more feet wide. Where the North Fork road crosses Sunday Creek the sandbars and pools are thronged any weekend the sun shines. For other accesses, take the roads to the trails for Sunday Lake and Loch Katrine (which see), and their crossings of the creek. On all roads after the first crossing, watch for grownover lanes going off right — some to the creek.

The thought that tantalizes on a hot day of late summer, when the creek is low yet icy, is to assume a costume of shorts or less and old tennis shoes and do a wet walk, right up the middle of the creek, making a round trip of up to 6 miles.

North Fork
Continue past the Sunday Creek crossing to Spur 30, at 10 miles from Spur 10, and park, elevation 1500 feet. (The spur is identifiable, just barely, by the "30" and arrow painted on a stump to the right at the junction.)

Headed south from here is the sideroad up Sunday Creek. On the north, ¼ mile up Spur 30, is the Spur 30 Gate, never open to the public and thus largely keeping Spur 30 free of wheels. Pass the gate and walk to the river and the first tempting stretch of riverbank. Just across the bridge Spur 30 turns downvalley. Frequent grownover sideroads invite messing around in the bushes to see what secrets they conceal. At about 1½ miles from the bridge take one or both of a pair of roads out over the full 1-mile width of the flat, by sloughs, oxbows, marshes, to the river.

While appreciating the windings of the river, look up the valley walls to the windings of the logging roads. Only in the past few years have such extensive road systems and clearcuts climbed so high on Cascade slopes. When will "commercial" forests regrow up there? Counting of rings in stumps shows trees 2 feet in diameter to be 250-450 years old. It'll be that long to the next "harvest."

Round trips 10 feet to 6 miles, allow a Sunday afternoon
High point 1500 feet, minor elevation gain
March-November

North Fork Snoqualmie River

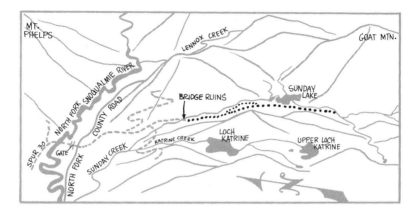

Sunday Creek and Lake (map — page 111)

If you're not prepared, this hike will give you a shock. Not the lake, which is nice enough, but in a land of hundreds of lakes has to be ranked run-of-the-mill. Nor even the creek, which is a jimdandy, but so are myriad others hereabouts. No, it's not the water. It's the trees. Accustomed as a hiker is in this area to tree-farm trees, cute little seedlings, vigorous Christmas trees, and the "big" second-growth that's half-a-century old, the sudden confrontation with old-growth virgin forest is enough to drop you to your knees. What explains this miracle of preservation? How did such forest survive at such low elevation? Someplace in the past of the U.S. Forest Service there's an unsung hero, someone who fought to keep this valley with its trees on while those all around were losing theirs. And now the Alpine Lakes Wilderness has assumed the heritage. So when weary of panoramas from clearcuts, come here.

Where Spur 30 goes left from North Fork County Road (see North Fork Lakebed), turn right on Sunday Creek road. At a Y in .7 mile, go right. In .3 mile more, where the good road curves right to cross Sunday Creek and climb toward Katrine Creek, a rougher road goes straight ahead, left. Follow it .4 mile (your car may request you to walk the last part) to wreckage of a bridge over Sunday Creek, elevation 1650 feet. A stringer remains as footlog, high in the air.

Several minutes upstream from the bridges is the former trailhead. A narrow, growing-in, washing-out road continues, the first portion a logging track, the remainder a relic of some mining idiocy in the lake vicinity. In 1 long mile the road-trail passes campsites and sidepaths to the lake. But there's a better way. Several hundred feet from the former trailhead, spot an old logging road going obscurely left. In a short bit, at the end of the logging, the start of virgin forest, it yields to genuine trail, none other than the ancient and honorable Sunday Creek trail. This is The Trip — a wilderness arboretum of mossy logs, fern-hung hillsides, cool-shadowy sitting spots beside the brawl and splash of Sunday Creek, and decadent old forest of fir, hemlock, cedar, hardwoods, and snags, a very different experience from a monotonous monocultural Douglas fir plantation of young, thrifty trees that never will grow old. Near the lake the trail rejoins the road.

The lake is worth a look. But since trees are the stars here, continue on. The trail goes up and down, rougher and skinnier, about ½ mile along the lakeshore. In another ½ mile it drops off the sidehill to cross the creek at 2000 feet and proceed onward, upward into the Alpine Lakes Wilderness. But the footlog crossing is perhaps far enough.

Round trip to footlog 5 miles, allow 3 hours
High point 2000 feet, elevation gain 400 feet
April-November

Katrine Loch and Ridge (map — page 111)

There's such a huge amount of air in the North Fork's glacial trough, and so little vegetation to obstruct views, the ascent of Katrine Ridge is a constant succession of gasps. The eye swings from peaks of the Alpine Lakes Wilderness to cows in Snoqualmie pastures to ferryboats on Puget Sound — and especially and dramatically down to the floor of the ancient North Fork Lake and across the valley to the strangely fascinating geometry of logging roads that climb to one of the largest tree mines in the Cascades. But there's a living lake, too, and a virgin forest, and one returns from a flirtation with its fresh face to a new perspective on the worn visage of the "tree farm."

This is the valley's simplest and shortest and most popular route to high views, for two reasons: (1) The road is not gated, is open to public wheels the year and clock around; (2) The fish in Loch Katrine keep the road in fairly decent condition. Unfortunately, whenever the road can be driven, it is, by too many vehicles to be a peaceful footroad. The trip therefore is recommended either for a weekday in summer or fall, or a weekend in spring, when patches of lingering snow halt wheels but merely refresh the boots.

Drive past the turnoff to Sunday Lake trail (which see) to the bridge over Sunday Creek at 1550 feet, 1.2 miles from the North Fork road. In early spring this probably is the proper place to park, because the road instantly turns steeply and roughly upward and in a mere .2 mile crosses Katrine Creek — which generally does a washout job every winter.

The next spot worth consideration as "trailhead" is at 2200 feet, 1 mile from Sunday bridge, where the road switchbacks right at the ravine of Katrine Creek. The road doesn't get any worse on the next stretch, but the views are already so terrific it's a shame to let the car whiz them past the eye too fast.

Here the second-growth forest (a plantation not by man, but Nature) has managed to grow higher than a hiker can reach since the logging in the 1960s, but by the next switchback, to the left at 2650 feet, the past two decades have produced nothing bigger than Christmas trees. The views that seemed so enormous below now are totally out-classed. The white gravel lane of Sunday Creek meanders along one side of the lakebed, the green-hedged lane of the North Fork along the other. The logging roads on Phelps Ridge climb the valley walls, top the crest, and reach almost to the foot of the rough cliffs of Phelps.

Sunday Lake

The road levels out to the edge of virgin forest at 2950 feet, about 1¼ miles from the 2200-foot switchback. A path leads into the forest — into the Alpine Lakes Wilderness — to the shores of Loch Katrine, a pleasant cirque lake ringed by wildwoods, an especially scenic destination in April or May, while its plain is frozen white.

Few folks will care to drive past here; the road soon grows steeper, narrower, and so airy the surveyor saw some car passengers with their eyes shut, and a few drivers, too. The crest of the ridge steadily narrows, the switchbacks tighten, the views expand to such dimensions they stretch the mind. At 1¼ miles from the lake is the last view, at 3800 feet, to the Olympics, to salt water, to Persis and Index, to Bare and Goat and Dog. A few steps higher, at 4000 feet, the road ends. Before descending the naked mountainside, step into the virgin forest for a few green thoughts.

Round trip from 2200 feet 5 miles, allow 4 hours
High point 3800 feet, elevation gain 1600 feet
Weekends March-June, weekdays to November

North Fork Vista (map — page 106)

Having looked up from the lakebed to the high ridges, the obvious thing to do is climb up there to look down to the pattern of meanders, sloughs, oxbow lakes. Go a little distance up or all the way to the top. If only a medium-high view is desired, be casual at the many twists and turns; all spurs lead to excellent perspectives. However, if the ridgecrest is the goal there is only one way, intricate, through the maze. So pay attention.

From the North Fork County Road walk past Spur 30 Gate (see North Fork Lakebed), elevation 1500 feet. Because this gate is never open to public vehicles, and there is no access from the Mainline except when West Spur 10 Gate is open, the wide, high-speed Spur 30 and the roads it feeds are free of wheels most days of the year.

Cross the North Fork bridge and in a couple of hundred feet turn right on a narrow, unused, just-nice-for-walking lane. At ¾ mile from Gate 30, where this road switchbacks left, it is deeply sliced by an admirable creek, the canyon a dandy wheelstop. The road ascends the creek to a T; go left (the right goes upvalley to deadend). At ½ mile from the canyon switchback, pass a sideroad (33A4) on the right, going upvalley to deadend; continue on the flat downvalley. Early on the views are fine to the lakebed and out the meandering river to the moraine. Then 30-foot-high second-growth closes in.

At 1 long mile from 33A4, at 1939 feet, the little-used road of the route thus far joins a more substantial road from downvalley, 33A (unsigned). Take the switchback right, upvalley, on 33A. Looking high up the mountain, spot a naked promontory — this is the goal.

In ½ mile, at 2400 feet, is a T. The right, 33A3, goes upvalley to deadend; go left, downvalley, on 33A2. Soon pass a spur right (33A2A) to a borrow pit and continue downvalley on the flat ½ mile to a switchback. Ignore the short spur left and make the switchback upvalley.

Shortly, swing into a creek valley and cross the boundary from sizable second-growth of 1950s logging into the stumps and shrubs of the 1960s. Views are now unobstructed and magnificent and continuous. And the road gets so rock-blocked as to discourage the rare razzers who venture this far.

Ascending out of the valley past granite walls and buttresses, in 1 mile from the 2400-foot junction the route reaches the destination promontory, 3100 feet, some 4½ miles from Spur 30 Gate.

East, the North Fork valley becomes a steep-walled U portal, beyond which is the division into two valleys, the North Fork proper and Lennox Creek. Across the gulf of air are deep-green preserved forests of the Alpine Lakes Wilderness up Sunday Creek — and clearcuts climbing the valleys of Katrine and Philippa Creeks. Out west, framed by valley walls, are foothills of Tokul Creek country and, beyond, the skyline of the Issaquah Alps. But mainly there is the view down down the windings of roads gashed in white and iron-stained granite to sinuous windings of the river across the enormous lakebed.

Round trip 9 miles, allow 6 hours
High point 3100 feet, elevation gain 1600 feet
May-November

To climb higher is to gain different but not superior views; in fact, by going too high on rounding slopes one loses the drama of the straight-down vertical look. However, the highland roaming may very well compel the long-leggitty to keep a-going.

At the promontory is a Y. The spur east goes to a deadend near the summit of Little (or Lower) Phelps, the fork west in 1 mile to a Y at 3350 feet. From here the east fork leads in 1 mile to a 4350-foot peak (bump on ridge) with broad views, including down north to the Tolt Reservoir; the west fork goes ¼ mile to a neat highland creek and, just beyond, to a 3450-foot knob offering a fresh angle on the lakebed and out the valley; from here it is less than 2 miles to Cascade Lookout.

Mud Lake

GREAT BIG WESTERN TREE FARM —
VIA ROADS BEYOND SPUR 10 GATES

West of the Cascade front, between the Skykomish River on the north and the Snoqualmie River south and west, are 150 square miles which have produced one crop of logs throughout, in most places a second, and in some spots are well along toward a third. The local community, the state and nation, must hope the farm continues in production permanently. That, however, is by no means certain. Though in 1985 King County adopted a General Development Plan aimed at confining development to specified centers and retaining large areas in open space, and a Farmlands Preservation Program to keep certain (cow and corn and peas) farms in operation, safe from the developers, it has not placed any significant restrictions on the right of tree-farmers to become, overnight, and at their sole discretion, land-developers, nor has it instituted a Timberlands Preservation Program. Until these two things are done, and so long as "the market operates" and "every property owner is allowed maximum use of his land," the tree farms near suburbia will be merely a clever way to dodge taxes. Already the urban frontier is pushing into the Great Big Western Tree Farm, and stumpranchers and wealthy recluses are settling in the very middle. If there is to be a GBW Tree Farm by the time the third harvest is due, the county/state/nation must declare the public interest in private forest lands.

To see how productive tree-farming can be at the elevation of the Tokul Plateau (mostly under 1000 feet — open to walking most of the year), tour the H.E. Morgan, Jr. Managed Forest, 50,000 acres of Weyerhaeuser land (part of its 347,000-acre Cascade Tree Farm). Named for a company official who sponsored the adoption, in 1966, of "High Yield Forestry," the 2.4-mile auto tour starts from Highway 202 just east of Snoqualmie Falls Lodge and goes through plantations and clearcuts of varied ages. Reader boards at vista points explain the techniques of intensive forest management on a 50-year (or less) cycle, including selecting superior seed, growing seedlings in nurseries, harvesting by clearcut, preparing the ground after harvest by removal or scattering of slash, planting within a year of harvest, fertilizing about every 5 years, thinning young stands, and protecting the crop from insects, disease, fire, and excessive brush.

South of the Tolt River the principal manager of the GBW Tree Farm is Weyerhaeuser. Some of the lands are hiker-accessible from the North Fork County Road and are treated in the preceding chapter. Here are those best done when the company's Spur 10 Gates are open to public vehicles.

In 1985 the company adopted a new gate policy, eliminating the long-time "tolerated trespassing" by wheels. The change was forced on the company by a dozen serious accidents in a single year, and by the advent of a fleet of trucks, used only on company roads, that have beds 12 feet wide and long enough to carry logs up to 110 feet — supertrucks that cannot share narrow, twisty roads with myopic Volkswagens which lack connection to the company radio system.

Rule One. No gates other than those at Spur 10 ever are open to public wheels. If you see them open it is either because the trucks are rolling or because the good ol' boys have got liquored up and enjoyed the favorite Saturday-night sport of "gate-busting."

Rule Two. No gates ever are open weekdays. Canny explorers, relying on the "tolerated trespassing," used to sneak in gates left open for truck use. However, *these physically open — but legally closed — gates may be closed physically at any time without notice.* The canny explorer must be prepared to spend the night locked in, or perhaps a weekend, or if his timing is really off, the winter. Moreover, when he trudges the many miles to the company headquarters to beg for release of his vehicle, he must be prepared to be cited for malicious trespassing — as may be done, also, by any of the company patrolmen who travel the roads every day of the year. Finally, when the big trucks are highballing, the drivers know via radio when they have a clear track, and though careful and expert and compassionate, on rounding a tight curve and confronting an unexpected civilian car, their choice may have to be between squashing the beetle or committing suicide by driving off a cliff. The price of being canny can be very high.

Rule Three. The two Spur 10 Gates, the West and the East, are open weekends (days only — no camping) from the start of fishing season through the end of hunting season — usually, April 1–December 15. *Except:* They are closed in the dry times of summer when fire danger is high — which in 1985 was from June to October!

Rule Four. In all seasons, on all days of the week, the public feet are permitted on these private roads. At your own risk, of course. If the rules seem restrictive, they indeed are; because of them an area in which true trails are next to nonexistent has hundreds of miles of dependably peaceful footroads. (For contrast, see the next chapter.)

Rule Five. Whenever in doubt about the gate situation, don't hesitate to telephone (during working hours) the Weyerhaeuser office in Snoqualmie, 888-2511.

The West Spur 10 Gate is the wheel access to the Tokul Plateau, the area's best example of a true, productive tree farm. As of the mid-1980s, much of it has newly seen its second harvest and is settling into the long and quiet growing time, when all but the main patrol roads revert nearly or entirely to trail, and the ones that are maintained become green tunnels. The beauties are subtle, few features fit for gasping and goggling. Next to the Canadian glacier, the major geologic force has been the beaver, which over the ages has dammed the country to a fare-thee-well. Most streams are greenery-over-grown series of lakes and ponds and marshes and bogs, some full of trout; the thousands of shallow depressions in the moraines are all one or another sort of wetland, full of birds. It's emotionally quiet country. As well as quiet quiet — the hundreds of miles of roads swallow up sport-drivers, most of whom are anyhow too spooked by wildness to venture far from the North Fork County

Road. Chances of solitude and peace are substantially better in the beaver marshes and third-growth firs than on, say, the Wonderland Trail of Rainier National Park or the Pacific Crest Freeway through the Alpine Lakes Wilderness. So let not the snooty purist scorn this road-walking.

It must be noted, though, that as of the 1980s the best part of the area, so far as a walker is concerned, the big old second-growth and mossy old railroad grades between the Mainline and the Tolt River, have only a few years left — by the mid-1990s the clearcutting will be complete to the river.

The East Spur 10 Gate is the wheel access through the transition zone from GBW Tree Farm to GBW Tree Mine. At higher elevations the forest composed mainly of Douglas fir (and associated western hemlock and western redcedar) yields to a forest dominated by Pacific silver fir, a species that is readily loggable, but difficult for man to regrow, and then only on a harvest cycle two or three times longer than cycles at lower elevations. Above that is a forest dominated by mountain hemlock, not a very valuable species and never part of any human management scheme because the cycle typically is 250-450 years to produce trees barely worth hauling off the mountain. At these elevations of 4000 feet and above there never will be a second "crop"; the farmers, however, take the attitude that while hoeing their potatoes in the valleys, they can't be expected to pass up gold nuggets on the hills. To look at the bright side, the post-clearcutting huckleberries are fantastic and the views stupendous. Wandering the wide-sky ridges is eerily reminiscent of another area that man skinned so completely the forests never have returned, the moors of Scotland.

USGS maps: Fall City, Snoqualmie, Carnation, Lake Joy, Mt. Si, Sultan, Index

For a free map of the company's road system, write Weyerhaeuser Company, Box W, Snoqualmie, WA 98065

Tokul Creek to Tolt River (map — page 120)

Cherish these old logging railroad grades and their green tunnels through half-a-century-size second-growth. As of 1986 they have just several years before the daylight comes glaring in from the big sky.

From West Spur 10 Gate (see Fuller Mountain) drive the Mainline north 6 miles. Turn left on road 3950, recognizable by its two entries with a tree between, 1 mile to a junction with road 3100, joining from the left.

As of 1986, 3100 may be worth walking 1 mile south, to the second of two old railroad trestles; when the trees come down in the second clearcut, so will these relics of the first clearcut.

Drive 3950 north 1.8 more miles, to where a grassy lane bends off right to a seemingly impassable blockade of fallen trees and brush. Park here, elevation 1199 feet.

The blockade proves to be impassable only to wheels, and thereafter the difficulties are a few logs to squirm over or under and some vine maple to thread through. Much of the grade is a carpet of moss or liverwort unmarked

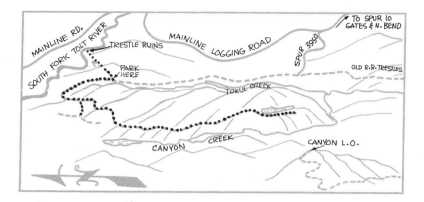

by so much as a game trace, no sign of passage since the lokies quit running in the mid-1930s or so. The forest is handsome big conifers, sloping down left to a marsh, then a creek. In 1 mile the grade runs out on a fill and ends in a litter of rotten timbers and rusty ironware, remnants of the collapsed trestle.

Drop off the fill on the left and descend an easy 100 feet to the river. Sit in the sand and muse upon the mossy boulders in the stream, the silvery alders on the bank, the dippers dipping, and, in season, the eagles feasting on rotten salmon.

Round trip 2 miles, allow 1½ hours
High point 1200 feet, elevation gain 100 feet
When West Spur 10 Gate is open

The longer walk from the same parking spot, the green tunnel, is a lovely brushfree stroll under the umbrella on a rainy day, the sociable conversation or solitary reflection occasionally interrupted by subtle spectacles of nature, such as mushrooms. It's too far from Spur 10 Gate for a weekday, and one doesn't want to try it during the hot passion of the lowland lakes in spring, when the lower classes of fisherfolk are out with their rubber rafts searching for where the Game Department hid the Easter eggs, or during the guns of autumn.

The dwindling lane makes a U turn around the end of a ridge and heads south. Soon one becomes aware of a sizable valley on the right — headwaters of Canyon Creek, tributary to Tokul. Across the valley is the ridge of Canyon Lookout. The road swings off into a sidevalley containing a large marsh at the foot of an imposing cliff that would have climbers fingering their jumars if it weren't rubbish. The road abruptly ends in daunting brush that discourages ambitions of pushing on along the unimproved continuation of the rail grade. By 1990 or so it will not have daunted the bulldozers and logging trucks.

Round trip 6 miles, allow 4 hours
High point 1200 feet, elevation gain minor

Canyon Ridge (map — page 121)

On the first survey, in 1977, Canyon Lookout gave views to the Cascade front from Phelps to Sultan, and to the Issaquah Alps, Seattle towers, and the Olympics. On the second, in 1985, there was no looking out at all, but much excellent looking in to moss and ferns and beaver-dammed creeks. Moreover, enough additional logs had fallen and vine maple woven together that the old rail grade hadn't seen a wheel in years. The wheels will return, and the views, as the harvesting advances north toward the Tolt River. For peace and quiet come quick.

From West Spur 10 Gate (see Fuller Mountain) drive left on the Mainline 2.3 miles. Turn right on the J Line, identifiable by two entries with a stump between, 4 miles to (the) Junction (of two old rail grades). In a few yards cross Tokul Creek and turn off right. All the following will change year by year, so carry the Lake Joy quadrangle and be alert, but the situation as of 1986 is: Drive 1 mile, passing a sideroad left, to a Y. Go right in a 1985 clearcut to the end of logging in .3 mile, then .4 mile more — 1.7 miles from the J Line — to where the road (not an old rail grade but a later connector between two such) steeply ascends 100 feet to a Y, elevation 1025 feet. Your car may wish to park below the top of the rise.

The road straight ahead is the way to Hull Lake. Look sharp for the Canyon

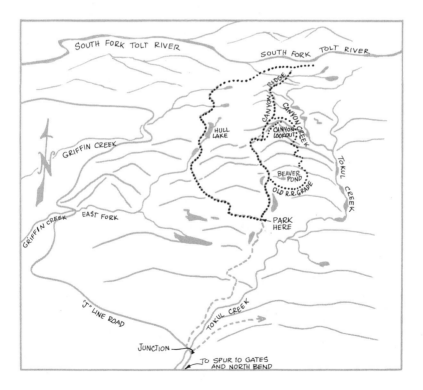

route, which begins in an obscure reverse turn right, then bends around to head north, into machineless peace. The way — now on rail grade — ascends an indistinct tributary of Tokul Creek, the valley distinguished by two large and birdy marshes (shown on the map as lakes) and a beaver pond. At 1 mile, 1160 feet, where a creek flows from a large beaver pond in a hillside bowl ¼ mile off the route, spot an overgrown grade on the right; remember it for future reference.

After a long arrow-straight stretch of grade, and a notch through a rib of andesite, the route bends right to a Y at 2 miles, 1375 feet. The railroad went straight ahead left; ascend the right fork, a truck road built to serve the lookout tower, a final ½ mile to the summit, 1691 feet, and foundations of the vanished tower, entirely ringed by tall young trees that permit views of naught but sky.

Round trip 5 miles, allow 3 hours
High point 1691 feet, elevation gain 666 feet
When West Spur 10 Gate is open

As a matter of fact, until logging reopens the views a walker would best forget the summit. The trip is the railroad. The surveyor was so weighed down by morels on his 1985 exploration he proceeded north from the 1375-foot Y only a short bit, the going slow, over logs and through vine maple, but not difficult and a constant joy. Since the rails and ties were picked up in the 1930s nothing has happened here except green things have been growing, and growing, and wild things roaming. The wheelfree walk in the tangle will survive some years. Where does it lead? The USGS map shows the grade proceeding northeasterly 1½ miles along Canyon Ridge to a deadend, and a spur looping back around the east side of Canyon Lookout some 2 miles to the creek (remember?) at 1160 feet.

Round trip on unimproved (1986) rail grades shown on map 3½ miles, allow a day or two

Hull Lake and Tolt Slopes (map — page 121)

Beaver valleys lead to a lonesome lake deep in second-growth at headwaters of East Fork Griffin Creek. The forest features cathedral cottonwoods and maples swollen up with moss sheathings. Frogs croak. Pond lilies bloom. Fish leap into creels. Then, beyond the lake, the forest gets darker and lonesomer as the old rail grade sidehills over headwaters of Griffin Creek to a deadend on the north tip of Canyon Ridge, where it falls off steeply to the Tolt River.

Drive as for Canyon Ridge (which see) to the Y, elevation 1025 feet — and as much farther as the road has been extended by the time you arrive. Thanks to agreement with the State Game Department, the logging will stop short of (and go around) Hull Lake, and that's a mercy, if a small one.

Go left from the Y, descending very gradually along a little valley, with a string of beaver ponds of great age but with the beavering still in progress. At

Beaver pond

one huge pond a path leads to the shore and a long dam centered on an enormous cedar stump. At a bit over 1 mile from the Y a divide is crossed (without ever leaving the valley) and the route is now upstream along East Fork Griffin Creek. In ¾ mile a long-ago-washed-out fill halts jeeps. Few motorcycles persevere over the fallen logs in the thorny salmonberry thickets. From dark fir forest the way opens out in a last ½ mile to the culmination of a series of beaver ponds, Hull Lake, 822 feet. Continue ¼ mile along the shore, scaring ducks into startled flight, to the far end, 2½ miles from the Y.

Admire mossy logs in the lake. Watch birds. Listen to the waterfall.

Round trip 5 miles, allow 3 hours
High point 1025 feet, elevation gain 200 feet
When West Spur 10 Gate is open

Why stop here? The railroad grade goes on, gouging through shaggy volcanic rock, following a narrow creekless valley from the lake through a pass to a slope above the (unseen) Main Fork of Griffin Creek, crossing its two headwater branches, both with waterfalls in rock slots, and then a third creek digging a nice gorge down toward the nearby (unseen) South Fork Tolt. Beyond the lake the grade is so little walked and treadless the boots sink silently in deep carpets of moss. There is no view — scarcely even up to the sky — as one burrows through the green tunnel. And at 2½ miles from Hull Lake, at about 900 feet, the grade abruptly ends. In the middle of Nowhere. Which to a solitude freak is really Somewhere.

Round trip from lake 5 miles, allow 3 hours

J Line to Tolt River (map — page 125)

The hiker who never stirs from the house except for alpine meadows and glaciers, a storm on the wilderness ocean, or old-growth forest by the square mile, will decline an invitation to the J Line. Admittedly, this isn't grand opera. The slow movement of a string quartet is more like it. Plain and simple, subtle beauties rather than spectacular. Quiet. The J Line has removed nearly every handy scrap of forest, has done it twice, once by railroad and once by truck, and has settled down to grow a third crop. The sounds of chainsaws and logging trucks will be rare hereabouts for decades. As for the racket of sport vehicles, most sports don't like to get this far from the bright lights. They need the noise of many vehicles, not merely their own, to be comfortable. And they're a-feared of getting lost and being et up by the b'ars.

From West Spur 10 Gate (see Fuller Mountain) drive left on the Mainline 2.3 miles. Turn right on the J Line, identifiable by two entries with a stump between, 4 miles to (the) Junction (of two old rail grades). Cross Tokul Creek and continue on the main road. Spurs (most of them unsigned) branch off this way and that, and most are worth a stroll, for the solitude if nothing more. There is more, of course — marshes and birds, creeks and beavers. However, the hiker a-feared to be alone with his thoughts had better stick with the sports.

J-1

At .6 mile from Junction, a spur to the right takes off at 750 feet and in 1½ miles ascends a sidehill to a deadend at 900 feet.

J-3

At 1.9 miles from Junction, a grownover spur to the right takes off at 667 feet. Not surveyed for this guide, it is shown by the map as winding around ridges and valleys, crossing a marshy branch of East Fork Griffin Creek, and proceeding better than 2 miles up another branch to a deadend at 800 feet.

Griffin Creek Mainline

At 4 miles from Junction, the Griffin Creek Mainline crosses Griffin Creek and climbs the valley wall to the Loop Lake plateau, a possible site of King County's next jet airport but until then offering little but 1980s clearcuts.

J-4-10

At 5 miles from Junction, a spur goes right at 600 feet, turns south, and runs along a fascinating little valley 1½ miles to a deadend at 700 feet, on a sidehill a few feet above East Fork Griffin Creek.

J-6

At 5.6 miles from Junction the J Line, having crossed Griffin Creek on a fill,

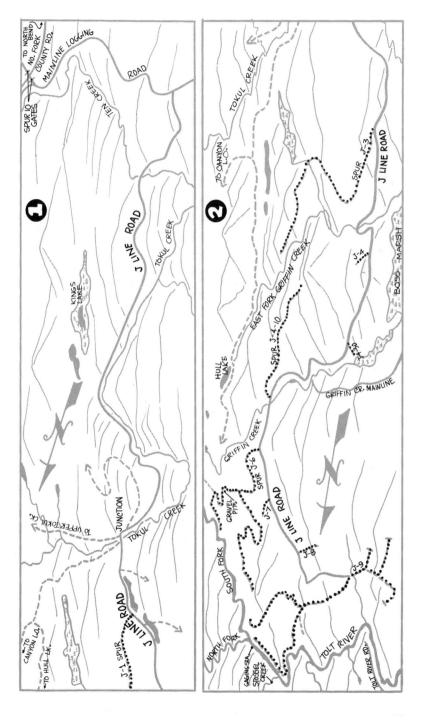

Tolt River from end of J Line

comes to a major Y at 580 feet. The J Line goes left. J-6 climbs to the right, in 1 mile reaching a Y atop a plateau, 720 feet. The left meanders 1.5 miles across the plateau to the brink of the Tolt River scarp; up-leaping trees have blocked the former view. The right goes to another Y in .4 mile; take the right, which descends past a gravel pit. In .3 mile more is another Y; go left and down .2 mile to a Y on the valley floor, at 500 feet. Park here and walk the right fork a few yards. Spot a rude fishermen's path to the South Fork Tolt, a lovely stretch of lonesome wild river, but nothing to do when you get there except go wading. (That is not an idle suggestion. In 1940 the Senior Scouts of Troop 324, in the course of escaping from a spell of disorientation in the chaos of the recently concluded railroad logging, went into the river a mile upstream of this point and waded by here and 1½ miles more downstream to the Tolt Forks, where orientation was regained. Try it on a hot August day.)

J-7

At 6.1 miles from Junction, a spur goes right at 620 feet, climbs the hill, and quickly deadends on a plateau at 680 feet.

J-8

At 6.6 miles from Junction, a spur goes left at 650 feet; it was not surveyed for this guide.

J-9

The J Line here has become quite narrow and rude. It bends left along the edge of the Tolt scarp, which is generally slumping toward the river, the road with it. At 7.2 miles from Junction is a Y at 620 feet. Park here. The left, straight ahead, is J-9, which once had views but now has only quiet amid the third-growth. A frittering of forks comes to several deadends in 1¼ miles.

The End of the J Line

Beyond the scarp-rim Y at 620 feet the J Line is undrivable as it slants steeply down to the valley bottom, trenching through 40-foot-high Douglas firs. In ¾ mile, at 460 feet, is a Y. The right goes 1 long mile to the absolute end of the J Line at a place where the morainal scarp slid out. Attaining so momentous a spot is some satisfaction. So is the beaver dam passed on the way, and the windows through the alders at the end, giving a look down to the Tolt Forks.

The left from the 460-foot Y continues downhill a few yards to another Y; go right, in ½ mile reaching the banks of the Tolt River at 410 feet.

A bang-up spot! The river, big trees of second-growth forest on the far bank, dippers flitting up and down the avenue — and, in season, bald eagles scavenging spawned-out salmon.

Now for something completely different. Wilderness! But not for those of delicate sensibilities. Follow the road upvalley to where it self-destructs in an old gravel mine become a lake. By the river find a game trail somewhat used by fishermen and for long stretches so decent one imagines it to be a regular maintained trail, until one notices it was engineered for creatures no taller than deer or beaver, both much in evidence. Avoid paths that head inland to a horrid jungle. Stick close to the river, eking out trail with gravel bars, plus some bits of silly stuff, beating bushes. In ½ mile Stossel Creek enters on the far side of the river and in another ½ mile rational progress is halted by the rock-wall portals at the Tolt River Forks (which see), just across from the gaging station below the old Boy Scout swimming hole.

Round trip from scarp-rim Y to Tolt Forks 4½ miles, allow 4 hours
High point 620 feet, elevation gain 200 feet
When West Spur 10 Gate is open

Mount Sultana (map — page 128)

Mt. Sultan, standing high above the Skykomish River, has long been a favorite view hike. But close to the south, at the opposite tip of the horseshoe ridge enclosing headwaters of Youngs Creek, is a companion peak that was totally scalped in the mid-1970s and so became one of the most stupendous viewpoints on the Cascade front. The lack of fame is owing to the unhandy location and the somewhat confusing approach on roads that have numbers on Weyerhaeuser's map but usually no signs. However, a person who keeps his routefinding wits about him will find the ascent a simple stroll.

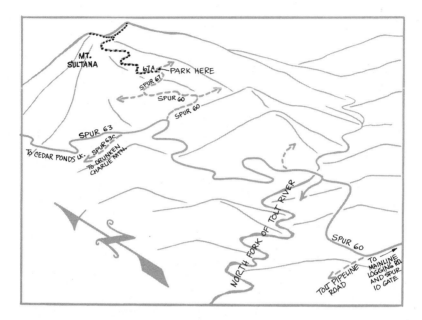

From West Spur 10 Gate drive north on the Mainline about 10 miles to a junction just past the crossing of the South Fork Tolt River. Turn left on Spur 60, in about 4 miles cross the North Fork Tolt, and in about 4 more miles reach a junction with Spur 63, elevation 2250 feet. (This point can be attained via Spur 63 by walking a long 4 miles from the closed gate at Youngs Creek — see Drunken Charlie Mountain.) Keep right on Spur 60 for .4 mile to a Y. Go left .4 mile more to a Y. Go right .5 mile to a Y where a fairly decent road proceeds straight ahead on the level in the clearcut valley of a nameless creek and a rough road turns uphill left. Park here, elevation 2600 feet.

Walk the rough road, 67A, uphill left, switchbacking along the crest of an indistinct ridge. At the start the second-growth dates from the 1960s and is some 15 feet tall; later it consists of scattered youngsters barely hiding weathered slash of the mid-1970s; ahead in the clearcuts can be seen the bald peak.

At the base of the summit mass, at a Y at 3800 feet, go right, east, along the sidehill; one last scrap of subalpine trees, and the huckleberry bushes and heather and mossy-licheny rockslide, remind of what all this high country was before being brought into production. At about 2 miles is a saddle at 3900 feet. Look down the other side to Youngs Creek headwaters. Turn left, west, ½ mile to the road-end and scramble a hundred feet up to 1976 stumps atop the 4206-foot summit.

Look north to the clearcut-virgin forest boundary on slightly higher Mt. Sultan. And Pilchuck, Baker, Monte Cristo peaks, Glacier.

Look west over odd little bumps and inane little valleys of the Tomtit Alps to High Rock Hills, Skykomish and Snoqualmie valley pastures, Monroe, Snohomish, Puget Sound, Everett, Seattle, Olympics, and sand cliffs of Double Bluff on Whidbey Island.

Look south over the Tolt River to Phelps Ridge, Fuller, Si, Rattlesnake, Issaquah Alps, Rainier, and what's left of St. Helens.

Look east to Persis, Phelps, Hinman, Daniels, Chimney, Bears Breast.

On the descent, at the 3900-foot saddle take the spur east ¼ mile to the 4000-foot east summit for perspectives on the Tolt headwaters.

Round trip 5 miles, allow 3 hours
High point 4206 feet, elevation gain 1606 feet
When West Spur 10 Gate is open

Spur 10 High Country (map — page 102)

Year by year, as the bulldozers have gouged their way up the Cascade front and the forests have been trucked down, the enlargement of the Great Big

Gunn Peak

Western Huckleberry Farm has been as awesome as watching a cloud of locusts descend upon Egypt, leaving only fields of stubble. A person cannot but feel an urge to climb there, above and beyond the frontiers of tree-farming, and roam the ridges as bare as Scotch moors, in gigantic views over the lowlands to cities and saltwater and Olympics.

A factor that makes the roaming less free and easy than it appears is illustrated by the surveyor's experience in 1985. This was the year, he decided, and this the edition, to tour higher than he had before, to definitively stake out the hiker's territory. All spring, while tramping in the vicinity, he watched the snowline melt upward. Then, just as the high logging roads were clear enough for feet, the long hot summer set in, the fires began, and Weyerhaeuser locked the gates the week around. Then, just as the rains came and the gates opened, the temperature dropped and the landscape was fouled by a hideous white substance. Why, you ask, is so much space taken here to report a failure? To hold space in the book for the next printing, because the surveyor vows to return when he can dodge through a window between snow and fire and gate closures.

A second discouragement is that only when the Spur 10 Gates are open, permitting some of the logging-road miles to be driven, are the remoter objectives within reasonable reach of the average foot. However, when the gates are open the ridges and basins are one enormous ATV park and shooting gallery. The ideal time for hiking is in May or June when snowbanks linger in cold corners, stopping wheels but not boots.

The following is partly derived from surveys before the frustrating spring-summer-fall of 1985, and partly from the USGS and Weyerhaeuser maps — a prospectus for the surveyor's planned explorations.

Calligan Highlands

Drive from East Spur 10 Gate to Calligan Lake (which see), elevation 2222 feet. How much farther can a rational vehicle be driven? Where must the walking start? That's what must be determined by the on-the-ground survey.

Spur 14 climbs from the lake northward to 4400 feet and broad lowland views, and atop the ridge connects to the Spur 16 roads from Philippa Creek (which see).

Spur 14-J climbs higher on the ridge overlooking Lake Philippa and also meets the 16 system.

Spur 14-F goes east from the lake to or near the top of a 5125-foot peak above Lake Philippa, on the edge of the Alpine Lakes Wilderness.

Hancock Highlands

Drive from East Spur 10 Gate to the Y shortly before Lake Hancock (which see), elevation 2172 feet.

Take the left fork ¼ mile to another Y. The right (straight) goes to Lake Hancock Hideouts, private summer homes, so leave it alone. Take the left, Spur 4300, which climbs through the big views at 3600 feet and northerly over the ridges to an overlook of Calligan Lake.

Spur 4333 cuts off and proceeds farther east, branching to peaks of 4700 and 4200 feet well to the east of the lake basin.

Take the right fork over Black Creek, continue eastward at lake level ⅓ mile, then switchback west and gain a lot of elevation in a hurry on a road that weeds out all but the sport-drivers. At 3000 feet, 1 mile from the creek, the road rounds a spur, losing the view (terrific) back down to the lake, gaining views southward (fantastic) to the Si scarp and North Bend and everywhere else and then some. This promontory may be quite far enough; however, it's hard to quit in this wide-sky country. Continue another 1 mile, bending left, climbing to a promontory at 3200 feet that has all the views, including a look straight down to the lake. This round trip is 4 miles from Black Creek, with an elevation gain of 1000 feet.

Especially if one has driven part of the distance, plenty of leg energy will be left. The main road heads southerly and connects to the Rachor Creek system. On the way it sprouts spurs east to or near peak 4702 and to a short stroll from SMC Lake, 3702 feet, just over the ridge from Lake Nadeau and Lake Moolock, which means the place is crawling with fishermen who surely have beaten paths to the shore of every lake, marsh, and puddle.

Rachor Highlands

Drive from East Spur 10 Gate to Rachor Vista (which see) and continue on, passing an impressive deep gorge in the moraine, .2 mile to a Y on the dissected floor of the drained lake, elevation 2300 feet.

The left fork climbs the ridge to the north and connects to the road from Hancock. On the way it sends a spur east which among its offshoots has one to a 4400-foot ridge above SMC Lake and another to 4400 feet on Green Mountain, apparently to within several stone's throws of the summit, 4824 feet.

The right fork forks again. The right — a narrow track too rough to drive, a dandy footroad — crosses the creek and climbs to 3500 feet on the northernmost ridge of Mt. Si.

The left, Spur 4220, climbs to 3200 feet in the basin beneath the northeast face of Teneriffe and may not be a practical route to anywhere.

On the way, however, it passes within ½ mile of Rachor Lake, 3500 feet, and thus may have a fishermen's path up the steep 1000 feet to the cirque. Since Rachor Lake was clearcut via a road dropping from the Teneriffe road (see Mt. Teneriffe) on the ridge just east of Mt. Si, this might be an amusing way to climb Si, and Teneriffe as well, and therefore should be studied for inclusion in the Mt. Si Conservation Area (State Park). A spur from the Teneriffe logging road drops to a clearcut in Rachor valley, and if a connection exists, this would be the hotshot route up Teneriffe.

Watch this space.

Tolt River Gorge

GREAT BIG WESTERN TREE FARM —
NORTH OF TOLT RIVER

The key difference between the portions of the GBW Tree Farm on either side of the Tolt River is that on the south the Weyerhaeuser gate policy makes the logging roads part-time footroads, and on the north the state Department of Natural Resources, having first thrown away the keys, then threw away the gates, keeping every road under its jurisdiction wide-open to any and every assemblage of wheels at any and all times of year and hours of the day or night. An area that until recently was a hikers' favorite, tramping the old logging railroad grades, has been abandoned by them.

The loggers will not be long in following, because in the lack of a Timberland Preservation Program, suburbia is invading from the Snoqualmie valley, sweeping past Lake Joy to Moss Lake and over the crest of the High Rock Hills, and from the Skykomish valley, totally privatizing the Tomtit Alps and inching up Elwell Creek. Stumprancher pioneers have parked their mobile homes and penned their pigs beside the Marckworth Freeway.

The one section of this province that can be unreservedly praised is the Tolt River, close to population centers and at low elevations, open all winter. Weyerhaeuser ownerships (and gates and patrolmen) and Seattle Water Department pipeline (ditto) exclude racketing public wheels but permit quiet public feet (and hooves). Moreover, King County might be convinced to restore the ancient and honorable Tolt River Trail, and citizens of the area are talking up the notion of volunteer reconstruction parties.

Of hikes that were in this chapter in the 1978 edition, a half-dozen have been cast utterly out and that many more demoted to quick stops on the Marckworth Freeway, which has been retained as a family-picnic Sunday drive, with about enough walking in total to burn off the calories in one chicken wing and a diet Pepsi.

The previous edition expressed a pious hope that land-managers would adopt a policy of multiple-use, closing some roads for the benefit of hikers and horse-riders, and setting aside a few choice beauty spots for the family picnics. That is not happening. A proposal is retained here to save the logging railroad grade and old-growth forest at Cherry Creek Falls, and the rail grade and old second-growth forest in Elwell Valley, but in general the chief value of the "Marckworth Forest" is as an embodiment of just about all the worst features possible (from the standpoint of a quiet recreationist) in a tree farm.

As for the mountain front, its two major peaks, Sultan and Sultana, are in other chapters which offer easier access. Two hikes on the front are included here, without enthusiasm, which the surveyor lost when residents of the Tomtit

Alps boobytrapped a public road and cost him $200 worth of tires, making Drunken Charlie the most expensive mountain he's ever climbed.

Stick with the Tolt, it's a grand old river.

USGS maps: Carnation, Lake Joy, Monroe, Sultan, Mt. Si, Index

For a free map of the company's road system, write Weyerhaeuser Company, Box W, Snoqualmie, WA 98065

Tolt River Trail (map — page 134)

Fifty years ago the Tolt River Trail was a thoroughfare tromped by troops of Scouts and mobs of fishermen. And it was far from new then, as testified by log cabins sagging to the forest floor, gnarled apple trees of homesteads being swallowed up in brush. By the late 1930s most entry was via a sidetrail from Moss Lake, but this path is long gone and so are all but vestigial scraps of the old river trail. However, intrigued by a proposal of the King County Urban Trails Plan for a reopening of the trail, and inveigled by a Weyerhaeuser forester's assurance that "fishermen hike it all the time," in summer 1977 the surveyor, after a previous winter defeat, set forth determined to win through to the Tolt River Forks. The day proved altogether fascinating — so much so that the surveyor spent 3 hours on the 3 miles to Stossel Creek. (Both ends of the route and the middle were resurveyed in 1985.)

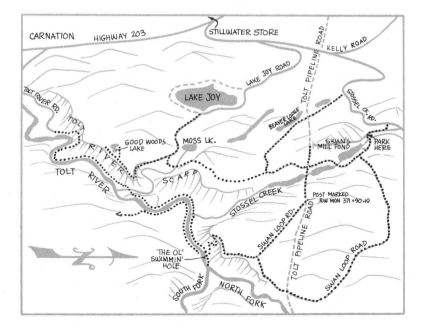

Tolt River from Tolt River Trail

It is true that fishermen hike here. But not always on trail — they wade a lot. Hikers willing to do so when jackstraws and salmonberry thickets are too mean, and able to navigate traces of tread that start and end nowhere, can reach the Forks. (In low water, anyhow.) Here is a splendid project for a youth group or outing club desirous of performing a good deed; surviving bits of old trail and new fishermen's paths could be linked by a few people running amok with machetes.

On Highway 203 in Carnation (nee Tolt, renamed when the Farms gained fame) turn east on Entwistle Street, which shortly throws off that quaint disguise and reveals itself as the Tolt River Road. Driving through stump-ranches and exurban mini-estates, on blacktop all the way, at 4 miles from town take a left at a Y (the right, NE 80th, goes to a public fishing access) and continue the short bit to the road-end turnaround, elevation 240 feet.

No attempt will be made to render a blow-by-blow account of the 3½-mile journey from road-end to Forks; until the benefactors swing those machetes the trip should be attempted only by experienced brushfighters and path-finders to whom excessive detail would be insulting. The rule is: When a trail in woods fades out, look for where boots have beaten a way to a gravel bar. When a gravel bar pinches out, look for where boots have entered forest. The rule works great except at several spots where the only answer is hurling the flesh at a thicket or partly immersing it in the river. Following is a brief outline:

Road-end to high clearcut, ½ mile.

This first section is a good-in-itself, with nice views down to the river and then an easy way down to its banks. From the road-end the boot-maintained trail goes a short level way to a log jam at the river's Big Bend. At a split here take the right, then dodge further rights. The way climbs, contours, climbs, and in ½ mile reaches the edge of a mid-1970s clearcut at about 400 feet.

High clearcut to upstream end of First Terrace, ¾ mile.

The much-used fishermen's path contours at the clearcut edge,then skids down the bluff to the river, reaching it at the downstream end of a large valley-bottom flat, clearcut in 1975 or so, enclosed in a meander arc. The loggers complied with state regulations by leaving a streamside strip of big cedars and spruces, huge cottonwoods, and arching vine maples. The combination of path bits and gravel bars allows easy travel.

First Terrace to start of Second Terrace, ¾ mile.

Wide flat and clearcut end in big-tree forest of a steep bluff. The way is along the toe of the slope, partly on a narrow flat, partly on gravel bars and a boulder-hop in the river (not in high water!), and finally, after a horrid floundering on a marshy sidehill, a wade nearly to the knees (low water only!). Moss-green twilight of gorgeous cedar-spruce-maple forest, old old campsites on benches, the purest wildness of the route, make this the climax of the trip.

Along Second Terrace, ½ mile.

The way emerges from forest and water onto a wide, long terrace clearcut in 1973 or so. A path shortcuts across the terrace on grownover logging roads, near the foot of the scarp, down which used to come the trail from Moss Lake. The route returns to the river at a lovely camp on a sandy point at the end of terrace and clearcut.

Second Terrace to Stossel Creek, ½ mile.

The old trail, clearly recognizable, enters a wow of an old forest of large firs and cedars on a narrow flat between bluff and river. Tread quits — or rather, dives into brush that cries out for a machete. The survey nearly was abandoned here; only a very few fishermen brave this stretch. The surveyor waded a side-channel to an alder island, at the head recrossed the channel to the woods, disliked that and tried more boulder-hopping. But the river bends sharply, deep swift water runs close against the bank, every trace of old trail has slid out in a bank of blue clay, not fishermen, not game have beaten a replacement, and the struggle is grim in clay and brambles. In despair the surveyor took to the river for a long, chilling wade in swift water over the knees — watched, from the other side of the river, by an incredulous doe and two fawns. But here the river is truly wild, the water avenue lined on both sides by lovely tall trees of mixed species. Concluding this bitter battle (which took the surveyor 40 minutes) are a gravel bar and (hurrah!) Stossel Creek.

Stossel Creek to Tolt Forks, ½ mile.

Forget-me-nots and other exotics escaped from some vanished homestead garden. A magnificent camp on sandy beach under spreading boughs of great cedar trees and cottonwoods. And trail! Downstream it disappears beyond remains of two ancient cedar bridges over Stossel Creek. But upstream it leads quickly to the Ol' Swimmin' Hole, elevation 360 feet, and on a hot summer day after a sweaty survey of the brush, looking and feeling mighty good.

Round trip to Forks 7 miles, allow 10 hours
High point 400 feet, elevation gain 500 feet
All year

Now for a completely different idea: Though the ancient trail route described above ought ultimately to be restored (probably — the environmental impact of thronging crowds must be considered) the cost would be large. A very inexpensive replacement — one possible for Scouts and other volunteers — could climb from the "high clearcut" to the tops of the scarp, proceed on old closed-to-wheels logging roads to Stossel Creek, and descend that valley to the river. Side-trails at one or two points could give access to the river. As of 1986 the idea is being kicked around Carnation. The project might be undertaken in 1987. Watch this space in the next revision.

Marckworth Freeway (map — page 141)

In the past decade, as the Great Big Western Tree Farm north of the Tolt River has been re-barbered, the central artery has so much improved from its previous primitivity that the ironic "freeway" has become virtually accurate. Though there still are few or no signs, and myriad logging spurs must be sorted out from the main route, the 15.8 miles nowadays can be comfortably driven in an hour in any season, except during the occasional deep snow. The Freeway therefore no longer can be recommended as a footroad, even on weekdays. Moreover, the logging railroad grades that formerly constituted a splendid trail system have been reclaimed for wheels, now rubber, at two, three, four or sixteen per vehicle. The suggestion is to pile the kids and the baloney sandwiches in the family car (4x4s not required) and make a day of it, doing this and that little stroll. The south-north drive is described here, points of interest noted in sequence.

On the Freeway, 2 miles; from Stillwater Store, 2 miles

At Stillwater Store (established 1900), north of Carnation on Highway 203, turn east on the road signed "Lake Joy." At a Y in 1.4 miles go right on Kelly Road, also signed for the lake. At a Y in .6 mile more, where Lake Joy Road goes right, keep left.

Moss Lake/Tolt River Scarp–Good Woods Lake

Turn right on Lake Joy Road 1.7 miles to a Y; keep left. In .8 mile go off left on a sideroad signed "Moss Lake." In .7 mile is a parking area by the lake, elevation 530 feet. Created from a peatbog by 1930s peatmoss mining, the lake lies in a subdivision-in-progress, but King County Parks may gain an access.

The road is drivable at least .3 mile past the lake, to a Y. The left turns east over the beaver-dammed outlet of the lake, bends northerly over hill and dale in a confusion of logging roads, and in a scant 2 miles intersects the Tolt Pipeline. Here in the clearcuts and plantations a hot-footed walker could loop himself to death.

The right leads (probably afoot) ¼ mile to the brink of the Tolt River scarp, 525 feet. In olden days a Boy Scout and fisherman thoroughfare dropped to the Tolt River Trail. In the late 1970s a skidpath could still be walked, but a thinning operation in young firs made such a mess not even animals can move about, except moles. The volunteers contemplating a New Tolt Trail envision restoring this side-trail. For now there are views down to the river, 300 feet, and across the wide gulf to more clearcuts.

Tolt Pipeline bridge over North Fork Tolt River Gorge

The road-trail goes another ¼ mile (at a Y, take the right) to a patch of tall trees grown up since railroad days, a mystery amid plantations of young firs. The explanation comes when one finds a path through the forest to Good Woods Lake, 520 feet, a beaver-dammed pond, the dark water sprouting huge old cedar stumps and snags, half-submerged logs nourishing linear gardens of salal and huckleberries. There are fish in the lake and by agreement with the State Game Department, and obedience to latter-day shoreline regulations, the shore will not be re-logged, will remain a marvel. The New Tolt Trail would continue west from here along the scarp, then drop to the Tolt River Road.

Back on the Freeway, 2.6 miles; from Stillwater Store, 4.6 miles

Where Lake Joy Road goes right, keep left 1 mile (to just past the crossing of the Tolt Pipeline — which see) to a Y; go right on Stossel Creek Road. At a Y in 1.4 mile, "School Bus Turnaround," keep right, from blacktop to gravel. In .2 mile the Freeway bends sharply left and a garbage-dump lane proceeds straight, elevation 504 feet.

Beaver Lodge Lake

The garbage lane, blocked by garbage, crosses a headwater of Harris Creek. Employing the road as a foundation for a line of dams, beaver have built a lake and flooded the road, forcing a hiker to do some tussock-hopping, brush-fighting, and wading. The water is covered with pond-lily pads, the blossoms a yellow brilliance in flowering time. Frogs croak. Ducks quack.

The way joins a better road from the left, at ¾ mile from the Freeway crosses the Tolt Pipeline, and in ¼ mile more comes to a lake ½ mile long, 550 feet. Descend the bank, by fir trees that were gnawed but not felled; when beavers turn teeth to conifers it usually means they're running short on good food and about to move along in quest of tastier deciduous salads. Walk out on sunken logs to within close view of the heaped-up brush of the abandoned lodge.

Back on the Freeway, 5 miles; from Stillwater Store, 9.6 miles

At 589 feet, .9 mile from the garbage lane, the 1940s Swan Mill Road goes off right. Just beyond, a 1980s logging road also goes off right. They join and proceed to Swan's Mill Pond and the Tolt Pipeline (see Tolt River Forks).

The Freeway passes through a saddle to the valley of Stossel Creek, here a mile-long marsh. At 1 mile from the Swan Mill roads a spur descends right to the marsh; take the binoculars and go after the ducks and blackbirds and beaver.

In .2 mile more a spur climbs left in a 1984 clearcut. In .4 mile more are the end of the clearcut and of Stossel marshes and a sideroad right to homes — pioneers of the suburbia that bodes ill for the Tree Farm. In .3 mile the Freeway crosses Stossel Creek and in .2 mile passes more private property on the right and a sideroad over the ridge to North Fork Creek. Still recalling the railroad grade it used to be, the Freeway passes Langendorfer Lake and marshes on the left, and then — recrossing the creek — more marshes on the right — these being the headwaters of Stossel Creek.

At 580 feet, 1.3 miles from the sideroad to North Fork Creek, a sideroad climbs left and swings around the sidehill to the valley of Cherry Creek. Having crossed a divide while staying in the same Pleistocene valley, in .1 mile the Freeway crosses Cherry Creek, 570 feet. Continue a bit to a gated *private* road right (to condos?) and park. Find a path down left to a delightful falls, the water tumbling over an 8-foot wall of hard rock.

In .2 mile more is a major junction, 571 feet. The left is the middle entry to the Freeway, via the Elwell Valley Railroad and Proposed Cherry Creek Park (which see). Keep right.

At a Y in .2 mile keep right .2 mile to a sideroad left, 620 feet. (Just before, in a 1984 clearcut, note a short spur to large concrete slabs, foundations of a 1930s mill.)

Elwell Wall

Astounding precipices are a specialty of this part of the Great Big Western Tree Farm, due to grinding by the glacier, though why the ice should have taken such fierce bites here is not apparent to a lay speculator. Anyhow, particularly appalling is the Elwell Wall, even steeper than suggested by the brown blur of contour lines on the USGS map — indeed, the cliff is partly overhanging and would have climbers a-twitter were the rock not utter trash. In addition to giddy gazing straight down there are fine views out, some of the best in the Freeway vicinity.

Drive the sideroad left, climbing to the crest of a 930-foot ridge. At 1.3 and 1.4 miles are the best spurs to the brink of the wall.

Look south to the Issaquah Alps, west to the High Rock Hills, north to the Skykomish River, Stickney, and Pilchuck, and east to the Tomtit Alps, Sultan, Sultana, and Drunken Charlie. Look down to the broad valley of Elwell Creek, some of it not yet (1986) re-logged. Look over the brink to a million-odd beer bottles and cans and a litter of broken cars that may or may not contain skeletons of Saturday-night frolickers.

Back on the Freeway, .4 mile; from Stillwater Store, 10 miles

The Freeway leaves the valley of Cherry Creek, snakes around in smaller glacial drainages, and at .4 mile comes to Marckworth Junction, 650 feet. A large reader board explains how the University of Washington is running an experimental forest, named for a former dean of the College of Forest Resources. The University actually has pretty well gone away because whenever a 40-year research project just got nicely started the plot was logged by the DNR. There is no income to the state from research; knowledge may be power, but cash spends better.

Cherry Lake

Turn south from Marckworth Junction .8 mile to a bridge over Cherry Creek and a campsite, 760 feet. The moody little lake in the woods is well worth the time. Before setting out, investigate the superb falls tumbling down a mossy rock scarp. In spring snowmelt season a person can take a showerbath in billows of spray while still yards distant from the plungebasin.

Back at the picnic table, spot the trail steeply climbing the dirt slope. Walk carefully, noting the twists and turns for the return, ascending the lovely little valley of Cherry Creek in fine forest (1986). In ½ mile (seeming thrice that) the trail reaches the outlet of the lake, 980 feet.

The rude path grows ruder yet and most hikers will quit at a gorgeous inlet creek, walking out on a log in the marshy lake for a look around. However, if tantalized by the tree-screened falls entering the lake head, fight on through the brush.

North Fork Creek

At .5 mile south of Cherry Lake trail is a Y, 800 feet. The right crosses a marsh headwater of North Fork Creek and proceeds 1.2 miles to a sideroad right, over the ridge to Langendorfer Lake, and continues 1.8 miles to a

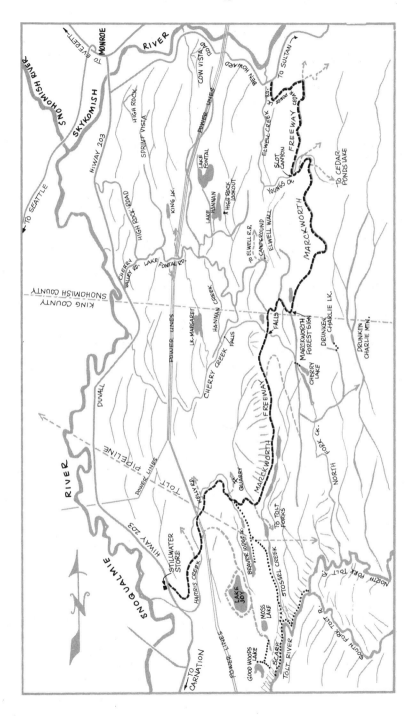

clearcut, 950 feet, of the early 1970s, with views over the Tolt River to the Cascade front and the Issaquah Alps.

Drunken Charlie Lake

From the above Y the left goes south 1.1 miles to a Y. A bit beyond on the right is the old Drunken Charlie trailhead, and the 5-minute walk along the rail grade, by ferny-mossy rock outcrops, beside a green-tangled creek, is enough to get a walker excited by the prospects. But then the trail ends, beheaded by the left fork.

So, from the Y drive the left, built in the mid-1980s, .7 mile to the ridge, 1200 feet. The road continues a bit to a gravel pit; survey flags indicate it will soon reach the lake. Find the path, wherever, climb in forest, as long as it lasts, and contour to the lake, 1380 feet, ¼ mile or less from the road.

The name proves to be the lake's most interesting feature. Who was Charlie? Why did he drink? The hiker who spends more than several depressing minutes at this somber little garbaged-up pothole may think he understands. (To answer the question, Charlie operated a still here, serving the local loggers, when he was not taste-testing his product.)

Back on the Freeway, 5.8 miles; from Stillwater Store, 15.8 miles

From Marckworth Junction the Freeway climbs the sidehill to its highest elevation, 740 feet, and drops back to the valley, now carrying Youngs Creek. More marshes are passed (in winter they used to flood out the Freeway). At 560 feet, 2.6 miles from the junction, Cedar Ponds Road goes off right to Tomtit Vista (which see).

At the turnoff, Youngs Creek flows under a bridge, over a falls, into a canyon. Park at the picnic ground by the bridge and walk paths along the top of the slot.

In .4 mile more the Freeway crosses a second bridge, 506 feet. Here are the best falls of all, in a deep dark dank mossy scary gorge. Park and explore — carefully! — paths upstream and down.

The Freeway emerges into the bright air of 1980s clearcuts and views over Elwell Creek, which receives the flow of Youngs Creek and occupies the northernmost stretch of the Long Valley that extends from the Tolt River to the Skykomish. Spurs lead off left to Elwell Creek.

In 1.6 miles from the gorge the Freeway becomes a maintained county road at the cow frontier. (If driving from the north entry, keep right at the Y here.) In a final 1.2 miles, here signed Cedar Ponds Road, it comes to a T, 106 feet, with paved Ben Howard Road, at a point 6.2 miles east of Highway 203.

One-way drive from Stillwater Store to Ben Howard Road 15.8 miles
High point 740 feet
February-December

Tolt Pipeline (map — page 144)

The cooperative arrangement by which the Seattle Water Department has made available to King County Parks the Tolt Pipeline Trail from Bothell to the west side of the Snoqualmie valley is described in *Footsore 1.* On the remain-

Moss-draped rain forest

der of the pipeline route eastward to the Cascades all private vehicles are banned and motorcycles specifically forbidden, but walking and horseback riding are tolerated on the service road — which is a de facto extension of the King County trail.

Western Segment: Snoqualmie Valley to Harris Creek

This segment is a near twin of the Bear Creek Plateau on the other side of the valley; notable features and views are few but the strolling is pleasant through second-growth, by the occasional horse farm or cow pasture or stumpranch. It is particularly attractive on a winter day when one wishes to visit the pretty snow but fears to venture on wheels off valley pavement up slippery hill roads.

Drive Highway 203 to 1.5 miles south of Duvall and park at Duvall Community Park, elevation 80 feet.

Cross the highway to the Tolt River Headquarters and the start of the service road. Though wide and well-maintained, it is driven only by the rare work vehicle and thus quiet all week, and especially on Sundays when motorcycles and fun trucks are racketing elsewhere. The road slants up the valley

143

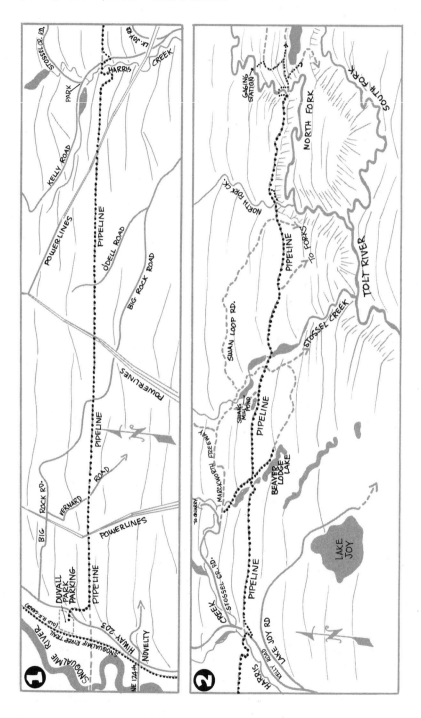

wall to the pipeline and thence runs a compass course due east for miles. With moderate ups and downs, mostly in woods, passing scattered homes, the way crosses Vernard Road, Big Rock Road, and O'Dell Road, all accessible from the Big Rock Road that goes east from Highway 203 at ¼ mile north of Duvall Park, all offering alternate starts for shorter walks. At 4½ miles the pipeline gives a view to Tolt headwaters, then descends to Harris Creek and the pastures and homes of Kelly Road.

Round trip 9 miles, allow 6 hours
High point 550 feet, elevation gain (going and coming) 1400 feet
All year

Eastern Segment: Harris Creek to North Fork Tolt River

Eastward from Harris Creek is something else. Inhabited land is immediately left, tree farm entered. Second-growth alternates with the broad-horizon third-growth of young plantations. Sidetrips are many. Saving best for last, at the end is the stupendous gorge of the North Fork Tolt, bearing comparison with the Green River Gorge.

As the Great Big Western Tree Farm north of the Tolt River loses its trees — and worse, its old railroad trails — and is opened up to every manner of public vehicle, the pipeline "trail" becomes more and more attractive. Not only is it officially closed to machines, it forms a policed barricade that guards some nearby logging roads and makes them footroads, and even protects a few genuine trails. Never is it more appreciated than in winter, when the playboys are out to see how much snow they can mess up with wheel tracks, leaving nothing for the foot-stomping pedestrian or cross-country skier — except this refuge.

From Stillwater Store on Highway 203 drive the Marckworth Freeway (which see) 3 miles to the Stossel Creek Road and park at the Y, elevation 336 feet.

Walk back down Kelly Road the short bit to the pipeline service road and climb the valley wall to the plateau rolling east to the mountain front. From young plantation see Tiger, Si, Phelps Ridge, and local foothills. At 1½ miles a small sideroad goes left into plantation; in a few yards its continuation goes right into woods; this is the way from Marckworth Freeway to Beaver Lodge Lake (which see). The sidetrip to the beaver lodge invites.

At 2½ miles, having descended nearly to the bottom of Stossel Creek valley, the pipeline is joined on the left by a 1980s logging road and a short bit farther along by the 1930s Swan Loop Road, marked by a white roadside fence and several large boulders; this approach from Marckworth Freeway is 1 long mile, 1½ miles shorter than the pipeline. (See Tolt River Forks.) Sidetrip ⅓ mile to Swan's Mill Pond. If in the mood, take loops hereabouts until you're dizzy.

At 3 miles, on the hill beyond the marshy bottom of Stossel Creek, Swan Loop Road diverges right to Tolt River Forks. Topping a 700-foot crest, at 3¾ miles the pipeline crosses Swan Loop again; the right is another way to Tolt Forks, the left another way to Swan's Mill Pond (see Tolt River Forks). The plateau is now ending, chopped up by taller hills and deeper valleys. At 4 miles the pipeline drops steeply to cross North Fork Creek.

Lulled by pleasant but undramatic terrain, the somnolent hiker is jolted wide-awake and yelling at 5 miles as the pipeline drops to a bridge over the North Fork Tolt River.

The view from the bridge is appalling. The river, which in most of its course from this point to the Snoqualmie is sliced in glacial rubbish, here is slotted in hard rock, at a couple of spots squeezed to a width of barely 6 or 8 feet, the water boiling-white. Upstream is a truly terrifying sight — spanning the gorge at the same high level as the bridge is a footlog! Apparently used by construction workers, it will not tempt any sane hiker; however, the approach trail is mandatory. Find the path in the woods just short of the bridge, walk to the log and breathe deeply several times at the thought of crossing, then continue — carefully — down to the river, reached at the upper entrance to the gorge. The sandstone walls have been scoured and polished by the water. Potholes up to 6 feet wide and 8 feet deep have been eroded by floodwater-swirled boulders. The river seems narrow enough to jump across. Don't try! Standing on end as it is, the stream is roaring a mile a minute.

Round trip 10 miles, allow 7 hours
High point 780 feet, elevation gain (going and coming) 1200 feet
All year

Walking is tolerated to the North Fork bridge, just short of the Tolt Regulating Basin, but not beyond. Too bad, because the barring gate could be moved ¼ mile east to a Y; blocking the right fork to the Seattle installation, assuring the purity of city water, it would permit walking to more splendors on the left fork, Weyerhaeuser road 6151. For example, at ¾ mile from the bridge is a ¼-mile trail down to a stream-gaging station. Here the wild and superb river features a pool many yards wide and more than a dozen feet deep. Gazing into the green-delicious depths stirs two thoughts: one, fling off clothes and dive in; two, dash back to Seattle, turn on a faucet, and get blissfully drunk on ambrosia.

Back on road 6151, a hiker would be able in ½ mile more to take the left at a triple fork and in ¾ mile reach the North Fork in still another gorge, at what will be the intake site if and when this stream is added to the South Fork as a Seattle water supply. And continuing on road 6151 from the triple fork, by this way and that one could in several miles walk to the bridge over the fearsome gorge of the South Fork, also little-known to the public. And so on to a number of destinations, the way providing a variant Sound-to-Mountains Trail, a pedestrian route from city to wilderness.

Tolt River Forks via Swan's Mill Pond (map — page 134)

In olden days the Tolt Forks was where Boy Scouts of the Seattle area learned to cook kabob and mulligan, build a bough bed and shiver all night in a wool blanket, and sing marching songs while soaking up the rain. Aside from the education there was fun — scrambling on rock walls, splashing around in the deep green pool of the Ol' Tolt Swimmin' Hole. When logging and brush and mudslides disrupted the Tolt River Trail (which see), the scene became lonesome. But on surveys in the late 1970s, and revisits through the mid-

1980s, it was found to be amazingly little changed from the 1930s and just as exciting — to an old Boy Scout, anyhow.

From Stillwater Store on Highway 203 drive the Marckworth Freeway (which see) 5.5 miles to where two roads go off right — the 1930s Swan Mill Road and a 1980s logging road. Take either one; they quickly unite. At .4 mile from the Freeway is a Y, the right a continuation of the new logging road to the Tolt Pipeline, the (virtually) undrivable left to the millpond. Park here, elevation 500 feet.

(The new logging road can be driven .6 mile to the blockade that forbids wheels on the Tolt Pipeline road, and the latter can then be walked left ¼ mile to join the route described below. This approach is a little quicker but misses one of the good parts of the trip.)

Walk left from the Y, cross marshy Stossel Creek on a sagging bridge which in 1977 replaced Swan's falling-apart bridge to permit several years of gypo clearcutting hereabouts. In ¼ mile, on the far side of the valley at 502 feet, are the two ends of the old Swan Loop Road. That on the left may be employed for a looping return.

Take the right, downvalley, leaving the clearcut and entering nice old second-growth woods (1986), the road dwindling to trail. The marshy pond that is Stossel Creek widens to a true lake. At the lower end the road-trail crosses an old dam that one is startled to realize is not a beaver project but a manmade earth-fill dam. Indeed, this lake is Swan's Mill Pond.

Swan's Mill Pond

Bob Swan, whose lumber company was headquartered in Carnation, operated a mill here until about 1947. He then departed to make a fortune in Oregon forests, simply walking away from the mill and all its machinery (located at the upvalley end of the pond), the bunkhouses and other buildings on the hillside, all the miles of railroad track, and even the locomotives. Salvagers and scavengers moved in; the only traces to be seen now are some big timbers, scattered rusty junk, and (of course) the dam and pond.

On the far side of the dam the path splits, each fork leading to a way over Stossel Creek, which at high water is best crossed, gingerly, on a log jumble at the lake outlet. The valley widens to a broad marsh, the far hillside clearcut in the 1970s.

At ½ mile from the 502-foot Y the path hits the great broad service road of the Tolt Pipeline. Turn left on this monster gravel swath, which for a way has obliterated the old Swan Loop, and follow it down into the Stossel valley and up the far slope. After a long ½ mile on the pipeline road, as it is very nearly at the crest of the ascent, spot a path angling off right, directly across from a yellow post marked "RW MON 371 + 90.19." This is the resumption of the Swan Loop, somewhat maintained by horseriders, so take it. Alternating between second-growth and young plantation, in a long ½ mile from the pipeline, at 720 feet, the way merges with a better road from the left—this, another segment of the Swan Loop, is the route of the alternate return described below.

Walk right a bit to the edge of the Tolt scarp and south along it ½ mile. The road now dives off the edge and becomes a trail — rarely gouged by razzers since their only access here is via the Tolt Pipeline which is forbidden to them and regularly patrolled. In a steep ¼ mile the road-trail ends on a bluff (side of the old camp) above the Forks, 2¾ miles from the car. Elevation at river level, 360 feet.

Three things must be done here. First, follow paths out atop cliffs above the river, which just here, below the Forks, passes between rock-wall portals. Second, find a path down to the gravel bar below the Forks, beside a broad green pool known to Boy Scouts of yore as the Tolt Swimmin' Hole, and to one troop of Girl Scouts arriving unheralded as their introduction to mass male skinnydipping. (On a survey early in 1977 the water was found frigid, but subsequently, in summer, the lone surveyor assumed the traditional costume and took the plunge. The water was still frigid. But good, but good.) Third, walk ½ mile down the river past the gaging station to Stossel Creek (see Tolt River Trail). The much-used camp in the grove of giant cottonwoods indicates many a Boy Scout (and Girl Scout) still finds the way here.

Round trip 6½ miles, allow 4 hours
High point 720 feet, elevation gain 600 feet
All year

The adventurer may wish to return on the other leg of the Swan Loop Road, the route only a mile longer but having some of the confusion inherent in clearcuts. To try it, at the 720-foot junction take the right a long ½ mile to the Tolt Pipeline. The resumption on the far side leads to a 1975-77 clearcut. Forge ahead past spurs left and right, following a series of side-valleys parallel to and elevated above Stossel Creek, passing a line of knolls. The way goes to a high point, then drops to a vale and a Y; go left, up a sidehill, down to a final vale, in which logging has obliterated the old road. Maybe find a meager path going left over the valley bottom and up the slope to a resumption of the Swan Loop, which steeply descends a tributary valley. At 2 miles from the 720-foot junction the loop is closed at the 502-foot junction by Stossel Creek.

Proposed Cherry Creek State Park (map — page 151)

In these pages, it is merely a proposal. On the ground, it must be made a reality. Are you listening, Government?

The middle entry to the Marckworth Freeway (which see) is notable in 1986 for three things: (1) the on-going completion of the re-scalping of the High Rock Hills and the concomitant reopening of smashing views in every direction, from Rainier to Seattle to the Tomtit Alps; (2) the area's last remaining good-walk stretches of old logging railroads; (3) the finest of the several falls of Cherry Creek, amid a patch of old-growth forest, connected to a lovely length of creek flowing through noble big second-growth, paralleled by one of those stretches of rail grade — the assemblage absolutely shrieking to be made a (state or other) park.

Drive Highway 203 from the north edge of Duvall 3.4 miles and turn east on Cherry Valley Road 1.1 miles to the junction with High Rock Road. Continue on their union, Lake Fontal Road, 1.9 miles to a Y; keep left. In .9 mile is a sign, "End of County Road," and in .7 mile more, a total 4.6 miles from the highway, a signless and exceedingly confusing junction, with a T and a Y. Stay alert. To reach the proposed park (and the Marckworth Freeway), you are going to turn right at the T.

(But first, for the benefit of high clearances if not necessarily 4x4s, following is a description of the left turn at the T: In a few feet is the Y. Take the left, straight ahead, and soon parallel and cross and recross a Bonneville powerline, in the earlier edition of this book described as the High Rock Hills Traverse, but no longer recommended for a walk. If all correct dodges are made and pitfalls and logging trucks avoided, in 3.3 miles the scenic drive reaches Cow Vista (which see). For more exploration, at the Y take the right .6 mile to another Y. The left goes .4 mile to Lake Hannan, 1094 feet, which only a fisherman or aluminum recycler could love, and another .5 mile to Lake Fontal, 1050 feet, just as rotten. The right, however, is worth driving. It passes the route to Hi Rock Lookout, 1463 feet, which now has only 10 minutes' worth of forest remaining and no views and thus has been dropped from this edition, and at 1.5 miles from the Hannan junction comes to a vast mid-1980s clearcut on the slopes of the Elwell valley, with magnificent views across to Elwell Wall, Sultan, and the Tomtit Alps, and over the Skykomish valley to Stickney and Wallace Falls.)

Back at Exceedingly Confusing Junction and the T, turn right. Pay attention — logging spurs sprout every which way. In .2 mile turn left, out into a 1980s plantation with an enormous view to the Cascade front from Si to Sultan, to the Issaquah Alps and Rainier, and to Seattle. In 1 mile more, go straight. In .9 mile more, at 760 feet, a total of 2.1 miles from Confusing Junction, the main road goes left (to Elwell Railroad and Marckworth Freeway). Turn right on a road that may still have a small sign, "600." Descend gently, then switchback steeply,

Lower Cherry Creek Falls

through a plantation with a Rainier view, 1.4 miles to the valley bottom and a narrow, brushed-in sideroad left. Park here, elevation 350 feet.

Virgin Forest and Falls

Walk the sideroad a few steps and turn right on old railroad grade to the big trees — old-growth Douglas fir up to 5 feet in diameter and cedars nearly as big. The place obviously has been a beloved campground and picnic ground for decades — from the era of railroad logging, otherwise the big sticks so handy to the rails would have been hauled away then.

The grade continues ahead, past little Hannan Creek falls, where a trestle used to cross; a bit of volunteer labor could brush out a path to let the hike proceed downvalley from here. But for the event at hand, find a steep path from the big-tree overlook at the top of the falls to the base at 350 feet. White water froths 20 feet down the moss-black vertical wall, a double plume on the left, a 30-foot-wide sheet on the right. The plunge basin is eminently suitable for wading and swimming.

Old Second-Growth, Railroad, and Creek

To avoid what presently is a mean crossing of Hannan Creek at the picnic grounds, from the sideroad drive the logging road .8 mile to a deadend at 360 feet. Clearcut is on the right and ahead downvalley; on the left is jungle (1986).

Retreat up the road to where the forest below is relatively brushfree and pick an easy route down to Cherry Creek at 270 feet. Very pretty, tunneling through mossy arches of maple boughs. Very wild.

Now return up the slope a bit to the railway crossed on the descent. Do not be discouraged by 2-foot trees in the middle of the grade, suggesting its age. Walking is slow but not arduous, threading through interwoven alders, maples, and cedars, past huge, mossy cedar stumps. The problems are the creek gulches where the bridges are long gone and the brush and muck and jackstraw are vicious. It was one of these that daunted the surveyor as he explored downvalley. It was another that terminated the survey upvalley, causing a climb back to the road.

Surely, in the second stripping of the Great Big Western Tree Farm to the altogether, the Gross National Product can tolerate sparing one little strip of second-growth, one ¾-mile stretch of historic railroad and wild creek, and adding these to the proposed park.

Round trips 2 miles, allow 3 hours
High point 400 feet, elevation gain 200 feet
February-December

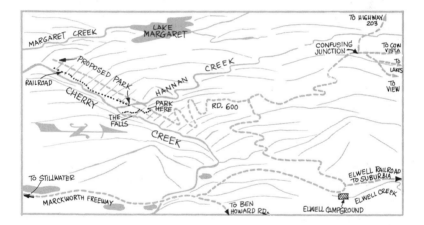

Elwell Valley Railroad (map — page 151)

Beginning before the turn of the century and continuing to the midpoint, engineers who never attended any college but that of the deep woods roamed the virgin forests, jaws full of snoose, carrying no maps (there were none) and no equipment except axes to blaze the routes for the lokies. When the last rails and ties were pulled up and the loggers — now traveling by truck — moved along, Nature was left alone to get on with her tree-farming. The second crop ready, the loggers returned, this time accompanied by college-educated transit-and-sliderule-equipped engineers — who found their job largely already done for them. Throughout the Great Big Western Tree Farm, a pass of a bulldozer and a topping of crushed rock have converted old rail grades to truck roads, and the poignant sound of the steam whistle has receded into history.

During the decades between harvests, the old grades were trails, and the second-growth forests of the GBWTF were thronged by pedestrians seeking fish, deer, mushrooms, or non-material rewards. But where the iron wheels rolled, now there are rubber. Footroads there may still be, though few enough of those; trails are a vanishing species.

As of 1986 one of the quintessentially best of the old grades survives. By 1990 — perhaps by 1987 — it will be gone. Come quick — a year or a month too late and you'll drive through the 3 miles of stumps in 10 minutes and wonder what ever could have been here to get a guidebook writer excited.

Though close enough to civilization for horns of modern trains in the Skykomish valley to be heard, the way never is in sight of any human activity other than that of First Wave loggers of a half-century ago. However, walking the grade doesn't require machetes or other weapons of war. It never is interrupted by harrowing tangles where ancient bridges have vanished. Staying on course requires watchfulness: what with 3½-foot cottonwoods and 3-foot maples and 2½-foot firs growing in the middle, one begins to doubt this narrow lane of flatness is truly manmade; flat lanes arranged by nature can lead one astray. There's enough bobbing and weaving, stepping over and ducking under, and some short detours around thickets, and a lone missing-bridge gap that must be skirted by swinging upstream and around, that a good steady pace nets 1 mile an hour.

But there's no sweat. Not in this cool greenery. Sometimes on level benches, sometimes on a sidehill, the grade penetrates typical lushness of a valley bottom, with old mixed-species forest growing toward the next harvest above gigantic stumps of the first reaping, with vine maple, devils club, ferns,

and carpets of ginger and festoons of moss, and small creeks (Elwell Creek itself is never neared) to entertain and please but not to entangle and torture.

Drive to the trailhead either from west or east: From Highway 203, continue easterly past the road 600 turnoff to Proposed Cherry Creek State Park (which see) 1.8 miles to Elwell Camp and Picnic Area, the recreational hub of Marckworth Forest. From the Marckworth Freeway (which see) at 9.2 miles from Stillwater Store turn west at the major junction, 571 feet, into a clearcut (featuring a new stumpranch, this far has the frontier advanced) and descend into forest, reaching the camp in 1.3 miles. Park by the entrance, elevation 429 feet.

Some 70 feet west of the entry sign, spot an obvious overgrown road diverging to the right; this is the grade. Forge on through the first thicket of vine maple and settle into the rhythm, not assaulting the green things, your friends, but insinuating your body among them.

At about 1¼ miles is a Y. The right, not surveyed, is shown by the map as deadending in a mile. The left fork continues about the same distance before being chopped off by Second Wave clearcutting and/or suburbia, which are advancing up the Elwell.

Round trip 6 miles, allow 6 hours
High point 580 feet, elevation gain 200 feet
February-December

Tomtit Vista: Low and High (map — page 154)

For such "little" country the Tomtit Alps are exceptionally dramatic. The Puget Glacier seems to have run amok here; the area abounds in pointy miniature mountains, surprising cliffs, hideaway lakes tucked in odd corners. It used to be enchanting to walk, rounding the shores and circling the peaks. It's still charming to gaze down upon. Two vista points, one low, the other higher, show the Alps at their best. And provide broad views of much else.

From Ben Howard Road drive Cedar Ponds Road (see Marckworth Freeway) 4 miles. Where the Freeway proceeds straight ahead, turn left over Youngs Creek, pass a logging road to the left, and in 1.3 miles reach a Y above the shore of Cedar Ponds Lake.

Tomtit Vista: Low

The elevation of the Y is 722 feet. The left fork, "Private," is to homes; other such warnings are proliferating everywhere hereabouts, as are "Keep Out" and "No Trespassing," suggesting a general irritation. The right fork (normally lacking signs, which are instantly torn down) is a public road, DNR, never upgraded to big-truck standards, meager and barely maintained, in timber so scrawny the next harvest is years away. The road is so rude that most family cars quickly beg for mercy, and most family nerves are severely racked.

It is, then, a splendid footroad — in winter and spring when washouts and windfalls halt kiddywheels. However, when the warm sun of the new year brings out the Good Joes in 4x4s to do their Good Deeds, opening the way with chainsaws and shovels, forget it. The residents never can, and the roaring

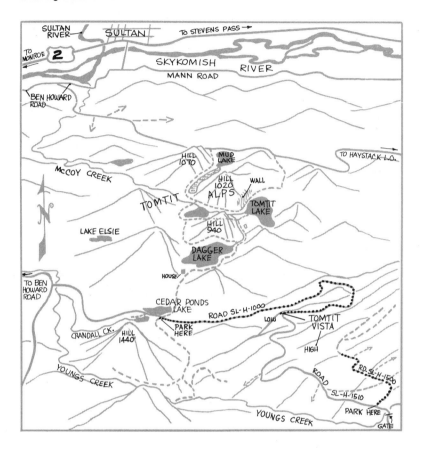

boys have driven them over the brink. On the surveyor's return from a 1985 tour — always on public roads, never molesting anyone's privates — he developed two flat tires. In the Cedar Ponds vicinity he had driven over a boobytrap that punched dozens of tiny holes in each tire. With towing charges and fruitless attempts at repair, the day cost him $200. He fully understands the feelings of the residents but thinks it's a shame they wreaked their vengeance on an innocent friendly.

The surveyor has recommended to the DNR that it gate the road to all public vehicles. If the residents want peace, they'll second the recommendation and stop committing felonies; their next "gotcha" may not be a mild-mannered surveyor but a fire-breathing yahoo who'll return to torch the neighborhood.

Anyhow, in proper season, walk the right fork. In 2 miles, at 1320 feet, the way switchbacks out of green tunnel onto a steep sidehill, traversing under one cliff and over another, screened views quickening the pulse. At 3 miles, 1700 feet, whammo, there it all is. For maximum effect scramble onto a bald knob above the road. Gaze: Straight down to Dagger and Tomtit Lakes and their Alps. Northerly to pastures and the hamlet of Sultan and beyond to Bald,

Dagger Lake from Tomtit Vista

Pilchuck, Three Fingers, and — well, a goodly share of what's seen from the High Vista.

Round trip 6 miles, allow 4 hours
High point 1700 feet, elevation gain 1000 feet
February-December

Tomtit Vista: High

Drive to Low Vista and continue 3.1 miles, shunning obviously lesser sideroads, to a junction a few yards short of a bridge over Youngs Creek. Park here, elevation 2410 feet.

The fork going uphill left is the route of the walk, a track become too rough even for sports. Ascend steeply a short bit to a Y; take the left, bending sharply left to an intersection at a scant ¼ mile. The left drops back to the road from Low Vista. The right, not surveyed, leads to upper Youngs Creek, slopes of Sultan, and perhaps the top. Go straight ahead through the intersection a scant ¼ mile to a Y. Take the less-good road left. (The right was not surveyed but leads toward Sultan and might provide an easy summit route.) In ¼ mile the way levels out at a 2840-foot promontory.

All the way from the bridge the view from the young plantation is terrific over the skinned valley of Youngs Creek to Sultana and up to Sultan and virgin forests lingering on National Forest lands. Now, on the promontory, the panorama is smashing from Sultana to Sagging Shanty Lake to Drunken Charlie Mountain to Youngs Creek Canyon to Elwell Valley and High Rock Hills, beyond to Si, Rainier, Issaquah Alps, Puget Sound, and Olympics, and out the Skykomish to cows and trains and river, and Startup, Sultan, Monroe, and Everett, and to Stickney and Blue and Big Four and Pilchuck. Just past the promontory and a deadend spur right is an all-year creek that provides water for the camp that gives a mind-blowing night experience of lowland lights.

On the initial survey in 1977 the route was investigated 1¼ miles farther, contouring spur roads to their ends at 2800 and 2850 feet in a plantation of the early 1960s, almost directly above Low Vista. However, the 1985 survey found the extension of marginal value, what with the young trees poking very slowly but steadily higher.

Round trip 1 mile, allow 1 hour
High point 2840 feet, elevation gain 500 feet
March-November

Drunken Charlie Mountain (map — page 158)

The low-elevation tangle of Marckworth Forest lakes and beaver marshes and peaklets and cliffs-in-the-bushes, now in the midst of Second Wave clearcutting, merges upward into new-skinned ridges and benches where First Wave clearcutting is just finishing and plantation shrubs are not yet tall enough to interfere with broad views. Marking the boundary is the long ridge and stunning scarp of Drunken Charlie Mountain. The view is fascinating. And the trip there through the tree farm is perhaps even more so, a pleasant stroll in Nature's (and only to a minor extent man's) plantations, mainly of hemlock and silver fir.

From the Y at Cedar Ponds Lake drive 6.2 miles to the bridge over Youngs Creek (see Tomtit Vista). Just beyond is a gate, always closed to public vehicles even when it chances to be left open for logging purposes — or busted open by frolicking joyboys and not yet repaired. To drive on is to break the law and take risks; see GBWTF — Via Roads Beyond Spur 10 Gates. So park here, elevation 2360 feet.

At the gate the road changes from DNR management to Weyerhaeuser and on the company map is shown as Spur 63 — a very good road, engineered for big trucks, but thanks to completion of the skinning of local hills, left lonesome — even though it can be driven by the public from Spur 10, when the West Gate is open (see Sultana).

At 1 mile from Youngs Creek take a sidetrip to "Sagging Shanty Lake." Walk the spur to the shore, turn north on the wet, spongy bog mat, pass silver snags (trees killed when the beaver flooded them out, decades ago), ancient gnawed stumps and logs, bleached silver, and continue through a field of aromatic Labrador tea to the old cedar-shake shanty, no longer sagging but collapsed.

Drunken Charlie Lake

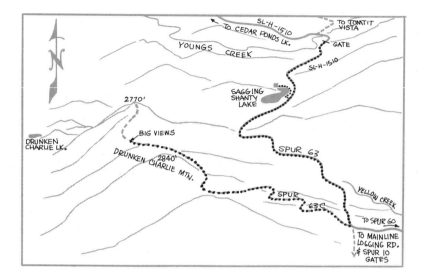

Look over lilypad-strewn waters to naked Sultana and Drunken Charlie Mountain.

Continue almost 2⅓ miles to two spurs right at 2350 feet. The first of these, the most northerly, heading uphill is Spur 63C (unsigned), the route to Drunken Charlie.

Spur 63C is easy to follow; though it sprouts sideroads, these obviously do not go to the top, which is the goal. Head northerly and up, through plantation; from this east slope the views are across headwater wetlands of Yellow Creek to Sagging Shanty Lake and the bleak expanse of Sultana and beyond to the upper valley of the Tolt and to Index. The way swings into a saddle-plateau, 2730 feet, almost 2⅓ miles from Spur 63. The road continues a bit to the north tip of the ridge, but the trees there are growing high; the saddle is the place, with panoramas on both sides of the ridge.

The view is from Three Fingers-Pilchuck to the north, over the Skykomish valley and High Rock Hills to Everett, and on down the Olympics, Puget Sound, and Seattle to Issaquah Alps and Rainier. Of special interest is Marckworth Forest and environs, of which this viewpoint gives the best overall perspective. Pastures of the bounding Skykomish and Snoqualmie valleys can be seen, and the north-south valley of Elwell-Youngs-Cherry-Stossel Creeks, and the broad green bay of Cherry Valley, and North Fork and Harris Creeks, and the Tolt River. And 1000 feet down the splendid Si-Sultan scarp at whose top one stands is the intricate vicinity of Drunken Charlie Lake. The lake itself very decently hides in its hole.

Round trip 11¼ miles, allow 8 hours
High point 2730 feet, elevation gain 500 feet
April-November

SKYKOMISH RIVER —
UPSTREAM TO THE MORAINE

In 1977 the Legislature designated the Skykomish as first in a state system of Scenic Rivers, protecting (to a degree, and to only ¼ mile from the water) public lands along the stream and two of its chief tributaries, the Tye and Beckler, from headwaters down to Sultan. This action at once recognizes the popularity of a splendid waterway and promises a future of enhanced hiking, kayaking, and other quiet recreations. Or so one would like to hope, because the valley below the moraine of the Canadian glacier is a half-hour and less from northern neighborhoods of Puget Sound City and has the potential for a wealth of all-year, close-to-home, wilderness-edge hiking. However, in a dec-

Skykomish River and Gunn and Merchant Peaks

ade as "Scenic River," no new recreational opportunities have been provided and some have been lost.

With several notable exceptions, the main attractions for hikers are not on or near the Skykomish but the tributaries. The Sultan River presents a spectrum of walking experiences from the old-growth forest and wild waters of its canyon, to the broad-view, mountain-edge clearcuts of Blue and Stickney, to the subalpine meadows of the Greider and Boulder cirques where state Department of Natural Resource (DNR) recreational policy shines at its brightest.

The next tributary east, the Wallace River, was mainly known to railroad loggers of the 1920s, then a scattering of fishermen and assorted brush-busters drawn by the lakes and the falls—until the past decade, when Wallace Falls State Park was given a trail system and instantly became nearly as loud with thudding boots as with falling water. So overwhelming is the popularity that plans are being noodled around to fulfill an original proposal for a "super-park."

When this grand park comes to be created, the adjoining tributary, May Creek, must be included. Here, where DNR recreational policy flickers at its dimmest, State Parks recoiled from trying to bring order to the tolerated chaos of every sort of loud machine and adopted the Wallace River as a defense line. However, as a demonstration of how much good can be done by constructive destruction, Mother Nature sent a torrent down May Creek, blew out the bridge, and something resembling peace and quiet descended upon the splendid forests and streams and waterfalls and vistas formerly such a riot that sensitive hikers flinched at mention of "May Creek" and "Reiter Road" and "RV City."

This is not to say that "Reiter" has become a lullaby for little babies, yet we see here that there never is cause for final dispair, not until the last nuclear bomb has been dropped. The super-park extending from near the Sultan River through Wallace River to May Creek and beyond, adjoining the high wilderness that in the next Congressional go-round will become the Ragged Ridge Wilderness, is a piece of good news worth waiting—and working—for.

USGS maps: Snohomish, Maltby, Monroe, Index, Sultan

Cow Vista (Barr Hill) (map — page 162)

There's a lot more than cows to see from this perch an abrupt 1000 feet above the Skykomish River; the panorama stretches from saltwater bays to volcano glaciers. But though a viewer is far enough above the valley for a broad perspective, he is intimately close enough to hear the cows moo and watch the dogs chasing the paperboys.

From Highway 203 just south of the Skykomish River bridge, drive east 3.4 miles on Ben Howard Road. At .2 mile east of Widman Road spot the turnoff of the 1972 logging road that scalped the ridge. Park on a turnout before the road turns steeply up the hill. Elevation, 70 feet.

Skykomish River from Cow Vista

The old question arises — why walk? Motorcycles and jeeps and even the sturdier family sedans drive to the top, rough and steep and narrow and airy though the road is, and the hang-glider fraternity parades up and down, yipping and howling, elbows out, and at night the hills are alive with the sound of breaking beer bottles. The answer is, walk because the view is so exceptional it can properly be seen only afoot and as a succession of steadily widening panoramas. Yes, walk — but never on Sunday. Midweek is the time. Winter is the season.

The road ascends from one gasper view to another, switchbacking along the spine of the ridge above Barr Creek, in 1¾ miles topping out on the 1180-foot summit.

From any or all of a dozen sitting-down spots on rock knobs and cliff brinks, see the Olympics, Everett, the Skykomish valley from Monroe to Sultan, Pilchuck, Blue, Vesper, Stickney, Ragged Ridge, Mt. Sultan. And farmers in the dell, fishermen on the gravel bars, boats in the river, trains on the track.

Round trip 3½ miles, allow 3 hours
High point 1180 feet, elevation gain 1110 feet
All year

Watch Fontal Peak, 1580 feet, immediately to the south and half again higher. The rude road from Cow Vista proceeds down and up in that direction, at ¾ mile reaching the powerline at the foot of Fontal. The peak is sure to be barbered by the late 1980s and will then put Cow Vista to shame.

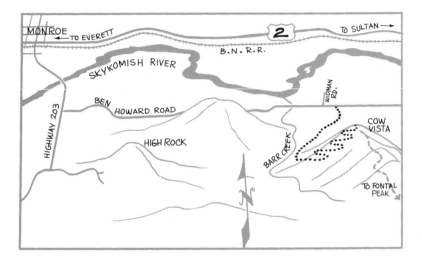

Buck Island Park (map — page 163)

Between the converging waters of the Skykomish River and Woods Creek lies a floodway tanglewood up to ⅓ mile wide and nearly 1 mile long. Though as a whole it's actually a peninsula, when the river is up and the sloughs are full, it becomes an archipelago — traversed on high by the abandoned grade of the Milwaukee Railroad, which proceeds across the river on the abandoned bridge. This Monroe city park offers two trips: high on the causeway; down low in the bushes and on the gravel bars.

For the high trip, park in the east end of the Monroe business district and walk Burlington-Northern tracks east ¼ mile to Monroe Junction. Here, where shiny rails proceed straight ahead to Stevens Pass and New York City, curve right on rusty rails. A bridge crosses the deep-shadow flow of Woods Creek. A fill runs through cottonwood forest and sloughs. See concrete footings and tottering trestles of ancient bridges of unknown purposes. A path drops off the fill right, a connector to the low trip (see below). The tracks go from fill to trestle to river bridge — safe now there are no trains to force pedestrians to take the high dive. Views are superb up and down the duck avenue.

For the low trip, drive Main Street east in downtown Monroe, turn right on Railroad Avenue, then right on Anne and left on Simons, passing through a log dump and down over Woods Creek to the center of Buck Island Park, .3 mile from the east end of the business district. Park here, elevation 50 feet, or drive muddy woods road onward to the river and turn left to the road-end at the railroad bridge, .4 mile from the park center. From any point along the road, explore forest paths where the wild things live. Walk upstream or down to gravel bars suitable for eating cucumber sandwiches and drinking iced tea. To connect to the high trip, walk inland along the railroad bridge to a path that scrambles up the bank to the rails.

Round trips 3 miles, allow 2 hours
High point 50 feet, minor elevation gain
All year

As of 1987 or so, there will be another entry to the park. Where Highway 203 enters Monroe from the south and becomes a boulevard, a park strip along the highway on the east overlooks Woods Creek and Buck Island. A trail is contemplated and presumably a bridge over the Creek. Access to gravel bars of the river may be excellent.

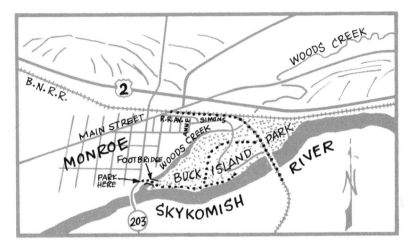

Echo Lake (map — page 164)

A tall showerbath of a waterfall, an entertaining zigzag of 50-odd switchbacks up an intriguing scarp, beaver ponds, miles of old logging grades linked by the work of Scouts into a cloistered trail through second-growth forest, the path defensively constructed to foil wheels, and at the end a lake that feels a million miles the other side of nowhere. The sort of walk on which a lone hiker may see, on a dark winter day, a bear or beaver, or a sasquatch.

From Highway 2 at Monroe turn north on Woods Creek Road (part of the way signed "Yeager Road") and follow the winding little valley 11 miles to a junction where the road goes straight ahead to Snohomish. Turn right, and in a couple of hundred feet right again, following signs for Lake Roesiger Snohomish County Park. In 2.3 miles, at a gas station-grocery, turn right on a gravel road signed "Camp Brinkley 1." In 1.3 mile, at a Y marked by a large signboard-map of the Cascade Reservation, go left. In 2.3 miles (17 miles from Monroe) see Explorer Falls close to the right. Just beyond, park in an old quarry, elevation 800 feet.

The trail crosses the South Fork of Woods Creek (in high water, cross it on the road bridge) and instantly starts up The Rim, a long scarp apparently

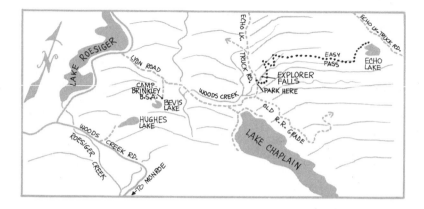

formed by a dike of resistant volcanics intruded in softer rocks. In seven switchbacks the trail attains the top of the falls. A perilous path to the brink offers a look down, and also a modest view (the best of the trip) to Lake Chaplain, Everett's water reservoir, and out to the Olympics.

Crossing the creek, the trail ascends to an old railroad grade with a trail running both ways. Turn right, leave the grade, and finish the switchbacking to Rim Camp Shelter, 1600 feet, 1 mile. (Since the camp is used on a reservation basis by Scout troops from Camp Brinkley, and since these Scouts have provided the trail, please leave the camping here to them.)

In a couple of final switchbacks the way tops The Rim and joins a railroad grade to proceed across a plateau with minor ups and downs through dense woods, by little creeks dammed by beavers. Despite some sharp turns the trail is obvious, most of the way on railroads cleared by Scouts, who also built the links between grades. (Ignore the many ribbons and notes; the area is heavily used for cross-country navigation and search-and-rescue exercises.) At 2¾ miles, on one of the trail links, is the highest elevation, 1800 feet, at Easy Pass. In 1¼ miles more spot Echo Lake down to the right. The trail continues but don't bother — it soon hits a road. Descend to the shore, 1675 feet, and go out on an old walkway of cedar logs for a look around the wooded shores, the forest of snags, and up to Blue and Bald Mountains.

Warning: Experienced hikers who stay alert find the trail "obvious." Some folks become totally disoriented; at least one became permanently lost.

Round trip 8 miles, allow 6 hours
High point 1800 feet, elevation gain 1100 feet
February-December

Mount Sultan (map — page 166)

Mt. Sultan rises as high above Sultan town as Mt. Si does above North Bend, and the panorama is equally grand — down to villages and pastures in the Skykomish valley, out over lowlands to saltwaterways and the Olympics,

Explorer Falls

south to Si, the Issaquah Alps, and Rainier, and north to Pilchuck and Three Fingers and Big Four and Glacier Peak.

The big "however": For many years a popular day hike, as of 1985 it's strictly for marathoners and backpackers. For whatever reasons (too many motorcycles? too many complaints from residents of the Tomtit Alps?) Weyerhaeuser has installed a gate exactly by the Ben Howard (county) Road, and this gate is never ever open to public vehicles, to wit — "Unauthorized Motorized Use Not Permitted . . . Non-Motorized Use Permitted." So here's the howdeedo — all the miles that used to be driven before donning boots now must be walked.

Why, then, does the surveyor retain the trip in this book? Because Mt. Sultan is too enormous a piece of real estate to be ignored. And because he feels sure Weyco ultimately will come to terms about this gate. For now . . .

At Sultan, turn south from Highway 2 across the Skykomish River, turn west on Ben Howard Road, and in 1.7 miles from Highway 2 (.4 mile after crossing McCoy Creek, unsigned) spot a gravel road making a reverse turn left — to the gate. Park here, elevation 175 feet.

The road climbs eastward onto a bench where Second Wave clearcuts have been in progress since the late 1960s, and continue, proliferating new roads that confuse the issue and defy useful description. The rule is, pick the one that seems "main," even though a haul road in use shows more signs of traffic. Play your cards right and in 3 miles from Ben Howard you'll come to marshy Mud (Lost) Lake, 617 feet.

Continue onward, passing new logging roads and old woods roads, 2½ more miles to the foot of the mountain at 900 feet. The road ascends eastward up a cliff to views of the Skykomish valley, switchbacks, and enters a narrow

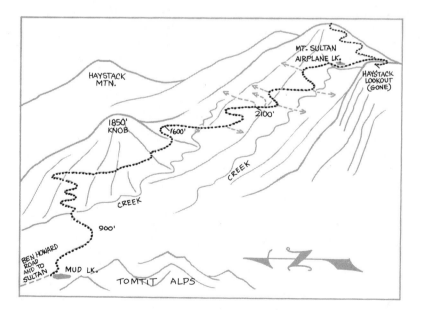

defile, a weird little canyon between an 1850-foot knob and the main mass of the mountain. After a short flat the climb resumes to a 1600-foot pass. A bit above here, where a waterfall-creek goes under the road in a culvert, about 1¼ miles from the 900-foot elevation, used to be recommended as the best place to begin the summit hike (though sports usually drove ¾ mile more), climbing east, switchbacking west, and at the top of a steep and rough stretch coming to a Y some 4 miles from Mud Lake, the roads beyond impassable to any sort of wheels. Elevation here is 2100 feet, and the distance from Ben Howard Road, 7 miles, with an elevation gain of 2000 feet—in a word, a pretty good round trip in itself.

Round trip from Ben Howard Road to Y "parking place" 14 miles, allow 9 hours
High point 2100 feet, elevation gain 2000 feet
February-December

But the heights call — and until well into summer the creeklets are plentiful for camping purposes, and the lowland lights at night are big and bright.

From the Y take the road heading straight ahead to the west, already in terrific views, with more of the same all the way in young forest dating from clearcuts of the 1960s and later. The many forks in the road are very confusing and it's easy to go astray. At the first fork, go right. At the second, where a grownover old road goes right, go left. At the third, just above a promontory, go right. At the fourth, just before a creek, go left. If all goes well, the curious little pothole of Airplane Lake is attained at 3040 feet. Here go right, sidehilling the naked ridge west 1 mile to the 3590-foot site of long-gone Haystack Lookout, out on the point of a ridge commanding views down south to the 1970s-skinned valley of Youngs Creek and down north to Skykomish farms and towns, and this way and that all around the countryside.

On logging roads, then in a last scrap of virgin forest (in the Mt. Baker-Snoqualmie National Forest), hikers can continue 2 miles east from the lookout to the 4400-foot summit of Sultan. After a long tramp in sun-blasted clearcuts the shadows of the old trees are delicious.

Round trip from Y "parking place" to lookout 5 miles, allow 4 hours
High point 3590 feet, elevation gain 1490 feet
May-November

Having said all *that,* it must be noted there's another way. The existence of the above "traditional" route has kept the surveyor from checking it out. However, if Weyco holds firm on the gate, next time around he'll hook up logging roads from High Tomtit Vista (which see) to the long-gone site of the Haystack Lookout. There's less than a mile to puzzle out, all on logging roads.

Sultan Canyon (map — page 169)

When a large tract of old-growth forest survived through the steaming and whistling of railroad loggers and the tooting and snorting of truck loggers, the assumption grew that the U.S. Forest Service had somehow missed it in the inventory. When Mt. Baker-Snoqualmie National Forest proved to know perfectly well the gorgeous trees were there, a petition was made to preserve them as the area's last sample of old-growth Douglas fir at so low an elevation. Petition was denied. In 1986 the road will be built and soon thereafter the trees will be on a ship bound overseas. *Most* of them, *not all.* As can be viewed from the summit of Blue Mountain (which see), partly for legal considerations and partly for practical, a miles-long strip of old-growth has been left along the Sultan River canyon. The new clearcut will be similarly minimally merciful. So, by all means take the walk — whatever remains of it when you arrive. At present the path to an abandoned stream-gaging station is the only moderately reasonable access to the canyon. Conceivably a trail — a very expensive one — could be built through the canyon. On the other hand, very possibly it ought to be left a Truly Wild Place for the noble survivors and the animals and the more rugged botanists.

On the east outskirts of Sultan turn north on the Sultan Basin Road and drive 5.2 miles to the City of Everett's pipeline swath. Just beyond a fence turn left on a gravel road along the swath and stay on it (with a jog left from one side of the swath to the other) .6 mile. Diverge left on a woods road, into a clearcut; at a Y .5 mile from the pipeline go left, into woods (and more clearcuts as time passes), and start climbing. Dodge harvesting roads, sticking to the "main way" (maintained as a watershed patrol road by Snohomish County PUD), and in 2 more miles (a total of 3.1 miles from Sultan Basin Road), just past a wooden bridge over a small waterfall-creek, come to a major switchback, elevation 1300 feet. Park here, probably.

The "main way" switchbacks 2.8 miles to the site of Blue Mountain Lookout, 2820 feet, and continues up and down the ridge crest 3 miles to "the place" of Blue Mountain (which see), most of the way in green tunnel, and much of the way uncomfortably rough for passenger vehicles, but a favored scenic drive for the 4x4s.

As of 1985, the way to the wild river begins at this first switchback on an ancient grade that soon deteriorates to bad old trail through magnificent old-growth forest, mainly big hemlocks but including some spruce and Douglas fir up to 6 feet in diameter. The new logging roads will diverge from "main way" somewhat higher on Blue, but cat roads, skidways and blowdowns can be expected to raise havoc with the present route.

The ancient grade crosses Big Four Creek in about ⅓ mile from the switchback and yields to trail, all of which presumably will be in the "protected" zone. If so, and if loggers' debris doesn't block the path altogether, follow the steep, poor trail to a fork.

The left descends ¼ mile to the abandoned gaging station, on the river at 780 feet. The right descends treacherously to the cable of the onetime gaging trolley. Either spot is wildness incarnate. Beyond the river the scarp of the Echo Lake plateau leaps 700 rough feet. On the near side the canyon walls are even higher. The trail (if it survives) permits relatively easy entry to the canyon; the cliffs and the turmoil of river forbid much in the way of exploration, upstream or down. No matter. Sit and watch the ducks and dippers fly by.

Round trip from switchback to wild Sultan 2½ miles, allow 3 hours
High point 1300 feet, elevation loss 500 feet
All year

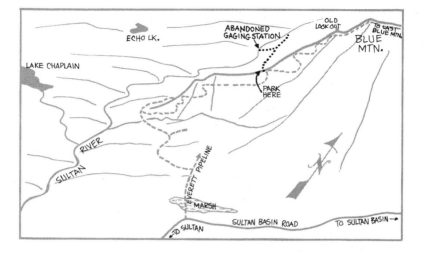

Stickney Vista (map — page 171)

Though not particularly high (only 5367 feet) and not at all famous, Stickney is among the most prominent peaks on the Cascade front as viewed from the Everett-Seattle area. (In winter it is the sharp peak rising from a huge apron of snow — the clearcut ridge.) Therefore the views from Stickney are broad — from pulpmill plumes of Everett and Port Townsend to towers of downtown Seattle, from the Olympics that way to Persis and Index the other, plus Sultan and Pilchuck and Rainier and a lot more. But what mainly captures the eye is the Skykomish valley — the meandering silver ribbon of the shining river, the bug-infested concrete ribbon of the highway, the railway, the farms and houses from Monroe to Sultan to Startup to Gold Bar.

On the east outskirts of Sultan turn north on Sultan Basin Road and drive 8.4 miles (1.3 miles past Olney Park) to an unsigned woods road taking off right, elevation 866 feet. In .2 mile is a gravel pit and motorcycle romper room. Park here, elevation 900 feet.

From the left edge of the playground a woods road goes ¼ mile to a creek, and from there, if not before, becomes too mean for family sedans or even Volkswagen beetles but a heady challenge to jeepers, though not in such numbers as to rule out the trip on a Sunday. Ascending steadily in second-growth dating from logging of the 1930s, in ½ mile the road switchbacks right, in ½ mile more coming to a Y. The straight-ahead fork leads to Wallace Lake. (Public vehicle access to the lake is *not* permitted, even when practically possible.) Go left on the switchback north. In another scant ½ mile, at a switchback right, is the first of the views, through a wide window out west to lowlands. After the next switchback the road levels at 2100 feet to round a marshy pond, passing another window west, and goes up and down across a little valley that contains, farther down, Jay and Wallace Lakes. At 2070 feet, 2½ miles from the start, a sideroad leads left in a few minutes to Shaw Lake, a

Mount Stickney from Stickney Ridge

minor thrill. The main road now quits messing around and starts up and up the steep cliffy slopes of Stickney Ridge, views becoming virtually continuous. Crossing a superb splashing creek, the road switchbacks repeatedly, becoming so rough that only the rare four-wheel sport continues, and not many two-wheelers either. At a promontory where is located a donkey skid of the 1940s the road turns into the valley of the creek previously crossed lower down and comes to a Y, 3150 feet, about 4 miles from the car; the left fork goes to the stream, a nice spot to have lunch before starting down on a second binge of gasping at views.

Round trip 8 miles, allow 6 hours
High point 3150 feet, elevation gain 2200 feet
April-November

The energetic and view-greedy can profitably extend the trip. At the creek Y take the right fork and climb moderately in young forest (from logging of the 1950s) screening views, then contour, views resuming, to a 3700-foot saddle in Stickney Ridge, some 1¾ miles from the creek Y. Added now to views south over the Skykomish are those north over recently logged Olney Creek headwaters to the summit of Stickney, to Three Fingers, Bald, Big Four, Vesper, and Greider.

But it's hard to stop at the saddle. One has a light-headed top-of-the-world feeling, and the road goes on, descending slightly. In 1 more mile, at 3600 feet, is the champion view of all, featuring a straight-down look at Gold Bar. Come this far and the round-trip distance is 14 miles. And worth it. From here the road

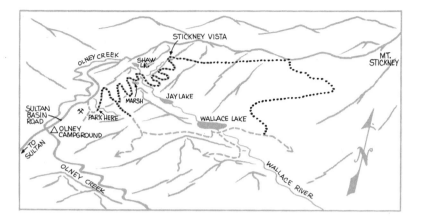

drops steeply to Wallace Lake, a fact that could give some hikers notions of a one-way trip, exiting via Wallace Falls State Park (which see).

Blue Mountain (map — page 173)

Teeter giddily along a tightropelike clearcut ridge, looking dizzily straight down to valleys on either side and across to peaks from Pilchuck to Bald to sharp summits of the Monte Cristo area and out over green lowland plains to saltwater shining in the sun. What's that — "teeter"? On a logging road? Well, so narrow is the crest one feels the log-truck drivers must have got the vertigo from it. But why walk the road, which though exceedingly steep and rough can be driven even by the smaller and tougher family sedans? Because once the views begin you've no spare time to wrestle a machine, you've got to concentrate on gawking.

On the east outskirts of Sultan turn north on Sultan Basin Road and drive 12.5 miles, .4 mile short of Olney Pass, 2050 feet. (If you reach the sign announcing the Sultan Watershed you've gone too far.) The obvious gravel road turns uphill left. Park on a handy shoulder.

The supersteep road shoots up the slope in tall second-growth. Windows open on the view south, stirring boots to speed. At 2650 feet the way tops the Blue Mountain ridge, adding views north. Now the road proceeds upward on the very crest, through clearcuts increasingly recent, the last completed in the mid-1970s, removing every green obstacle to 360-degree panoramas. At 2 miles is a 3050-foot summit of Blue. Beyond here the crest dips a bit and rises, dips and rises again to the highest summit of Blue, 3080 feet, at 2½ miles.

Now, what's all the fuss about the view? Well, it includes but is not restricted to: down to Olney Creek and Pass and across to Stickney and the basin of Wallace Lake; south to the Skykomish valley and the towns of Gold Bar and Sultan and the peaks of Index and Persis and Sultan and High Rock Hills and Rainier; out to Everett smokestacks and Seattle towers and Puget Sound and Olympics; down to the Sultan River and its strip of preserved old-growth forest along the canyon, the long wide reservoir of Spada Lake that drowns Sultan Basin, over to headwaters of the Pilchuck River and the line of peaks from Pilchuck to Bald to Big Four to Vesper to Del Campo and on.

Because most of this vista is first attained at not much more than 1 mile from the Olney Pass road, the trip is a fine snowline-prober. In fact, when a few snowbanks block wheels the walk has the added reward of peace, which can't be guaranteed on a summer Sunday.

Some weekday, walk up for the sunset. Serene quiet is probable. And you'll certainly be struck dumb. Bring a picnic supper and stay for the city lights and farm lights and sky lights.

Round trip 5 miles, allow 3 hours
High point 3080 feet, elevation gain 1200 feet
April-November

Bald Mountain from Blue Mountain

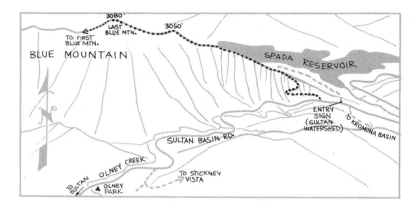

Kromona Basin (map — page 176)

Lacking valuable forests and minerals, abundant lakes, and faddish peaks to attract loggers, miners, fishermen, and climbers, the Ragged Ridge country, though at the Cascades edge, remains one of the purest trail-free wildernesses in the range. This hike leads to close looks at the heart of the wildland from the vicinity of the Kromona Mine, active until 1975.

From the east outskirts of Sultan drive the Sultan Basin Road 13 miles to Olney Pass, 2050 feet, and a sign announcing entry into the City of Everett's Sultan Basin Watershed. Take the righthand of the three roads departing from Olney Pass, signed "primitive road." At a Y in .3 mile keep left, contouring in young second-growth with many big windows out to Spada Reservoir in Sultan Basin and across to Del Campo, Vesper, Big Four, Bald, and Pilchuck. Given a vehicle-barring gate, this would be a superb trail — and the thought occurs that a person coming in early spring would find snowpatches doing the job of a gate, permitting peace to exclaim at the scenery.

At 3.1 miles from the pass the road goes from second-growth of the 1960s to a scalping of 1980, and slices across a slope so steep that to a person in a car it has the feel of a cliff. Because of the airiness — and the chance of a washout or rockfall at a spot where backing-up would be hysterical — and the eye-opening, jaw-dropping views, it is a very good idea to park here, elevation 2225 feet, in a commodious quarry-landing — the last place for .5 mile to turn around without the pulse rate going very high.

So, walk, looking across the valley to granite domes and slabs of Greider and up the North Fork of the South Fork to untrailed headwaters and to the granite splinters of Ragged Ridge. Proceeding beyond the 1980 barbering into virgin forest, then into open avalanche slopes, at 1½ miles from the quarry-landing the road crosses the Middle Fork of the South Fork Sultan River, 2480 feet, a long 4½ miles from Olney Pass. Should you choose to drive to this point, park before the bridge; on the other side there is no road worth the name.

Across the bridge the road splits, the left going downvalley a bit to the

173

Kromona Basin

dismantled mill of the Kromona Mine, the right upvalley a bit to the bottom
terminal of the tramway that led to the mine.

Look up the tramway swath to the mine buildings. The rough, steep,
wheelfree path climbs there in ½ mile — straight up to 3350 feet on the side of
Prospect Peak. Marvel at the preposterous energy required to haul artifacts up
here. Admire the backside of Stickney, then again enjoy, on the descent, the
forest of silver fir, cedar (both red and yellow), and hemlock (both western and
mountain). This country was proposed for inclusion in the Washington Wilderness Act of 1984 but didn't make the cut. Nevertheless, there someday will be
a Ragged Ridge Wilderness because there must be, and the boundary will be
right here, if not a couple of miles back along the road from Olney Pass.

Round trip from quarry-landing 4 miles, allow 3 hours
High point 3350 feet, elevation gain 1200 feet
May-November

Greider Lakes (map — page 176)

Genuine mountain lakes in the long-winter country, the Greiders perhaps
don't really belong in this book. But heck, after all the road-walking in clearcuts, one hankers for a genuine trail in a genuine virgin forest. Especially when

thoughtful defensive construction has made impossible any intrusion by wheels.

From Olney Pass (see Kromona Basin) take the middle of the three roads and drive down into Sultan Basin, by Spada Lake, passing logging spurs and the Williamson Creek road, 7 miles (20 miles from Sultan) to the Greider Lakes trailhead, 1500 feet. The picnic ground and trail are the work of the state Department of Natural Resources, bless its often maligned heart.

Signed "foot trail only," the path passes a beautiful little loop around a pair of marsh ponds and starts up a forested precipice, a magnificent hemlock-cedar forest well worth a walk even if too much snow or not enough energy rule out a climb to the lakes. Higher, still in superb trees, the trail dodges under cliffs — then over cliffs. Walk, don't run. The way flattens into the hanging valley and at 2 miles reaches the outlet of Little Greider Lake, 2900 feet. Pleasant. Not spectacular in the high alpine way, but nice, ringed partly by big-tree forest and

Deer in velvet

partly by subalpine meadow and rockslide, and with a look up to the rock horn of Greider, 4897 feet. (The DNR altitudes disagree with the USGS figures used here.)

The trail rounds the basin to a Y. The left drops a bit to the outlet of Big Greider Lake, 3000 feet. The right climbs meadow-brush slopes and heathery rockslides to a vista point 1 mile from Little Greider at 3600 feet. Slow down. From the vista knoll a cliff drops dizzily to the cirque of Big Greider, with slabby rock walls, meadow shores, and the dominating horn peak.

Round trip to vista point 6 miles, allow 6 hours
High point 3600 feet, elevation gain 2100 feet
July-October (for the great forest, May-November)

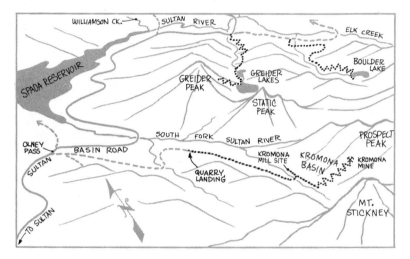

Boulder Lake (map — page 176)

In 1977 the state Department of Natural Resources completed a trail to Boulder Lake, previously virtually unvisited, lacking fish as it does. But there are heather meadows.

Drive past the Greider Lakes (which see) trailhead a short bit to a Y; take the right, road SL-S-7000. At 1.2 miles past the Greider trail is the Boulder Lake parking area, elevation 1650 feet.

The walking starts on a closed-to-wheels logging road in a clearcut of the 1960s, replanted in 1970. A short bit uphill is a Y; go left, crossing Boulder Creek (worth a pause on the descent to admire torrents gushing over rock slabs into cool pools). The road makes a long switchback up the clearcut, with views across the valley of Elk Creek to monster clearcuts. In 1 scant mile, at 2400 feet, on the brink high above Boulder Creek, road ends and trail begins.

Clearcut brush merges into avalanche-slope brush, both gaily decorated (in season) with flowers or a variety of berries. Switchbacks commence, then

Boulder Lake

deep forest of big hemlocks and firs. At about 1 mile from the old road-new trail transition, valley and trail bend 90 degrees eastward; the opposite valley wall features Sierra-like exfoliating granite slabs. Now switchbacking doggedly, in forest except for one small subalpine meadow (butterwort, marsh marigold, elephanthead, shooting star, bog orchid, tofieldia), the way climbs steeply, then levels into a hanging cirque and proceeds over the flat to the outlet of Boulder Lake at 3 miles, 3750 feet.

The outlet is a garden of red and white heather, partridgefoot, lovage, and the like, ringed by subalpine forest of lichen-draped hemlocks, amid which are the new-built campsites. Boots may be expected to eventually beat a path around the shore to the rockslide on the far shore and perhaps to viewpoints on the 5000-foot ridge above.

Round trip 6 miles, allow 5 hours
High point 3750 feet, elevation gain 2100 feet
July-November

Wallace Falls

Wallace Falls State Park (map — page 180)

Spotted from the Skykomish valley below, the white line high on the green slopes long has drawn explorers. Since the trail improvements that came with the 1977 dedication of the state park a hiker needn't be an adventurer to experience the spray-billowing gorge and earth-shaking thunder of Wallace Falls. Moreover, though the 11 separate plunges in a single awesome white-water canyon are drama sufficient for an exciting day, there are quieter beauties as well in the park forests, grown up since railroad logging in the World War I era and now well advanced into the stage of deep shadows, green moss and ferns, and woodland flowers.

Drive Highway 2 to Gold Bar and turn north, following state park signs a long 1 mile to park headquarters, picnic ground, and trailhead, elevation 300 feet. Also here are six walk-in tent-camping sites.

The trail (barred to any sort of wheels — such motorcycles as sneak in are relentlessly hunted down and ticketed) follows a powerline swath ¼ mile to the edge of a bluff down to the Wallace River, with broad views to Baring, Index, and Persis, and then turns into the woods to a split. From here it is 2¼ miles to the falls via the Woody Trail, 3¼ via the Old Railroad Grade Trail. Each has its beauties; the neat plan is a loop.

Woody Trail

The path begins close by the river, with boulder bars for picnicking, pools for chilling hot feet. The valley narrows and steepens to a gorge and the trail switchbacks high above the stream, then returns to it in 1 long mile, joining the Old Railroad Grade Trail; the two, united, drop to the rustic bridge over the North Fork Wallace River, 650 feet.

Old Railroad Grade Trail

The trail — an old logging railroad grade — ascends steadily and moderately, switchbacking twice. It enters a valley and at 1 mile from the split crosses a creek. Note remnants of an old trestle. Just beyond is a Y. The left goes to Wallace Lake (which see); go right. Nearly flat and straight, the old grade swings out on a steep sidehill above the Wallace River. As it nears the gorge the trail leaves it, descending steeply right to rejoin the Woody Trail at 2 miles from the split.

Onward Together

The North Fork bridge is so pleasant a spot that many hikers, especially those with toddlers in the party, are content to picnic here by the tumbling river and return. However, the falls call.

The wide, safe trail climbs steeply in handsome forest of mixed conifers, not as big as the stumps left by the 1920s logging, but getting there. The happy thought is that this forest will not again be logged, but decade by decade will move toward cathedral quality. Moreover, being in a park rather than a tree farm, it will exemplify Nature's Forests — fir, hemlock, cedar, and other conifers and a variety of hardwoods mingling, in contrast to the monotonous single-species monoculture of Man's Forests.

Crossing a ridge to the gorge of the South Fork Wallace River, the one with the falls, the trail ascends to a picnic shelter, 1200 feet, and railing-guarded overlooks of falls directly below and a vista of the main 250-foot falls farther up the gorge. Continuing on, mostly up, the way passes Middle Viewpoint, with an impressive close view of the main falls. Finally, at 1500 feet, 1 mile from North

Fork bridge, the trail ends at Valley Overlook. The brink of the main falls is below, a giddy sight to see. Out the slot of the gorge is a broad view of the Skykomish River, the villages of Gold Bar and Startup, Mt. Sultan and the High Rock Hills, the Olympics.

Round trip 5 miles (Woody Trail), 7 miles (Old Railroad Grade), allow 3-4 hours
High point 1500 feet, elevation gain 1200-1500 feet
All year

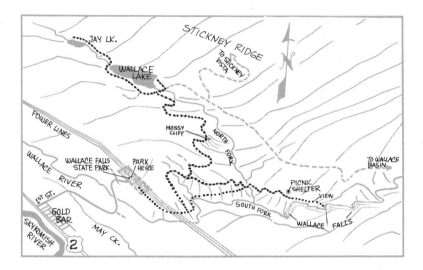

Wallace Lake (map — page 180)

Neither a lowland nor truly a mountain lake, yet indubitably a lake and a big one, Wallace Lake has much good lake-type stuff, such as reflections of Stickney Ridge, sun-sparkles, ducks a-swimming. Actually, though, the walk's the thing, not the endpoint — the pleasure is everywhere along the way in the gradual ascent through handsome second-growth forest.

At 1¼ miles on the trail to Wallace Falls (which see) turn left on a thoroughly blockaded woods road (to keep motorcycles away from the Wallace Falls trail system; they are equally illegal at Wallace Lake and are ticketed when caught). In ¼ mile is a T with the old road to Wallace Lake, now closed to the public by private property owners. Turn right. Not much happens — just a succession of old stumps and continuous dense second-growth, and ferns and shrubs and herbs and creeks, the road gently climbing, several times switchbacking.

If a short walk is wanted, at about 3 miles, 1300 feet, a mossy cliff rises 100 feet above the road. Beat through the trees on the backside for a view over screening trees to Mt. Sultan. Picnic and turn around.

Wallace Lake

In the next 2½ miles the road twice comes alongside the white-water North Fork, the second time while nearing Wallace Lake.

Here is a T with a private, gated road maintained by a timber company, used by park staff for maintenance, but closed to the general public. Two directions present themselves, right and left.

Turn right on the lakeshore road, cross the outlet (1844 feet), and in a short bit reach a Y. The right goes ¼ mile to a second Y, the right here going to Wallace Basin, the left climbing the side of Stickney Ridge to views of Sultan, Persis, and Index, and connecting to the Stickney Vista (which see) road. Back at first Y, turn left into a large campground beside a creek entering the lake. A nice spot for lunch. (As a legal requirement to supply substitute recreation resources for public lands flooded by Spada Reservoir, Snohomish County PUD may build backpacker campsites here in the late 1980s.)

Meanwhile, back at the T, turn left on the lakeshore road ⅓ mile to a Y. The left is the private (gated) road up from the Sultan River; go right on a narrow lane leading in ¼ mile to an inlet creek at the north end of the lake and the best picnicking of all, on a gravelly shore with fine views of the lake, Stickney Ridge, and Ragged Ridge.

Across the inlet stream a grownover green tunnel of a road leads in 1 mile to Jay Lake, 1900 feet, which only fishermen and birdwatchers could get really excited about. However, this is the only place in Wallace Falls State Park where trail camping presently is allowed.

Round trip to Wallace Lake outlet 14 miles, allow 7 hours
High point 1844 feet, elevation gain 1544 feet
March-December

Wallace Basin (map — page 184)

Wallace Lake ought to be in Wallace Basin, but isn't. Wallace Basin just has the Wallace River (and at that, only the South Fork), second-growth dating from logging of the 1930s, and, in a hanging valley guarded by a moraine of the Puget Glacier, a fine feeling of isolation.

In fact, the question may arise, why bother with the basin at all? It's a very long walk for very little excitement. True, but in future there could be a trail system from here to heights of Stickney and Ragged Ridge and into the proposed Ragged Ridge Wilderness. Presently there is solitude, never more complete than, say, in a quiet winter snowfall, the white blanket freshly tracked by animals of the feline, canine, and rodent styles.

From Wallace Lake (which see) outlet, 1844 feet, 7 miles from the Wallace Falls State Park trailhead, follow the ancient logging railroad-become-trail ¼ mile to a Y. Take the right, which contours the valley wall of the North Fork Wallace River some 2 miles to a junction at 1746 feet. The straight ahead leads in ½ mile to the South Fork and the site of a bridge, long gone, at the top of the gorge of Wallace Falls. Take the left and ascend into Wallace Basin, rounding gravels of the Puget Moraine, then flattening into the wide valley, passing lovely pools in the river, views up to cliffs and crags. At 3 miles from the 1746-foot junction the trail comes to virgin forest and ends.

Round trip 24 miles, allow 12 hours
High point 3150 feet, elevation gain 3000 feet
April-November

Wallace Vista (map — page 184)

A person of the pedestrian persuasion cannot look up from the Skykomish valley to the shaggy mountainside above Wallace Falls without wondering how it would be to look down from there. The answer is: terrific.

At "Isabel Junction" on the route from May Creek Campground to Lake Isabel (which see), elevation 1050 feet, 1¾ miles from the campground, proceed straight ahead west on the old logging railroad grade. Creeks splash, windows open in the forest down to the Skykomish and to RV City and out to Sultan and Persis. In ¾ mile is The Washout, where a trestle across the base of a 250-foot cliff has rotted away. Great views from here out to Monroe.

In another ¾ mile, at 1500 feet, is a creek distinguished by an old trestle below in the woods. Just before the creek, a road-trail switchbacks right, providing a pleasant woods-and-marsh variant route that leads in 1½ miles to a four-way junction, discussed below. Just after the creek, a trail goes left, first on an old railroad grade, then plunging straight down the hill past Wallace Falls, giving perspectives unfamiliar to walkers across the gorge on park paths.

The main road-trail now begins to climb, passes a look down to Wallace Falls, ascends a promontory ridge with clear views east to Index and west to Monroe, and in a scant ½ mile from the Trestle Creek reaches Four-Way Junction, 1700 feet. To the left is a stub grade to the site of a bridge over the

Canadian dogwood or bunchberry

uppermost brink of the falls; the river cannot be crossed here. To the right is the longer variant trail from Trestle Creek. Go straight ahead ⅛ mile to Switchback Junction, 1750 feet. An old railroad grade goes a scant ¼ mile to the Wallace River, 1750 feet.

Turn right on the switchback and climb-climb-climb the steep and narrow remnant of a road dating from some halfwit logging operation of the 1950s. The way switchbacks onto slopes high above Wallace Basin, to views out windows provided by avalanches and rockslides to Stickney — and more. Switchbacking out of the valley, at about 2950 feet the road comes to a ridgecrest promontory and — zounds — more of the more. But merely pause, don't stop. Continue up a couple of zigzags to 3150 feet and — pow — Wallace Vista at its best, 2 miles from Switchback Junction. The cat road goes up ½ mile to 3450 feet but does not surpass the pow view.

Look precipitously down the stumps of logging and snags of burning to Wallace Falls canyon, the thunder rolling this high. Look from the mile-high

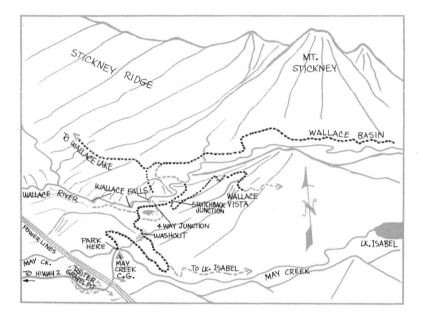

wall of Index to Persis, Sultan, Tomtit Alps, High Rock Hills, and the Olympics. Look along the valley from Monroe to Sultan to Startup to Gold Bar — and straight down to RV City. And the Skykomish River winding out of its canyon sliced in the Puget Moraine.

Round trip 11¾ miles, allow 9 hours
High point 3150 feet, elevation gain 2700 feet
April-November

Lake Isabel via May Creek Camp (map — page 186)

The lake, yes, it is big and wild, a blue gem beneath Ragged Ridge, and well worth a walk. However, the magnificent waterfall the trail closely parallels, the one climbing as steeply as the other is falling, is even more exciting. And lakes are plentiful, but such giant cedars as are featured here in the virgin forest are rarities nowadays.

Drive Highway 2 east from Gold Bar to .3 mile past the fire station and turn north on Reiter Road. In .7 mile the blacktop bends left; go straight on Reiter 1 mile, past RV City, to the far edge of the infamous Reiter Gravel Pit. Here the Trout Hatchery road goes straight ahead downhill; turn left on a chuckhole-and-mud lane along the flat. In .2 mile pass a powerline service road and in .1 mile more the sideroad right to Copperbell Mine. In .7 mile more, 1 mile total from the gravel pit, is large, undeveloped May Creek Campground, elevation 475 feet. Park here.

The big old bridge over May Creek blew away late in 1977. Getting across now can be simple when the water is low or somebody has rigged a footlog, or impossible when floods are roaring. But do not complain. Until the blowaway the four-wheelers and two-wheelers racketed in regimental strength every fair Sunday and hikers shuddered to hear the name, "Reiter." As of 1985 virtually the only wheels on the far side of May Creek are those from RV City, which has installed a private bridge, closed to the public. Four-wheeling is rare, two-wheeling mainly confined to the idiotland low down, close to the valley, and on high trails ordinarily doesn't endanger reason.

Once across the creek a hiker has two choices. The first, on old logging road, is pleasant walking and the route is surefire. The second is pure trail, much shorter, but routefinding may confuse the inexperienced or unwary.

Road-Trail

Walk the footroad westerly from the campground ½ mile and switchback easterly. Cross pretty little creeks and at about 1¾ miles switchback west. (Note: Throughout this area the hiker will spot sidetrails going off in every direction. Few go anywhere significant, most simply loop around, providing terrain to rupture blood vessels in the brain, developing that vacant look medically known as "Biker's Stupor.") In a few yards from the switchback, at 1050 feet, is "Isabel Junction." The road straight ahead goes to Wallace Vista.

Take the sideroad switchbacking east, an abruptly and distinctly steeper track. In about 1¼ miles the way flattens out in the hanging valley of May Creek and comes to the junction with the alternate route at 1700 feet, 3 miles from the campground.

Lake Isabel

Trail-Trail

Immediately after crossing May Creek at the campground find a good trail upstream, at the start well-used by boots, rarely by wheels. The route is a bit confusing in the upper portions because motorcyclists there have created loops within loops. However, the hiker who keeps his destination in mind will have no trouble making the right choices — which usually are the right forks.

The way switchbacks through huge old stumps and pleasant second-growth. At 1000 feet the trail T's with an old logging grade; turn right the short way to the end at a splendid series of falls, a lovely deep-woods campsite. Wreckage of a bridge calls attention to a motorcycle trail on the far side, leading to Copperbell Mine (which see). Steep trail resumes, switchbacking to hit an old cat road-become-gully. At 1700 feet the way flattens out and joins the road-trail at about 1½ miles from the campground.

Onward Together

The old road, made a boulder-bed by a blowout flood in 1976, nears the stream and passes from second-growth into creekside virgin forest, including snagtop Douglas firs 6 feet in diameter. At 1950 feet, ½ mile from the reunion, is the remains of a log bridge over the creek — a glorious cool spot on a hot summer day. On the far side the trail from Copperbell Mine comes in. The road switchbacks right, then left, and right again.

A few steps beyond this final switchback is Crucial Junction, 2250 feet, a scant ½ mile from the bridge. The road continues straight ahead to a sporadically active mining claim; a blowout gully near the "mine" provides a window out on the Skykomish valley, lowlands, saltwaterways, and the Olympics. The trail to Lake Isabel turns left up what appears to be a creekbed, then in a few steps left up a granite staircase onto tread. An alert person isn't going to miss the junction, which has a fire ring, cut trees, garbage, and usually a mess of ribbons.

Once an elaborate miner's trail but for decades maintained solely by boots of doughty fishermen, the way is now much-used and even maintained a little, but is totally wheelfree. It begins as a green tunnel in young trees but soon enters splendid virgin forest of Mt. Baker-Snoqualmie National Forest, which

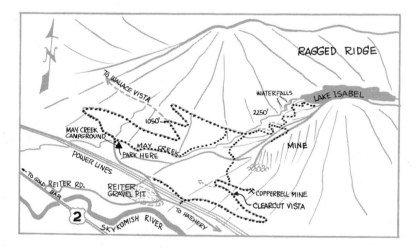

has been urged to place the boundary line of a Ragged Ridge Wilderness precisely here. Several times the tread peters out or splits; the novice is liable to get lost but the wily traveler will back off, cast about, and easily find the route. At ½ mile from Crucial Junction is a delightful camp in big trees at the base of the falls. The trail distance from here to the lake is just about identical to the waterfall distance. And the walker's route is just about as steep as the water's. The ladderway of roots, passing within inches of the falls at several points, is no place for little kids to be running around loose. Or for big folks to try to make speed. None too soon the ladderway ends at the very outlet of the lake, elevation 2842 feet, ¾ mile from Crucial Junction. In virgin forest beneath rock knobs of Ragged Ridge, if the lake is not put in a Wilderness there's no justice.

Round trip from May Creek campground 6 miles (trail-trail) or 9 miles (road-trail), allow 5-6 hours
High point 2842 feet, elevation gain 2400 feet
May-November

Lake Isabel via Copperbell Mine Vista (map — page 186)

The shortest and most popular way to Lake Isabel is via the Copperbell Mine, from which a trail little more than 1 mile long leads steeply up to the hanging valley of May Creek, the whole distance in deep forest, including some magnificent old-growth, and passing interesting logging artifacts. — But this is two trips in one, because views on the road to Copperbell Mine are worth the price of admission by themselves.

Copperbell Mine Vista

Drive from the edge of the Reiter Gravel Pit toward May Creek Camp .3 mile, .1 mile past the powerline service road, to a sideroad making a reverse turn right at an elevation of 450 feet. Park here. (Alternatively, at the powerline swath turn right on the service road and drive it .4 mile to where the powerline passes a belt of rock slabs and walls. Park here and follow a motorcycle path the few yards up the rocks to the Copperbell road.)

Walk the sideroad east, first on the flat, then climbing, paralleling the powerline. The road is solid-bottomed but very narrow, prone to washouts, and with few turnouts — a dandy footroad. But also beloved of the sports, so walk here on Sunday at the risk of your sanity.

In less than ½ mile is the first vista, beside the powerline, where the road is blasted from the side of granite buttresses. The alternative parking spot is just below. See Index, Persis, Haystack, and Sultan. Open all year.

The road now leaves the powerline and the view, ascending into second-growth, crossing tasty little creeks, passing myriad motorcycle courses. At a long mile is a switchback west, and in ½ mile more the big window provided by a 1980s clearcut, 1000 feet. (The road continues, in ¼ mile more switchbacking right shortly reaching the road-end at Copperbell Mine, 1100 feet.)

The views are over the moraines of Deer Creek Flat, over others to Index, Persis, Anderson Cirque and Proctor Trough, and Sultan, and down to the river

Copperbell Mine

and highway and out to the lowlands. The mine has a couple of minor holes in the ground and some rusty junk but hardly is worth the time.

**Round trip from May Creek Camp road to clearcut 3¼ miles, allow 2 hours
High point 1000 feet, elevation gain 550 feet
All year**

Lake Isabel

The entire 2 miles to the mine the road has only several turnouts spacious enough to turn around, and not many more where two cars can squeeze past each other. Nevertheless, it is drivable by most tough little vehicles, and thus can offer quite a quick trip to the lake.

After making the final switchback to the mine and immediately upon reaching the excavated flat of the mine workings, spot an obvious foot trail up left. Disbelieving, climb straight up a hundred feet and be convinced by a blaze, a sawn log, and then the commencement of good old tread, happily not good enough for wheels, which snarl below in frustration.

The way climbs through choked second-growth, passing skidway gullies and the rusty boiler of a steam donkey. May Creek is a white ribbon of cataracts plunging through the green gloom. The character of the forest begins to change, becoming older and wilder, and the explanation is made by the massive log foundation upon which the donkey engine rested. Marked by a 5-foot Douglas fir, virgin forest begins and continues to trail's end. Beyond the donkey foundation windfalls old and new obstruct the way, but fishermen feet pound down easy enough detours, though a certain amount of clambering must be expected. In 1 long mile, at 1950 feet, the way joins the road-trail from May Creek Camp just where it bridges the creek.

Have lunch at the lovely creek and turn back. Or proceed onward to Lake Isabel.

Round trip from Copperbell Mine to Lake Isabel 5 miles, allow 5 hours
High point 2842 feet, elevation gain 1800 feet
May-November

Skykomish River Rail Trail (map — page 192)

The frustrating thing about the Skykomish River in the moraine area is that the low elevation promises lots of good walking in winter. But the promise is broken; private property squeezes out the public almost totally. Aha, not quite. Because of the railroad, one can walk for miles beside the river even when the awesome walls of Mt. Index hanging over the route are plastered white.

Drive Highway 2 east from Gold Bar to .3 mile past the fire station and turn left on Reiter Road. In .7 mile the blacktop bends left; go straight on Reiter 1 mile, to the far edge of a gravel pit. Here the May Creek Campground road turns left; go straight and down .4 mile and turn right on the Trout Hatchery road .5 mile to the end by the rearing ponds, elevation 328 feet.

Tour the hatchery ponds, see the little leapers, and gulls and ducks waiting for a bite, and in season the adult fish returning from the river to the hatchery outlet creek. And look up to Sultan, Persis, and Index. Walk upriver ½ mile to a water intake at Austin Creek. Across the creek continue on the abandoned (1962) railroad grade; signs ban motorcycles from the hatchery area. Slopes of the Puget Moraine leap abruptly up on the left as the river makes a big bend south. In a scant 1 mile the living railroad crosses from the other side of the river and the way henceforth is on a trackside path. (Just where the living railroad joins the route, spot a path climbing the slope to a pleasant overlook.) The river makes a big bend southeast, toward Index, and now the moraine also leaps up abruptly on the right. The head-on look at Mt. Index and Anderson Creek cirque, the precipice standing a vertical mile above the river foreground, is the classic low-valley view of the peak. In 1 long mile more the river curves north to views of Merchant and Baring. Here, 2½ miles from the hatchery, where the Gold Bar-Index Road comes down to the railroad tracks, is a good turnaround.

Round trip 5 miles, allow 3 hours
High point 550 feet, minimal elevation gain
All year

The abandoned railroad grade goes downvalley from a bit before the rearing ponds, gated and barred to vehicles. If not posted against trespassing, the path can be walked 2 miles in pleasant forest by the river.

North Peak of Index and Skykomish River

SKYKOMISH RIVER —
THE MORAINE AND ABOVE

In the canyon sliced through the great moraine, on river banks at just 400 feet above sea level, yellow violets and trillium bloom in fresh-greening maple groves; there, it's balmy springtime. Meanwhile, on the precipice above, avalanches rumble from the corniced summit ridge of Index more than a mile straight up; there, it's still bitter winter. No other highway in the state displays so dramatic a contrast or such overwhelming verticality. At the moraine, the single most impressive heap of Canadian rubbish in Puget Sound country, there is a distinct change in character, a definite sense of a gateway from lowlands to mountains.

To report the bad news of the past decade, since the surveyor began his pokings about, a number of trips have been eliminated from this chapter because the young trees grew up and blocked the views from clearcuts, or because the DNR-sponsored Reiter Razzers have done such violence to the land a hiker cannot pass through, even when the razzers are not on the scene, without weeping, yowling, or throwing up. All that has been kept is condensed in "Index High Rise," where the moraine nearly overtops a hard-rock rib thrust out from Ragged Ridge. Further sad news is that Anderson Cirque, as wildly violent a scene as the locality knows, has been removed from the realm of reasonable hiking by human neglect — the privately owned path to the creek has been let grow up, the blown-out bridge over the creek has not been replaced. Since this is part of the Alpine Lakes Management Area, the Forest Service may, or may not, be heard from.

The good news is that the province continues rich, and richer, in near-city, low-elevation, wilderness-edge trails and footroads (the surveyor found several exciting additions for this edition). The final three hikes in the chapter — in the book — flirt with the Alpine Lakes Wilderness, and the last plunges right on in. This honest-to-gosh trail through real-life preserved old-growth wilderness forest has great value in helping us keep perspective: it's all very well to learn to stop worrying and love clearcuts and plantations but one should be reminded they're not the whole picture; otherwise one will find oneself declaring how much one loves cheerful, thrifty, vigorous young forests, how much one detests gloomy, rotten, decadent old forests, and one will no longer be smiling ironically.

USGS maps: Mt. Si, Index, Baring, Grotto, Monte Cristo, Snoqualmie Lake

Index High Rise (map — page 192)

Grownups should know better than to go birdwatching in a kindergarten playground. However, when the wheelkids' racketing and hollering cease, songs can be heard, and that's why the ridge rising high above the town of Index cannot be totally abandoned to pleasures of the puerile. It demands a visit — but never, ever, on Sunday.

From the trout-hatchery turnoff (see Skykomish River Rail Trail) continue straight ahead on "Primitive Road" 1.3 miles to a Y. The right fork is the road to Index; go left, passing myriad deep-rutted motorcycle roads and a bewilderment of arrows and numbers and paper plates. (Where do all these miles of wheel-built runways go? Nowhere. And they stink of gasoline and scorched rubber and moldy French fries.) At 1.1 miles from the Y is a (formerly) stupendous corner; the brush is growing up and closing off the views, but the head-on look into Anderson Cirque, between the masses of Index and Persis, still rates a pause. In .6 mile more the road crosses a powerline swath with a panorama west to lowlands.

Vertigo Rim

At 3 miles from the Index road a narrow sideroad goes off right, on the flat, .3 mile to an ancient bridge over Deer Creek. Park here, elevation 1700 feet.

Walk across the bridge (wheels ford the creek) a short bit to a Y. The right fork has lost its views to the trees; keep left ¾ mile to the end. Carefully, oh ever so carefully, push through the screen of pine trees to the mossy granite knobs of the brink.

Gulp. Retreat into the trees until the fainting sensation passes. Then find a secure place to sit (clinging to a pine?) and enjoy, if you can, the view down to rooftops of Index town, to white riffles in the North Fork Skykomish River, to the railroad tracks making a big swing up the North Fork valley, to dogs chasing bicycles, to climbers reeling out of the tavern after a day in their gymnasium.

Do not, in the spirit of fun, drop rocks or little children off this cliff — you may dislodge a climber whom you cannot see clinging to the wall but whom you will hear as his "YAW-AW-AW!" recedes.

To see more climbers, bring a telescope and train it on the North Peak of Index directly across the Skykomish valley; this is the best viewpoint of the standard climbing route.

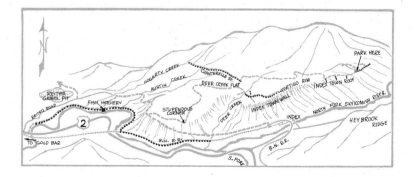

Baring Mountain

Chanterelle Street
At .3 mile from Vertigo turnoff, go left (walking, or you'll miss the chanterelles) on a narrow flat sideroad, elevation 1800 feet. In ½ mile the road is washed out for four-wheelers and in ½ mile more comes to pretty much naught at Gogarty Creek. The views are all inward — to green-dim cloisters of second-growth and (in fall) mushrooms. The creek is a nice splash for a picnic on a hot summer Wednesday (never Sunday).

Index Town Roof
At 1.3 miles from Chanterelle turnoff the main road makes the second of two big switchbacks, ascending from Deer Creek Flat and its morainal material to a rock-hearted spur thrusting from Ragged Ridge. As the road cuts the sidehill it has no forests on the right, only air; a succession of viewpoints offer drama and variety unsurpassed in the Skykomish.

At .6 mile from the upper switchback, stop the car and push through the screen of brush to see down to the Skykomish River, across to Index, out to the Olympics, east to Jumpoff, Gunn, and Hinman-Daniels.

In .1 mile more, find a path a few feet to a look 2000 feet down to Index town and across the valley to the North Peak of Index.

In .2 mile more, especially admire the north wall of Baring in profile, and in another .2 mile, again.

North Fork View

At 2.9 miles from Chanterelle turnoff the road goes through a saddle and is half-heartedly barricaded. Park here, elevation 2800 feet.

The road straight ahead can be driven, sort of, but to little purpose. Neither is it much worth walking, what with scrub trees growing up since the logging in the 1950s and 1970s.

However, the road to the right goes out into huckleberry bushes, by granite outcrops, and seems likely to stay quite naked of trees for decades. At the end in ¼ mile are views over the North Fork Skykomish to Jumpoff and Baring, and up the valley past Spire to Goblin and Columbia and other peaks of the Monte Cristo group.

Round trip 4 miles, allow 3 hours
High point 2800 feet, minor elevation gain
April-November

Headwater cirque of Proctor Creek

Persis Panoramas (map — page 195)

The Proctor Trough is among the momentous geological spots of the Cascade front. The glacier from Canada passed through here. So did the Big River (Skagit plus Stillaguamish plus Skykomish) that was dammed off from the ocean by the ice and slid southward, searching for Grays Harbor. For a time a Great Lake received waters and sediments from both the Cascades and the Canadian ice. Evidences of all this are plainly to be seen from high on the side of Persis — as well as panoramas north to Pilchuck and Ragged Ridge and Everett, south to the Issaquah Alps and Seattle.

Drive Highway 2 east from the Gold Bar fire station 3.7 miles. Several hundred feet past the 1933 highway bridge over unsigned No Name Creek, turn right on the great, wide, gravel log-haul road, elevation 400 feet. (If Weyerhaeuser installs a never-open gate here, this is where the hike will begin.) The road climbs steeply up the moraines, excellent views starting in 3.3 miles, and levels out in the flattish valley of the trough, now used by several creeks, including Proctor. At 3.5 miles, 1650 feet, is a Y. Go left on road 2701 and climb from excellent to glorious views. At 2350 feet, 1 mile from the Y, the main road goes ahead and a rotten remnant of a road turns steeply and undrivably uphill left. Park here, elevation 2350 feet.

Low Pan

Ascend the overgrowing road to a junction at a landing. Take the right fork a

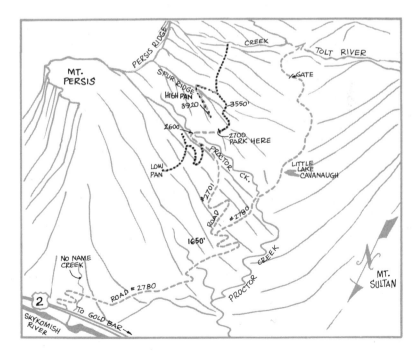

few yards to a fine creek sliding and splashing down slabs from a dark canyon in virgin timber above. Then return and take the left fork, ending at 2800 feet.

Steeply below, past the clearcut of 1960 or so, the second-growth still shrubby, is taller forest dating from logging of the early 1940s. The floor of the glacier trough appears as flat as the old lake. Across is Sultan, an island mountain completely surrounded by low valleys. Out the trough north are Ragged Ridge, Stickney, Blue, and Pilchuck, and in the distance, saltwater-ways. Out the gap south is Seattle and more saltwaterways.

Round trip 5½ miles, allow 3 hours
High point 2800 feet, elevation gain 450 feet
May-November

High Pan

Continue on the main road into the head of Proctor Creek, cut deep in the side of Persis, 1 mile to a Y, 2600 feet. The left climbs toward Persis cliffs. Keep right, over the creek — or, in spring with much snow above and lots of water tumbling down, park and walk.

At 2700 feet, .7 mile from the Y, views are terrific out to the Skykomish valley and Pilchuck, and the road begins to be so steep and airy that most cars, and many people, will wish to park here, as did the surveyor, whose dogs were whimpering.

Walk, therefore, improving the lungs and calming the nerves. Look down to the lakebed, across to Sultan-Sultana, cut off from the rest of the Cascades by the glacier's works, and north to Pilchuck, Three Fingers, Blue, Stickney, Everett. The road switchbacks to still bigger views — views that will last indefinitely because this is a "tree mine" and nothing "commercial" will regrow in these 1976 clearcuts for centuries — unless the market for huckleberries and Christmas trees goes crazy.

At 3550 feet, 2 miles from the chickening-out spot at 2700 feet, the road rounds the tip of a spur ridge and enters splendid old virgin forest. To the broad views north now are added views south — in windows through the splendid old forest — to the Tolt River, Issaquah Alps, and Seattle.

The road continues, now gently descending, to a Y. Take the left, steeply uphill, to the end at 3920 feet on the tip of the spur ridge at 1 mile from the 3550-foot rounding of the same ridge. The views here are still of the window variety. Will they ever grow bigger, as the trees come down? If not, why was this road built? Did The Company belatedly count rings in logs and find the 2-foot-thick mountain hemlocks were 250-450 years old? And that the bigger trees, much older, were conky, not worth hauling to the mill? Do tree-miners ever think about these things?

Round trip from 2700 feet 6 miles, allow 4 hours
High point 3920 feet, elevation gain 1220 feet
May-October

Bridal Veil Falls

The Mountaineers are honoring the request of Forest Service personnel that we not give directions on how to find the old trail to Bridal Veil Falls, which is en route to Lake Serene and which the Forest Service now considers dangerous. In 1987 or some year soon following, the Forest Service will construct a new trail.

Bridal Veil Falls

Mount Index, left, and Mount Persis, right, from Jumpoff Vista

Jumpoff Vista (map — page 199)

From a perch high on craggy Jumpoff Ridge, look over the North Fork Skykomish valley to Ragged Ridge and across the main Skykomish valley to Index, Persis, Puget Sound, and Olympics. Between old clearcuts and new ones are lingering scraps of virgin forests where waterfalls plunge from snowfields.

East of Gold Bar on Highway 2 turn left at Index Corner onto North Fork Skykomish River Road and drive 3.7 miles to an old logging-type sideroad on the right, firmly gated to four-wheelers and dwindled to a trail. The road can be identified by a look straight up (bend your neck) to an arrogant finger of gray granite. Park just a bit in from the highway, elevation 800 feet.

Beginning in second-growth dating from the 1940s, the road soon grows steep and commences switchbacking. A small creek in a waterfall alcove provides a pleasant rest. Windows in the roadside greenery give views from Heybrook Lookout to Index to Persis and across the North Fork valley to Index Town Roof. That view is lost as the way leaves a 1950s clearcut and contours around a shoulder into the valley of Bitter Creek, where commences a different view, to the valley head. The creek is crossed in lovely forest at 2200 feet, about 2½ miles from the start.

In a long ¼ mile from the crossing is a Y; the road straight ahead is to a 1977 clearcut; take the switchback left, into a clearcut of 1970 or so, another ¼ mile to a landing, 2600 feet, at the head of Boss Creek. This landing — or a switchback a few yards beyond — is a satisfying destination. The view out is not as broad as that obtained earlier. But the view upward is grand — to the head of Bitter Creek cirque, water-gleaming granite slabs, waterfalls, snowfields, and rough summits of Jumpoff Ridge. Come in spring and watch the

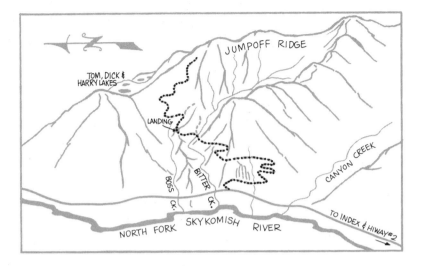

avalanches, which judging from the vastness of alder-jungle must be enormous.

Round trip 6 miles, allow 5 hours
High point 2600 feet, elevation gain 1800 feet
April-November

The landing is "far enough" — but doesn't provide the big picture. For that one must spend some more sweat and suffer some nonsense.

Continue sidehilling up the clearcut nearly to the road-end. Note a rude cat road switchbacking left and scramble up this track to the clearcut top. Here, at 2800 feet, the track switchbacks right and ascends extremely steeply into cool virgin forest. At 3200 feet it comes to an upper clearcut and ends. Continue up in steep, open forest on the left side of this clearcut. When trees end, pick a careful way through brush a short distance to the top of the logging at about 3800 feet. Sit on a granite outcrop and admire.

Index, Persis, Sultan, High Rock Hills, Olympics, Index town and Index Town Wall and Roof, Ragged Ridge, and, up the North Fork valley, Spire Peak and a mess of Monte Cristo summits. That's the big picture.

Jumpoff Valley (map — page 200)

Companions of Persis and Index and Baring, the crags of Merchant, Gunn, and Jumpoff (West Peak of Gunn, it was once called) are familiar components of the neck-stretching, eye-opening view from the Stevens Pass Highway. This hike leads up a lonesome valley, by a fine mountain stream, through logging mostly very old, past artifacts of a mine, to the wild side of these rough peaks, ending at the boundary between second-growth wilderness and virgin wilderness.

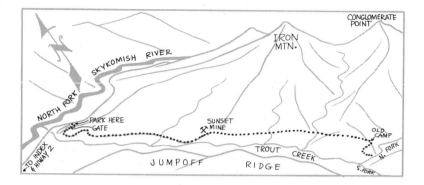

East of Gold Bar on Highway 2 turn left at Index Corner onto North Fork Skykomish River Road and drive 6 miles to Trout Creek. A bit beyond the bridge turn right up a gravel road to a parking space. Elevation, 840 feet.

Ignore a short deadend road going toward Trout Creek and walk the other way up a road which can be driven the 1½ miles to the mine — but don't do it unless you really hate your car. The way ascends steadily to a clearcut of the 1970s (at a Y in a scant mile take the right fork), levels out high above Trout Creek, and gently descends to reach the creek at 1½ miles, 1350 feet. On the right is the superb stream roaring through great granite boulders. On the left is (was) the Sunset Mine. Salvagers have hauled away most of the lovely junk shown in the photograph, but concrete foundations remain.

Beyond the mine the terrible road gets worse, barring four-wheelers and all but the most fanatic motorcyclists, and even they quickly are discouraged by obstacles. Pass sideroads left and right and proceed ahead, the deteriorating road nice for walking, and after one last small logging patch of the 1970s, entering second-growth dating from the 1950s. First climbing, then flattening, the road-become-trail passes a succession of delights — excellent creeks tumbling down mossy-black slabs or granite staircases, views straight up to dramatic Jumpoff Ridge, upvalley to Merchant, then Gunn.

At 2125 feet, 2½ miles from the mine, the trail ends at an old landing (and camp) on the brink of a steep bank down to the North Fork Trout Creek, here rushing to join the South Fork. On the other side of the creek is the start of virgin forest, untrailed, really wild.

Round trip 8 miles, allow 5 hours
High point 2125 feet, elevation gain 1300 feet
May-November

Mineral City and Poodle Dog Pass (map — page 201)

The Silver Creek valley reeks of history. Little remains to be seen. However, much can be felt, especially if the hiker is equipped with *Guide to Monte Cristo Area,* by Harry Majors and Richard McCollum, published in 1977, and *Mining in the Pacific Northwest,* by Lawrence K. Hodges, published in 1897. With one or both in hand, a person can breathe the atmosphere of two major settlements, 2500 mining claims and hundreds of holes in the ground, and major trails over several passes to Sultan Basin and Monte Cristo.

The first prospector arrived in 1871 and by 1891 some 75 miners were at work between Galena and Mineral City. A flood that washed out much of the trail along the North Fork Skykomish, and completion of the railroad to Monte Cristo, pretty well depopulated Silver Creek, and the rush to the Yukon and Alaska pretty well depopulated the North Cascades. However, hiking up the valley in the spring of 1942 the surveyor passed a cabin of very great age. Peering from a window was a very aged and very shy man who evidently hadn't rushed anywhere, except here, and that very long ago. Returning downvalley next day, the surveyor found displayed on a roadside log a row of magnificent quartz crystals; the shy smile in the window showed they were meant as gifts, which were accepted with a smile. Because of the exchange of smiles, the surveyor feels somewhat connected to the olden days of the valley.

From Index Corner on Highway 2 drive North Fork Skykomish River Road 8.8 miles, to just past Howard Creek, and turn left over the river. At .2 mile from the bridge turn right on a road signed "Road closed 1.3 miles ahead. No turnaround." (The latter is not so.) Pass a sideroad right to the site of Galena, founded in 1890. At 1.6 miles from the bridge the Silver Creek road is barricaded by large boulders. Park here, elevation 1500 feet.

Mineral City

The barricade is quickly explained by a cliff of rotten rock where keeping the road open to wheels would cost more than anyone currently cares to spend. (This was true, too, in 1942, when the surveyor parked his Model A here and hoisted Trapper Nelson.) One hopes it remains a footroad — and is made more completely so by excluding the two-wheelers and three-wheelers that pretty well rule out the hike on summer weekends, at least as far as Mineral City.

On weekdays there is no lovelier and more peaceful walk in the area. Though loggers entered the valley in the mid-1940s and by the end of the decade had slashed their way virtually to the meadows of Silvertip Peak, and periodically have returned, most recently in the early 1980s, much of the lower creek flows in so deep a canyon the virgin forest has been let alone — Douglas fir and hemlocks up to 4 feet in diameter. There are trees, and there is water.

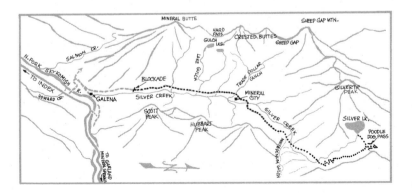

When a hiker isn't tiptoeing to the road edge to look down into white-roaring slots in the rock, he's pausing to exclaim at the waterfalls that splash down Pole Gulch, Moore Gulch, Lockwood Gulch, Cascade Gulch, and Lake Gulch — this latter the route of the miners' trail over Hard Pass to Sultan Basin. Springs ooze from cliffs, their drippings followed down by lines of saxifrage and hanging ribbons of twinflower. Several holes in the ground are passed, and a rotting cabin, and a rotting Seattle bus ("10 Capitol Hill").

At 3 miles, 2180 feet, the road enters the wide sidevalley of Trade Dollar Gulch, route of the (gone) trail over Sheep Gap to Sultan Basin, and site of Silver City, founded in 1873, reestablished in 1890 as Mineral City, and in 1896 boasting two hotels, two saloons, two stores, and five other buildings. Nothing of these was visible in 1942, but there were several buildings of later vintage — occupied, in fact, until the draft or high-paying jobs in the shipyards called the miners away. The surveyor camped in the main house, borrowing a can of peaches for his dessert, and explored the mine, gathering crystals of brilliant-red, glassy-transparent arsenic pyrite. Nothing was to be found of houses or mine on the surveyor's next visit, in 1985.

Round trip 6 miles, allow 4 hours
High point 2180 feet, elevation gain 700 feet
March-November

Poodle Dog Pass

In summer the best walking is beyond, where motorcycles are quickly left in the lurch and subalpine beauties begin to compensate for the barbaric logging done in the 1940s and after. Until the railroad was completed from Barlow Pass, this was a main supply route for the heavy action at Monte Cristo — and in fact was the way by which that area's vivid mineralization was discovered in 1889. Again, most of the history is in the books. But there are flowers.

A first discouragement — to boots as well as motorcycles — is Trade Dollar Creek, which lacks a bridge and is a mean wade in early summer. The road dwindles to trail as it crosses Silver Creek — on a bridge — and climbs in alder, then avalanche brush, but partly, too, in patches of virgin silver fir. The waterfall of Molybdenum Gulch is as pretty as they come, and the views grow of Sheep Gap and Silvertip and other peaks. A mine can be seen across the valley in Red Gulch. In 1942 the surveyor saw several buildings high on that wall. On the trail (the road then ended at Mineral City) he passed an old cabin that had been occupied and a mine that had been worked very recently. Scores of ore sacks were piled beside the cabin, filled with chalcopyrite, galena, and sphalerite, the fruits of years of "high-grading" — hand-cleaning the ore with a rock hammer — the only practical way to mine these thin seams, and only worth a man's time in a Great Depression.

At 2850 feet, 1½ miles from Mineral City, the logging road-trail crosses Silver Creek — without a bridge. By late summer the wading or boulder-hopping is no longer life-threatening. Having plowed straight up in snow in 1942, and having turned back in 1985 due to a cowardly dog who felt her life was threatened, the surveyor can report of the route beyond only that the last of the clearcuts is reached in ¾ mile, at 3200 feet, and the abandoned trail, maintained by many fishermen's boots and draped with plastic ribbons, then switchbacks 1 long mile to Poodle Dog Pass, 4380 feet. From the junction here the historic trail descends to Monte Cristo (see *100 Hikes in the North Cas-*

cades). The path left leads in a short bit to Silver Lake, 4260 feet, set in a cirque scooped in the side of Silvertip.

**Round trip from Mineral City to Poodle Dog Pass 7 miles, allow 5 hours
High point 4380 feet, elevation gain 2200 feet
July-October**

Heybrook Lookout (map — page 204)

Where there's a fire lookout tower there's a lot of country to see. This one is particularly famed for the close view of Index, rising a vertical mile above the Skykomish River. But that's not even the half of it.

Drive Highway 2 east from Index Corner 2 miles to a large sign, "Mt. Baker-Snoqualmie National Forest." Park on the shoulder, elevation 800 feet.

Widening of the highway in 1985-86 obliterated the start of the route, which nevertheless can be found without much trouble and by 1987 will be reestablished, perhaps with a formal parking area. The unsigned but excellent trail begins (or did) on the flat, along an old grade, then turns up the mountainside and climbs steadily through second-growth so sizable it could pass for virgin were it not for mossy old stumps. Granite boulders litter the forest floor, which

Heybrook Lookout, Mount Index, left, Mount Persis, right

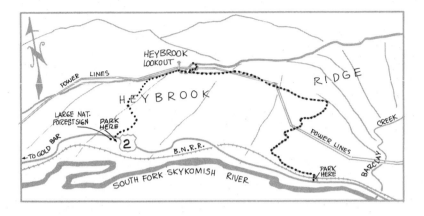

at last is broken by granite walls and slabs. The way attains the crest of Heybrook Ridge and turns right, gentling, and bumping into a granite buttress. One trail goes around to the right, another straight up to the lookout tower, 1701 feet, a long 1 mile from the highway.

The views are great from the foot of the tower, better from the 73-foot top. Look down to the Skykomish River, across to the three peaks of Index, the cirque of Lake Serene, Bridal Veil Falls, west to Persis, Sultan, the lowlands, and the Olympics.

For more views follow the service road down into the woods. Where it proceeds ahead to the right, take the undrivable left fork up ¼ mile to the powerline and granite outcrops of a ridgetop knoll, 1800 feet. The chief spectacularity here is the strange trough of Barclay Lake, framed on one side by the spires of Jumpoff and Gunn, on the other by the astounding north wall of Baring.

Round trip 2½ miles, allow 3 hours
High point 1800 feet, elevation gain 1000 feet
March-November

The service road also can be walked to the lookout. It begins 2 miles to the east along the highway, poorly marked, with poor parking, and much molested by wheels. Of the two entries, one has an ancient wire-mesh gate, the other a small sign, "Do Not Block." The little road immediately crosses the railroad tracks and heads uphill into the woods. The distance from the highway to the tower is 3½ miles.

Barclay Lake (map — page 206)

For generations one of the favorite valley walks in all the Cascades, in 1969 most of the Barclay Creek trail was desolated by a wall-to-wall clearcut. Only a remnant is left of what is often described as "virtually a true rain forest." But it's no mean remnant. Rest too long in this dank dark hole in the mountains and moss will grow on your boots and mushrooms sprout from your ears. For many

Barclay Lake and cliffs of Baring Mountain

months of the year the sun never touches these trees. Above is Something blocking it out — a Something so horrid that when it is revealed to you at the lake you may cry out in fright.

Drive Highway 2 to the hamlet of Baring, and turn north on Barclay River Road. Pass between houses, then wind steeply up and across a powerline swath, through second-growth dating from the 1940s. The road rounds a corner into Barclay Creek valley — and one can understand the wail of dismay that went up from hikers in 1969 when this desecration was perpetrated. Gasps at the desolation (the plantation is springing up thriftily, delighting fans of tidy Douglas fir even-age monoculture, saddening folks who prefer Nature's sloppy mixture of species and ages — including the very old and decrepit) compete with gasps at the first look at the profile of the Baring Nordwand. At 2350 feet, 4.3 miles from the highway, is the trailhead.

The path drops into clearcut but soon enters pristine forest. It's slow walking, what with ceaseless ups and downs, rocks, mud, and slippery roots. All the better for enjoying nurselogs, hemlock roots sprawling down to enclose a huge boulder, and gravel bars of the main creek, and moss banks of a tributary, and all manner of pleasing things to be found in green twilight. In about 1 mile the trail drops from the sidehill to cross Barclay Creek, then climbs the opposite slope. In 2 miles is a Y. The left continues up the lake. The right drops to a mass of enormous boulders tumbled about the lakeshore and the outlet stream. Keep a tight grip on yourself and look up. There's the Something. Where these boulders came from. Horrors.

Round trip 4 miles, allow 3 hours
High point 2400 feet, elevation gain 400 feet
May-November

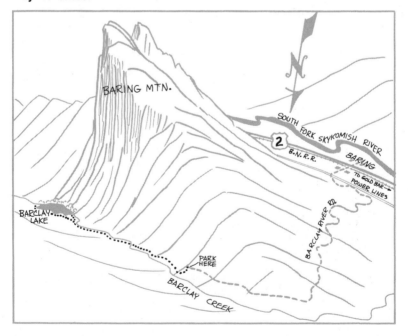

Baring Vista (map — page 208)

Glaringly prominent high under cliffs of 6125-foot Mt. Baring, a clearcut of the 1970s offers views up and down the Skykomish valley and across to Mt. Index. The rarity of wheels is a further attraction to peace-loving pedestrians. The bevy of splashing creeks, crossed first in forest, then in sky-open clearcut, are at least as entertaining as the views. An ideal time for the walk is a sunny spring day when cornices still hang above the great face of Index yet the snowmelt is storming.

Drive Highway 2 east from Baring Store 2.1 miles and just past the bridge over the railroad turn hard left on a road signed only "No. 6028," if that. It ascends west .7 mile to 1000 feet, switchbacks east under powerlines, to a junction at 1375 feet, 1.4 miles from the highway. In a clearcut where the better road contours straight ahead, turn steeply uphill left, through a quarry, to a gravel barricade, 1.7 miles, 1500 feet.

Wheels roll over the barricade, to no good purpose, since the way is shortly and quite thoroughly washed out by the first of the excellent creeks. Here, too, starts the virgin forest, Douglas firs up to 3 feet in diameter, the accompanying moss and ferns and creeks wildly green and white to match.

In 1 mile, at 2025 feet, is the edge of the huge clearcut, which at last is growing tiny trees but will have broad views well into the next century, and not a second crop for another century. The views begin — to the Main Peak of Index and the skyline of the Middle and North Peaks, beyond the bulk of Philadelphia Mountain; out past Persis and Sultan to haze-dimmed lowlands; up the valley to the Miller River and glaciers of the Hinman area.

Four more creeks are crossed on the ½-mile traverse to the west edge of the clearcut, on a promontory at 2180 feet. The views here include those off the cliff brink to the hamlet of Baring, the highway, and river.

Baring Mountain from Baring Vista

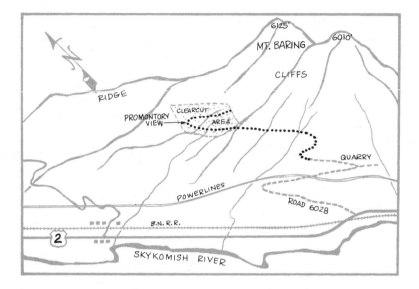

The road switchbacks east ½ mile under Baring's shaggy cliffs to the end at 2500 feet, adding little new in the way of views but all those wonderful creeks to soak your hot head in.

Round trip 4 miles, allow 3 hours
High point 2500 feet, elevation gain 1000 feet
March-November

Money Creek – South Fork Tolt River Pass
(map — page 210)

A white-water creek, virgin forests, old mining garbage and the bed of a narrow-gauge mining railroad, two subalpine lakes, and in season flower gardens or bushels of blueberries. When the miners get too gimpy to crawl around underground, or find other hobbies, the upper valley should be transferred from the Alpine Lakes Management Zone to the Alpine Lakes Wilderness and the road permitted to revert gracefully to trail. It does so now, just about every winter, and for some months is an excellent footroad. Later, when the boulders are cleared away and the floodwater gulches filled in, there are enough wheelfree excursions to fill out a day — including a brawl with the bushes in a genuine roaring wilderness (if not Wilderness).

Drive Highway 2 east from Index Corners 10 miles and turn right, at a sign for Money Creek Campground, on Old Cascade Highway. At a Y in 1 mile turn right on Miller River Road. At another Y in a few yards, go right again on Money Creek Road, signed "Lake Elizabeth." At 4 miles from Miller River Road are a fine view to waterfalls tumbling from Goat Basin, scooped in the side of Lennox Mountain, and a popular riverside picnic spot. In .4 mile more the road enters a

Mine shaft near Lake Elizabeth

gorge; in early spring the road is likely to be slumped out or rock-blocked here, making a good start for a peaceful walk. Elevation, 2100 feet.

In .8 mile more through a patchwork of 1960s clearcuts and virgin forest of silver fir, hemlock, and cedar, the road switchbacks right; take a sidetrip on the grownover lane straight ahead to an impressive heap of rusting machinery and rotting timbers, once the terminal of the tramway to Apex Mine, high above.

In 1.2 miles more, the way now partly in subalpine meadows, look for grownover cedar puncheon of the railway, a timber dam with a filled-in reservoir, and a falling-down bridge over Money Creek. The surveyor feels there must be a trail up to the Apex Mine but has failed to find it.

In .4 more mile is the little dot of Lake Elizabeth, 2880 feet, a beaver marsh converted by a low dam into a lake, a pleasant reflecting pool for the meadows and big, old trees. A path circles the shore.

In .2 mile more is Money Creek-South Fork Tolt River Pass, 2960 feet. A sideroad climbs left a short bit to rubbish of the Damon Mine, some ancient, some modern. With ridges of Phelps Peak and Red Mountain rising on either side, the fall colors are spectacular, both in the avalanche swaths made by Nature and the silly clearcuts made by man; since the logging in the 1950s the slopes have barely grown a handful of Christmas trees—but if the tree-farming is a joke, the blueberry-farming is a huge success.

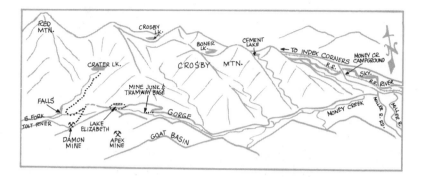

The road contours a final .4 mile above meadow-marshes of the Tolt headwaters to an end at 2960 feet, 7.4 miles from the Miller River Road.

Now for the sweating and groaning. From the road-end a path plunges through huckleberries to virgin forest and a Y. The left is down to the river (creek). Go right, on a rocky and rooty and slippery and bush-crowded and log-blocked and creek-eroded remnant of what once was a major thoroughfare, but which hasn't seen a trail crew since the 1920s. Crawling over the 15th log, one wonders why boots have kept the route open. In ½ mile — and ½ hour — the splendid waterfalls of Crater Creek seem the explanation. Certainly, the glorious old forest to this point, and then the lovely spot to sit and eat potato salad and fried chicken, manifestly demand pedestrian access.

Then one spots a scramble path, supposes it to be purely for views of the uppermost of the several falls — until at last the light dawns. In ½ mile, gaining 600 feet, the path reaches Crater Lake, 3520 feet, in a cirque at the foot of 5440-foot Red Mountain. The surveyor turned back a few minutes from the lake, having discovered he was missing a dog who hadn't crossed all 15 logs and subsequently bivouacked overnight with the coyotes before being found. The map suggests the lake might be very pretty, what with virgin forest and cliffs sharing the shore.

Round trips (not including footroad) 3 miles, allow 4 hours
High point 3520 feet, elevation gain 600 feet
June-November (footroad February-May)

West Fork Miller River (map — page 212)

Along the valley of the West Fork a long finger of "Management Zone" thrusts deep into the Alpine Lakes Wilderness. Presumably the boundary was drawn to exclude the patented mining claims that have been intermittently worked by one generation of fools after another, each convinced the next stick of dynamite may blast through to the Mother Lode. The valley ought to be Wilderness because it surely is wilderness. The road that was drivable by ordinary vehicles until the era of World War II has been let go, unmaintained, and now is so rough a trail that only the most indefatigable stuntmen torture their motorcycles here, and rarely. The very few four-wheelers are either witless prospectors or amateur archaeologists come to plunder the middens of nigh onto a century of witless prospectors.

This is the best valley in the area to study old idiocies, old middens, and old junk. In addition there are miles of virgin forest — fortunately not extensive enough to be worth logging (one prays), due to the steep walls and narrowness of the valley and the swaths cut by avalanches and alluvial fans. The river is a steady delight, the water sometimes sheeting over granite slabs for all the world like the High Sierra, sometimes quietly flowing through limeade swimming holes.

Drive Miller River Road (see Lake Dorothy) 3.3 miles to an unsigned and not rationally drivable sideroad. (If you come to the West Fork bridge you've gone several hundred feet too far.) Park here, elevation 1291 feet. The "road" deteriorates (improves) to trail. Impressive granite cliffs rise high above. Mossy maples on rockslides alternate with groves of old forest featuring 5-foot Douglas firs.

Look for miners' junk here and there, remnants of camps and cabins. At 1½ miles a Monarch range marks the site of the Silver Dollar Mine, located up the

West Fork Miller River

slope in the brush; in 1944 the surveyor surveyed the tunnels, then only recently abandoned, the miner having been drafted. The way continues past a 7-foot cedar, deep forests of 5-foot hemlocks, fields of bracken with views to ridges of Cascade Mountain. At 2½ miles, 2050 feet, a sidetrail takes off right up the valley of Coney Creek; the map shows it going to a nameless mine at 3100 feet. At 3¾ miles, 2200 feet, is "Cleopatra City." The surveyor didn't spot the map-shown "jeep trail" climbing to the Cleopatra Mine at 3400 feet, but in the broad field are ruins of two cabins and many rusty or rotten artifacts; the star attraction is a truck some 50 years old. A bit beyond here the road-trail, the whole distance never more than ¼ mile from the Alpine Lakes Wilderness on both sides, at last enters the Wilderness and at 4½ miles, 2400 feet, ends in a final flurry of holes in the ground. Somebody has been busy here recently, as evidenced by an elaborate new privy in the woods above a mine tunnel. Somebody or other has been busy here for decades — the rotten logs of a cabin must date from the turn of the century.

Round trip 9 miles, allow 5 hours
High point 2400 feet, elevation gain 1110 feet
February-December

Note: For a miles-long glory of meadow flowers in bloom, do the trip in late spring or early summer.

Lake Dorothy (map — page 212)

Clearcuts and second-growth have their beauties, and machine-dodging is sporty, but now and then one longs for a walk in genuine racket-free wild-woods, secure from tree-farmers and wheelfreaks. That's why this trip is included despite its going deeper into the mountains than is really quite proper for this book. Of all the hikes in the two Skykomish chapters, it's the only one that explores big-tree virgin forest that has a firm guarantee by Congress to be there next year.

Drive Highway 2 east from Index Corners 10 miles and turn right, at a sign for Money Creek Campground, on Old Cascade Highway. At a Y in 1 mile turn

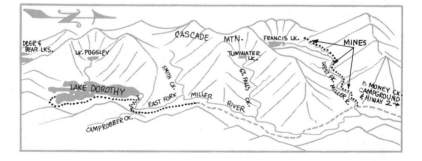

right on Miller River Road and follow it 8.8 miles to its end, and the Lake Dorothy trailhead, at 2200 feet.

In glorious forest the whole way, the trail soon enters the Alpine Lakes Wilderness and in a scant 1 mile crosses a bridge over Camprobber Creek, both it and the Miller River frothing down walls and slabs of granite. The path now switchbacks up a valley step and at 1½ miles reaches the outlet of Lake Dorothy, 3058 feet.

For generations among the most popular "Boy Scout lakes" in the Cascades, until quite recently the lake was 7 miles by trail and thus was a five times grander walk. But things could be worse — also until recently there was an official public plan to build the "Lake Dorothy Highway" over the ridge and down to the Middle Fork Snoqualmie.

Nearly ½ mile wide and 1¾ miles long, this is among the largest of the Alpine (in this case actually subalpine, of course) Lakes. For perspectives on the enclosing ridges and on the islands to which Boy Scouts used to raft, take the 2-mile up-and-down trail to the head of the lake and the large meadow-marshes there.

Round trip to outlet 3 miles, allow 3 hours
High point 3058 feet, elevation gain 900 feet
June-November

Lake Dorothy and Big Snow Mountain

INDEX